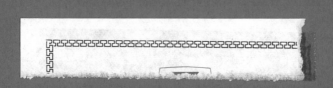

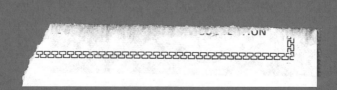

The Woodwards

DOUGLAS E. HARKER

The Woodwards

THE STORY OF A DISTINGUISHED
BRITISH COLUMBIA FAMILY

1850-1975

MITCHELL PRESS LIMITED

VANCOUVER • TORONTO • CHICAGO

Canadian Cataloguing in Publication Data

Harker, Douglas E., 1911-
    The Woodwards

    Includes index.
    ISBN 0-88836-012-6

    1. Woodward family. 2. Woodward Department
Stores Limited. I. Title.

HF5465.C24W643   338.7'61'6588710922
                    C76-016060-0

Contents

I dedicate this book to the spirit of merchandising integrity and enterprise, ever protective of the people it serves, needed by today's embattled consumer as never before and evidenced by the Woodwards for a hundred years.

D. E. Harker

Foreword

By Colonel the Honourable Clarence Wallace

I have read *The Woodwards* with much interest and am pleased to have an opportunity to express my admiration for the contributions which this remarkable pioneer family has made to British Columbia, Alberta, and indeed to Canada.

I did not know Charles Woodward well, but I remember that in the 1924 Election he was elected M.L.A. for Vancouver and headed the polls. I also remember that two or three years later the Young Liberals urged Premier Oliver to make him Minister of Finance. I think the Oliver government would have been wise to follow that advice. My father, who also was a Vancouver pioneer, admired Charles Woodward greatly.

Billy and Puggy Woodward were among my closest friends. On the day Billy learned he had been appointed Lieutenant-Governor of British Columbia he came straight to my house to tell me the news first, not only because of our friendship but also because he knew that, like himself, I was a keen monarchist and a strong supporter of British institutions and traditions. To be the Crown's representative for British Columbia was the highest honour Billy could wish for, and he discharged his duties with devotion and distinction.

Though Puggy was less in the public eye, his gifts to the University of British Columbia and many other concerns have seldom been equalled in the annals of the Province, and his business skills were of the highest order. The present Chairman of the Board, Chunky Woodward, Billy's son, continues to uphold the family traditions of first-rate merchandising and public service.

I admire the courage, industry and high principles of the pioneer men and women who have built our province, and I would place the Woodwards in the forefront of such people.

C. Wallace

THE WOODWARDS

In 1852 in Wentworth County, Ontario, a man was born, destined to revolutionize merchandising in Western Canada. This is the story of Charles Woodward, his sons the Honourable W. C. Woodward and P. A. Woodward, his daughter-in-law Ruth and his grandson C. N. W. Woodward, their families and their fortunes, and the times in which they lived; of the events and policies which led to the development of the Woodward chain of department stores and of some of the personalities who made outstanding contributions to that remarkable enterprise.

CHAPTER ONE

Charles' Boyhood

Thousands of settlers came to Canada from Britain in the 1840's and 1850's. Grinding poverty, long hours of work, a class-ridden society and overcrowded and disease-ridden habitations drove an ever-increasing number of middle-class and working-class families to seek sunshine, air and opportunity abroad.

One such settler was John William Woodward who emigrated from Lincolnshire in 1850. He was a wheelwright, 26 years old, enterprising and self-reliant; his total possessions on arrival were two sovereigns. More by chance than by plan he made his way to Mono in Beverley Township, situated some forty miles northwest of Toronto and rapidly becoming part of a rich farming district. Immediately he was able to establish himself in his trade and find work on a farm as well. Before that first year of his immigration had ended, he married May Culham whose family had come to Mono from Wales.

John Woodward had good reason to be pleased that he had decided to settle in Canada.

The stories of the early settlers' hardships, of stubborn land that had to be cleared with inadequate equipment, of log shanties without doors, of battles with wolves, intense cold and hunger, are legion. In the 1840's fifty-acre lots were given away to anyone foolish or brave enough to want one. But the flat fertile land abounded in rivers, lakes and creeks; by 1850 its farming potential was realized and the place was beginning to thrive. Where John Woodward farmed, the only road was a "mass of soft mud, improved by laying logs side by side across the roadway to prevent the wagon wheels from sinking into the mire. These were the corduroy roads. Wagons had no springs and often settlers preferred to walk rather than be bounced about in such vehicles over rough and bumpy roads." (*Orangeville. 100 Years of History.*)

Five miles to the west of Mono was Orangeville, the largest village within twenty miles. Orange Lawrence, the United Empire Loyalist who was its first postmaster and leading citizen, had energetically promoted its growth. The first public school in the district was built there in 1859. A stage line for mail and passengers was established between Orangeville and Brampton. Before long there were six churches in Mono Township. Another man whose family was to become famous in British Columbia, Maitland McCarthy, was practising law and would soon be Orangeville's first mayor.

John Woodward worked both as a wheelwright and as a farmer. He had his own farm and by diligence and careful planning he was able to provide for his family and save money. In 1863, the year when Orangeville was first incorporated as a village, he moved there from Mono. The population was over 2000 and was steadily increasing every year. He and May had two sons, Charles, 11, and William, 6.

When Charles was fourteen he persuaded his father to allow him to leave school. Though he no longer had to walk that long dreary road from Mono every day he found little pleasure in his books. He was shrewd and conscientious but he considered the whole business of schooling a waste of time.

Already he was nagged by a discontent which was to pursue him throughout his life wherever he was living and whatever he was doing. Even when he had become the founder of one of the most successful businesses in Western Canada and a millionaire at a time when a million dollars was indeed a large sum of money, he was dissatisfied and looked back nostalgically to his early life in Ontario.

"I would give a lot if I could live those days over again," he wrote to his friend C. J. Winkler, sixty years later. "They where the hapiest of all my life." (He never learned conventional spelling.)

Yet in fifteen working years in Ontario he changed his occupation ten times.

John Woodward's decision to let his son leave school soon after his fourteenth birthday was more easily reached than would be the case today. In his Reminiscences Charles recalls:

"When I was thirteen, being the oldest child, I could not be spared from the farm in the summertime and practically all my education was obtained in two winters, travelling often through deep snow 2½ miles after doing two hours chores and the same chores had to be done by me on my return.

"The teachers had no special training and often no certificates. The schoolhouses were made of logs chinked and cracks stuffed with moss. Ventilation was poor and sanitary conditions very bad."

He was practical and strong and had more talent for marketing his father's produce than any other member of the family. It was he who thought of hurrying to Orangeville on market days before any competitors arrived on the scene, even though it meant rising at 4.00 a.m. It was he who gave careful consideration to the positioning of the wagon so that it was the first to be seen by customers coming from Caledon or Mono. It was he who insisted on selling the grain and vegetables just a little cheaper than the other farmers and who posted clear signs advertising price and quality above the produce. In such matters he was his father's superior and was both trusted and relied upon.

But there was no lack of discipline in the home.

"As a boy," Charles recorded, "I was very mischievous and for those days perhaps a little wild for at the age of twelve I had learned to drink and smoke. Where we lived, very few of the farmers had any education. I thought they were fine men and wished to follow their example and do as they did.

"There never was a better provider or a more reasonable parent than my father until he was aroused by some of my mischievous tricks. Then he would punish me with the utmost severity, because he wanted to make me manly and honourable."

That first year when Charles started to work for his father as a full-time helper, 1867, the year of Confederation, was one of the most satisfying of Charles' life. It was a year when he did not suffer feelings of frustration. The excitement of trading, the joy of competition, the challenge of the market place were his and they thrilled him. As the eldest of the children he was the most likely to inherit the farm which was becoming more and more successful.

3

In fact his diary records that his father was worth $10,000 at this time. But deep within himself Charles knew that his destiny lay in other channels.

Life on an Ontario farm in the 1860's was one of unremitting toil. Though marketing the produce was Charles' special joy, other activities took far more of his time. The tractor had not yet been invented and animal power had recently replaced human power in the tilling of the fields. Better ploughs, tillage tools and harvesting equipment designed to be drawn by animals were being developed. Charles helped look after horses, mules and oxen. He planted and cultivated, fed the chickens, spent endless hours with seeding machines and harrows. He learned to use the new combined harvester and thresher, the 'combine' which had originated a few years earlier in California and was now being used by some of the more enterprising farmers in Canada. He kept records and helped his father plan for maximum yields. Life on a farm meant a thousand chores from which there seemed to be no remission. Charles' father permitted no new development to slip by without examining it and determining whether he could profitably use it. He was one of the leading farmers in the area.

"My father was a good citizen and very much respected. He helped many a poor neighbor with seed and feed. Indeed I have known him refuse to sell seed and hay because he knew there were farmer neighbors perhaps less provident than he who would need it for their stock during the winter months."

This was no overstatement. The Historical Atlas of Wellington County published in 1906 one year after his death, recorded: "John W. Woodward raised and educated his family, helping all his sons to start in life. He was a School Trustee for some years, a member of the English Church and a Liberal in politics. He left a commendable record of which his family and the whole community are proud."

The year 1873 was momentous for the Woodwards. John had close friends who lived at Arthur, 22 miles west of Orangeville, the Andersons. Donald Anderson, a Scot from Ayrshire, insisted that the land around Arthur was better farmland than could be found in Orangeville and told John that Lot 8 Concession 7 consisting of 92 fine acres was for sale at a reasonable price. The homestead

4

Mr. and Mrs. Donald Anderson who emigrated from Ayrshire, Scotland, in 1850 and farmed at Arthur, Ontario. Charles married their eldest child, Elizabeth.

was a two-storey, square, stone house, solid and sturdy, with a new red roof. A deep creek ran through the property which was enclosed in open rolling hills. John decided to buy it and move there with his family, now comprising four children, Charles 21, William 16, Hannah 7, and John Culham (Cull) 2. He rejoiced to think that he who had come to Ontario with just two sovereigns could become the owner of such a farm. Arthur, named for the Duke of Wellington, was a smaller but no less thriving village than Orangeville. Its merchants did a large country trade and great numbers of its oxteams hauled supplies along the Owen Sound Road to Mount Forest 15 miles away.

That same year Charles proposed to and was accepted by Elizabeth, the eldest of the nine Anderson children. The eldest son of one prosperous farmer was to marry the eldest daughter of another. The omens were good. Fortunately Elizabeth Anderson could not foresee the tribulations that lay ahead of her.

Both sets of parents gave their permission reluctantly.

" 'How do you expect to get along at your age?' asked my father. I said we had no fear and we were married the next Wednesday . . . We built a board house on the south half of the farm and moved in. The house was not plastered and was cold but we were happy." (Charles' Reminiscences)

His father gave him $1,500 for a wedding present. He used the money for the purchase of forty-two acres of good arable land to start his own farm. Farming had been his whole life; it seemed inevitable that it should be his means of livelihood. Before two years had passed he had made an additional $1,800.

"I got very inflated ideas about myself," he wrote in his diary, but the achievement did not bring him any real satisfaction.

A chance remark overheard in a general store in Arthur changed his destiny. Whenever he came to town Charles never failed to visit this store. He enjoyed the atmosphere and the talk. He observed the relationship between proprietor and customer, listened to the banter and the gossip, noted that underlying all was the serious purpose of net profit. He envied storemen, agents and travelling salesmen who seemed with little capital of their own to make a better living and have an easier life than farmers could afford. On the auspicious day that was to alter his life Charles happened to overhear a manu-

6

facturer's agent say to a friend as they proceeded together down the wooden steps of the store:

"My wife and I have been over to Owen Sound for a vacation. It was lucky I came back to-day. That one new line will bring in as much profit as the other three together."

Profit! How hard Charles worked for his and how slender it was. Holiday! When would he ever be likely to take Elizabeth away for a holiday? Acting on impulse, as he was often to do in years ahead and more than once with catastrophic results, he turned, went back into the store:

"I'd like to learn to be a merchant," he said, " will you take me as an apprentice?"

The store proprietor sized him up. He had known Charles since boyhood as an energetic, reliable youth. He knew him to be honest and of excellent family background. Now he saw before him a young married man, fair of hair and complexion, sturdy and compact, experienced in marketing and eager to learn. The proprietor considered that he could not lose and a bargain was struck. Charles was to commence work the following Monday morning. He was to receive a salary of $200 per annum and a thorough grounding in the mercantile business.

Elizabeth, who believed implicity in her husband, heard the news with equanimity and helped him launch into the first of many unsuccessful ventures. He sold his land, crop and stock. The profits of his first two years as a farmer and the proceeds of the sale of the farm would be used to supplement the $200 yearly salary which even in 1875 was very little with which to support a family.

For many years Charles' business ventures would take him far afield and involve many changes of abode. He was always in a hurry, always totally concerned with whatever project was currently absorbing his vast energies and restless spirit. On Elizabeth fell the burden of looking after their family. Fortunately for her, Grandfather Woodward was a kindly man with a great love for children and often she would bring the two oldest, Jack born in 1875 and Maggie in 1876, to stay with him for long visits at the old homestead near the town of Arthur.

Almost next door, with just two intervening farms, lived Elizabeth's parents. Henry Anderson, her youngest brother, and Cull

Woodward, her youngest brother-in-law, were only slightly older than her son and daughter. The four children played happily on the farm and Grandfather kept a loving eye on them from his new house on the north half of the farm across the lane.

In summer they fished in the creek which ran through the farm. In winter they coasted over the snow-covered hills on the sleds and wagons which skilled wheelwright John Woodward made for them. They explored the huge stone fireplace which took up half the living room and examined the nests made each summer by a colony of rooks. Henry Anderson, who lived to be 92 and became the grand old man of Sault Ste. Marie, was the recipient of a sleigh made by him and commenting on these happy days remarked:

"This sleigh I prized and used for years and I never forgot his kindly thought and the hours he must have spent in making it."

On the first day of his career as a merchant Charles reported to his new employer with an eagerness which he could scarcely contain. Soon he thought he would be permitted to wait on customers and would learn at first-hand more of the secrets of the art of trading.

The store owner failed to keep his part of the bargain. He used his apprentice for chores which he himself found tedious or distasteful. Charles packed butter, stoked furnaces, pasted labels on bottles and ran errands. He was not allowed to serve behind the counter, though to meet the public as a salesman was his burning ambition. The store owner imparted almost no information, either because his pupil already knew as much as he did, or because he wished for his own reasons to prolong the apprenticeship. Even the meagre salary had been misrepresented and Charles found that he was being paid $8.00 per month. The owner misjudged his man.

At the end of three months Charles resigned. They must have parted on good terms for this same merchant helped Charles select goods and stock his own store at Manitowaning two years later.

His next venture was in Northern Ontario. The Ontario Government had opened up the Parry Sound and Lake Nipissing District and the land there was reputed to be equal to any in the south. Settlers were moving in fast. Charles and two of his brothers-in-law decided to hurry there before the spring rush started. They took the train to Toronto where they had their first set-back. A taximan

8

offered to drive their luggage from the Union Depot to the Northern Railroad for seventy-five cents, but on arrival demanded, and by means of threats and abuse succeeded in obtaining, three times that amount.

"I was astounded," said Charles, "and soon became fighting mad."

Less than half a mile from the little town of Commanda Creek, one hundred and fifty miles north of Toronto, they secured two hundred acres of land. Their property was covered by two feet of snow but it adjoined the Government trail which was to become the main highway. The three young men congratulated themselves on obtaining such a convenient location. When the snow melted they found it was of such poor quality that it could not be used for farming. They managed to sell at a profit the supplies of oats, potatoes, bacon and flour which they had brought in. Then they walked out, sadder but wiser, 120 miles to Gravenhurst, the nearest point from which they could take the train to Toronto and thence back home.

At the Union Station they met with more misfortune. An unhappy looking young man told them that he had his railway ticket, cash and overcoat stolen from him on the train coming from London. He borrowed the price of a fare to Orangeville. As security he gave Charles a heavy gold ring. Then he disappeared forever. The ring turned out to be brass.

"I was so smart," lamented the diary.

Back at home Charles obtained work on a farm. This time it was not his own farm nor his father's. He could not endure working for another man so he did not stay long.

CHAPTER TWO

The First Woodward Store

Charles heard that good farmland was being sold at bargain prices on Manitoulin Island. He was told stories of Indian corn ten feet high, of rich crops of grain and fruits, of great ranges for cattle and sheep.

The Manitoulin, said to be the largest freshwater island in the world, had hundreds of miles of coastline, most of it facing the open waters of Lake Huron. There were fine beaches and it had always been a favourite haunt of sailors. Until the treaties of 1862 it belonged to the Ottawa Indians. Shortly after 1866 the land was put on the market. There were difficulties at first because the Indians near the Mission at Witwemikong opposed the treaty and would not recognize it but an agreement was reached by which the eastern part of the island would remain Indian land. It is still the largest unceded Indian Reserve in Canada.

Manitoulin is 100 miles long and in some places 40 miles wide, has 100 inland lakes, numerous streams, a well-drained soil and the greatest growth of mixed grasses east or west of the Rockies. So favourably endowed was the Manitoulin that the Indians were convinced it was the home of the Great Master of Life, Gitchi Manitou and named it accordingly.

In the early seventies the township of Gore Bay was organized, mills were erected, schools started and roads built. The settlers were able to boast: "The best sheep and wool are produced on the Island. Manitoulin turkeys bring a five cent per pound premium over southern birds. The Little Current cattle sale is the largest one-day sale in North America."

But all these developments were well in the future. When Charles decided to move to the Manitoulin it was just beginning to grow. Whether by good luck or good judgment, at least four times in his life he picked a place about to undergo an unexpectedly large expansion. Manitoulin Island was the first of such places. In 1875 there was no railway, no newspaper (the first issue of the *Manitoulin Enterprise,* the Island's first paper was published in November, 1877), no judge and no gaol. Mail came in summer by canoe or boat from Collingwood or Parry Sound, in winter by dogteam, giving at best a three-week service. Today Manitoulin Island has a population of 6500 whites and 2500 Indians but at that time the Indians greatly predominated.

Charles' employer gave him two weeks off work and he went as fast as he could across Georgian Bay to the Island. His ticket cost $2.50 and he slept on deck. As the crew was shorthanded he made some money working as a deckhand. SS *Manitoulin* docked right in the Main Street of Manitowaning, a small village on the east coast and an unexpectedly bustling port with frequent steamers coming and going. He was told that its name meant "Home of the Manitou" and was pronounced 'Man-it-war-ning' rhyming with 'darning'.

It was autumn and the beauty of the place was impressive. The vivid colouring of the maples, beeches and golden birches through which as he walked about he caught occasional glimpses of the bright blue bay was lovelier than anything he had ever seen. (Later Manitoulin became known as the Rainbow Country.) Even more important were the reportedly substantial opportunities for prosperity. He was so impressed that acting as usual on an impulse he bought sight unseen two hundred acres at Bidwell, on the east shore of Lake Manitou, twelve miles northwest of Manitowaning.

He wrote in his Reminiscences: "I then returned to the farmer with whom I was working. I explained everything to him and he let me off. I immediately moved up on to the Island. We freighted our chattels for eight miles where it was dumped. The other four miles was a bad trail by oxen and a rough sled called a jumper."

When Charles saw the acreage at Bidwell which he had bought sight unseen, even he was momentarily daunted. Huge boulders covered the ground. A wide expanse of raspberry bushes growing rank hid more and more stones. More than half the 200 acres were green bush. The man from whom he had bought them had promised, "there were not enough stones to line a cellar." Once again he had been tricked. He started to clear the land determined to get in thirty acres of crops before the spring but he, a farmer and the son of a farmer, knew that such an achievement was impossible.

"There were thousands of acres of good rich farming land on Manitoulin Island and I failed to secure any of it," he said with some bitterness. Little did he realize that his misfortune would prove to be a blessing.

The Woodwards had a one-room log cabin for their abode, unsuitable for a woman, however gallant, with a one-year-old child and another on the way. So Elizabeth returned to Arthur to stay with Charles' parents at any rate until their second child was born.

In no way discouraged, the indomitable Charles decided to abandon his fruitless battle with the stony soil and invest 500 of his dwindling dollars in merchandise. He would become a trader with the Indians and the few white families who were beginning to settle at the west end of Lake Manitou.

If he could get them to come over to Bidwell Landing in their sailboats or canoes he could save them a long journey to Manitowaning. So the ten by twelve foot cabin became a trading post and he built a log house for his family. He bartered mats, baskets, fish, furs, grain, potatoes, berries or any other commodity which could be turned into a dollar. He succeeded beyond his expectations but it was impossible to make an adequate living in such a seasonal market. He must move to a larger place with more people.

"I must get to some centre where boats call and people congregate," thought Charles.

He remembered Manitowaning, that busy port on the east shore, though at that time its population numbered barely two hundred. He had accumulated a capital of $2,000. He took as partner his young brother-in-law who knew nothing of merchandising but was able to contribute another $1,000. There were already two general stores in Manitowaning and another man had announced his decision to start a third. Such competition made no difference to Charles' plans. His chief concern was to have his place open for business before the newcomer. He realized that four stores were

Charles and Elizabeth Woodward with their two eldest children John and Margaret. Margaret died aged 16 and John aged 25.

Manitowaning Village, Manitoulin Island, 1879. Charles' store was in High Street, a few doors beyond the buildings shown in this picture.

too many for such a small village but there was a big country around it. Moreover, right across the bay was Wikwemikong, the unceded Indian Reserve with its Catholic Mission. There was no store in the Indian village and their trading was done at Manitowaning.

Full of optimism and confidence he built a two-storey frame building on High Street sandwiched between S. G. Winkler, Hardware and Tinsmith, and Alec Mitchell's Blacksmith's shop. Charles maintained a correspondence with the Winklers all his life.

"I often think of the years we lived so close together," he wrote to Sam Winkler in 1926, "with a partnership-well dug on the line-fence between us and not a jar or bad word between us."

He went to Toronto to purchase merchandise and the proprietor of the store where he served his brief apprenticeship went with him.

"The stock was well assorted and not a surplus of any one thing," he recorded.

Charles' partner was his brother-in-law, John Anderson. The two young men were enthusiastic and the store of Woodward and Anderson was well received by the people of Manitowaning.

During the six winter months the waters round Manitoulin Island were frozen and no freight could be brought except by sled over the ice. A six months' supply of goods had to be accumulated while navigation remained open, and often until the ice broke up the islanders were on short rations. During those long winter months mail was despatched from Parry Sound every three weeks and had to be carried one hundred and fifty miles over the ice by Indian guides who ran great risks and suffered extreme hardships. Sometimes they lost the mail and their lives as well.

Unexpectedly a representative of one of the Toronto firms arrived and persuaded Charles to buy additional stock for the winter.

"Leave it all to me. I know just what you want. You are doing a good business and it is going to grow."

He ignored Charles' list and before long some nine thousand dollars' worth of unwelcome merchandise started to come in.

"This mean and unscrupulous man loaded us up with all kinds of goods which his firm did not carry and which he had to procure from outside firms and on which he got a percentage or profit. This kind of trickery I was not used to," lamented poor Charles.

15

At the close of navigation, business on Manitoulin Island dropped; some days the partners took in less than five dollars in cash. Merchandising conditions could hardly have been more difficult. The final blow was a cheque for $600 accepted from a customer and passed on to a creditor. The cheque was not honoured. Charles was ruined; his partner resigned. The sheriff came over from the Mainland and closed the store. Both Charles' and Elizabeth's parents owned farms free of debt or encumbrance and were comfortably off. The creditors agreed to accept their farms as security. The debt was $5,000 and had to be paid in one and a half years with six per cent interest. Not only did Charles' father guarantee his son's debts but he also lent him $3,000 to replenish the empty shelves of his store.

"As the stock dwindles and becomes incomplete, one does not have the same chance against competition," Charles reflected.

His father offered no word of criticism or admonishment but continued to show the same strong trust in him that he had always shown.

This disaster taught Charles a lesson which was to stay with him all his life. He was sincerely fond of his parents and shaken at the troubles he had caused them. His pride was hurt. With the utmost determination he resolved to make his store a success and repay his father every cent he had borrowed, within the shortest possible time. As the author of all his woes he saw the abominable practice of buying or selling on credit. From now on everything would be on a cash basis. He would pay cash for his stock, he would demand cash from his customers, he would never again overspend his budget. The Manitowaning store was renamed Woodward's Cash Store. To the end of his life the word 'credit' was so abhorrent to him that even when buying on terms had become a North American way of life which no merchandiser could afford to ignore and when Woodward's had become a multi-million dollar store in Western Canada, such dread words as 'credit' or 'charge-account' were never used in his presence. Seventy-five years later the Credit Office in every Woodward Store was still known as the Finance Bureau.

At first he had to contend with many difficulties. He had to meet his payments every three months on his extension notes. His credit was bad, his reputation tarnished. One of the three rival store-

16

keepers (the diary gave his name as 'Mr. James' and indicated this was a pseudonym) was an experienced businessman who was continually seeking underhand ways to outwit and cheat his competitors and with whom Charles had frequent clashes. All these problems he steadily overcame. The experience of failure was what he needed to build business acumen.

"I was soon becoming a rising merchant and I found when a person is successful financially or otherwise the astonishing number of persons there is to flatter and fawn upon you. I was developing character, confidence and a certain amount of hardness," he wrote.

Several incidents had conspired to bring about that hardness: the agent who had landed him with $9,000 worth of unwanted goods; the worthless $600 cheque; the young man with the gold ring; the misrepresented land in Commanda and on Manitoulin; the taximan at the Toronto railway station . . .

One hundred cords of wood which Charles had intended to sell to the steamboats when they commenced operations in the spring were stolen by a business competitor. He sued the thief in the small debts court. A customer who forged another man's name on the back of a note Charles had committed and sent to gaol. He was greatly changed from the trusting young farm boy he had once been.

CHAPTER THREE

Another Wild Adventure

Charles worked long hours, cut expenses to a minimum and built a reputation as an honest merchant who sold good products for low prices.

His advertisements began to appear in the *Manitoulin Expositor,* modest at first but as the months and years went by, they grew larger, the type bolder and blacker, the claims more extravagant.

May 24, 1879. The Store lately occupied by Woodward and Anderson will re-open in a week or so. Look out for our advertisement.

September 20, 1879. Charles Woodward carries on alone as per the last two months. Credit is out on and after September 29. Goods to be bought at lower figures for cash.

October 18, 1879. Great Bargains at Woodward's Cheap Cash Store. Since adopting the cash system we have bought goods very low for cash and will offer the same. We give you a list of a few things that can be bought from us. Large plug tobacco 4¢ a plug or 45¢ a pound and in 5 lb. lots greater reduction will be made. We have the best selection of sugars ever brought to the Island at prices that defy competition. Our teas are acknowledged by all to be a Specialty. We have thousands of articles used every day that we are selling cheaper than any house we can think of.

We sell Cheaper than can be bought in Toronto!

Goods Marked Down At Rock Bottom Prices!

Soon he was able to afford the front page of the *Expositor* and was offering:

. . . a full range of Winceys, Cottons, Flannels, Fullcloths, Tweeds, Lustres, Ladies' Clouds and Scarves. Scythes, snaths and cradles. Everything needed for Teaming and Livery . . .

as well as more readily identifiable articles such as:

Crockery, Glassware and Harvest tools.
Syrups, Dried Apples and Raisins, Butter and Eggs.
Men's long boots $1.50 to $4.00, Women's laced boots from $1.00 up.

In his determination to have a cash business he pulled no punches:

All outstanding Accounts and Notes must be paid or arranged for before the 10th of April or they will be sued irrespective of persons.
Pay up and save yourself unpleasant dunners!
1% interest per month to be added to those who haven't paid their overdue Notes and accounts.
All debts not settled before April 15 will be positively placed in Court for collection.
After September 20 the books will be closed against credit and all will have to pay up promptly.

Charles attacked his competitors as aggressively as his creditors:

Jan. 17, 1880. $100 Reward to any person proving that Woodwards have two prices in their store or sell to one man dearer than another. Their goods are all marked in plain figures with a uniform profit not as is the custom in some stores, one article at cost price to make the public believe they sell very cheap, while other goods are sold at 100 per cent. So don't be deceived by a great show of bargains but go to Woodward's and Realize The Truth.

At times he seemed to be resisting an inclination to throw in his hand:

May 29, 1880. Owing to the numerous requests of our numerous patrons we have resolved to continue business in Manitowaning . . .

Within eighteen months of his new start he had settled every debt completely and by mid-1881 his records showed that he had

19

made an additional $7000 nearly all in cash. His business had become well-known and well-established and he decided to expand:

> May 6, 1881. "A considerable addition is to be made to the Woodward Store," reported the *Expositor* editorially, "by tearing down the partition in the rear and extending several feet further back."

Then his old restlessness and driving ambition dislocated the career he was building and sent him on a wild adventure eight hundred miles away.

That year Winnipeg had been joined by rail to Eastern Canada. Speculators and settlers from all over the country flocked there and Manitoba enjoyed an unprecedented land boom as wild as it was sudden. The mass hysteria of buying and selling which characterizes real estate fever spread over the Province. The stories of the huge wealth being amassed overnight in this Western province reached the shores of Manitoulin Island and sent many men off to seek their fortunes. Charles heard the rumours, too, and decided with his usual impulsiveness to risk all on a 'get-rich-quick' venture. It failed completely but it taught him another lesson which much later he was to put to good advantage. His friend Thomas Parkinson had long been wanting to buy into his store. Now he sold him the complete business. Elizabeth and their four children moved across the Inlet to stay on his father's farm while he was away. Then he bought two carloads of oxen and shipped them to Brandon. He knew about oxen. He had dealt in them before as a farmer. Everything he had heard about the prices they would fetch in Manitoba encouraged him to believe that here was a way of making more money in six months than he had made in five years in Manitowaning.

But he did not stay in Manitoba for six months. Before the middle of April, 1882, the bubble burst and the boom collapsed. Misrepresentations and chiselling, competition from other developing provinces and a flooding of the Red River, the worst flood in Canadian history, were contributing factors. Real estate values which had been immense one day were worthless the next, fortunes were lost overnight, suicides abounded. Charles considered himself fortunate to be able to sell his oxen at a nominal price.

"I lost heavily when the boom burst," he recorded, "and returned to Manitoulin Island, a wiser and poorer man."

The lesson he had learned was that there were no quick easy paths to wealth or if there were they were not for him. Hard work, honest practice, diligent and unremitting endeavour, steady regular habits . . . these were the tools with which to build a fortune. Though he remained impulsive and a gambler he never again expected to become rich in an easy way.

The two principal towns on Manitoulin Island were Gore Bay and Little Current. Charles heard of a merchant at Gore Bay who had gone bankrupt and was desperate to sell his store if the purchaser had ready cash. Charles had not lost all his money in Manitoba. He had salted some away in the bank of Manitowaning and he had waiting for him enough capital to make a deal. There were several stores in Gore Bay but he had proved himself well able to cope with competition. His observations of local storekeepers led him to believe that they mostly preferred to chatter and gossip with their customers and that they seldom thought of ways of increasing their business or improving their methods.

After paying a visit to Gore Bay and making sure that the property was worthwhile, he set off for Toronto where the purchase papers had to be signed. By a coincidence Mr. James, the cunning and unscrupulous rival storekeeper from Manitowaning, was on the same train on exactly the same mission. Each was anxious to conceal his intentions from the other and neither would admit the object of his journey. Charles won the contest by slipping out of the baggage car as the train was pulling into the Union Station, rushing to the Sheriff's office and making his deposit. There was a tragic end to the story. Mr. James and his brother returned to Manitowaning on the steamer *Asia* which was wrecked on September 21, 1882. All but two of the 140 passengers were drowned. Thomas Parkinson who had bought Charles' store was another of the victims.

Soon thereafter the *Expositor* reported:

> Charles Woodward was a passenger by the 'Africa' on her down trip Tuesday. He is about to start business in Gore Bay in Thompson's old stand.

Gore Bay, Manitoulin Island. Charles had his third store here and operated it so successfully that he soon built another at Thessalon. W. C. Woodward was born at Gore Bay.

He found a house near the store where he could establish his wife and children. In the spring of 1882 their fourth child, Donald Anderson, had been born and as usual, Elizabeth had gone back to their parents at Arthur for the event. Charles was now thirty and anxious to resume living a regular family life. So far he could not claim to have achieved much success as a businessman, but there was no sign that his several catastrophes had cost him one particle of his self-assurance. He was as cheerfully dominating as ever.

Gore Bay, named for the then Lieutenant-Governor of Ontario, was the most centrally located town on the Island, being fifty miles from Meldrum Bay, the most westerly point and fifty-two miles from Manitowaning, the most easterly point.

In 1883 in Gore Bay, Manitoulin's District Town, you could buy a whitefish for a dime, a sack of potatoes for 75 cents, a side of beef for 7 or 8 cents a pound. If you visited the "very elaborate Barbershop" of Mr. Charles White and paid him an extra 25 cents, you could use the large, round bathtub which he had recently installed in his backroom. A Canadian invention called the telephone had just gone into service between New York and Chicago but you would not be using it on the Manitoulin for another twenty years.

You could attend a service conducted by the Reverend W. M. Tooke at All Saints Church built in 1882 and lament the fact that the small congregation (24) was due to a "Methodist attraction". (Charles Woodward was the Secretary-Treasurer of the Methodist Church.) Your annual taxes on two good-sized lots on Phipps Street would have been $4.08 but you would have had to pay a small monthly sum to the school for each pupil. If your suffering and your courage were sufficient you could visit Mr. Cole, the dentist, and allow him without anaesthesia to give you a taste of his gigantic drill.

In winter you could stand on the high bluffs above the bay and look across the ice onto the distant haze which concealed Darch Island, twelve miles away and called the Halfway House; Little Detroit, another six miles on; and finally Cutler, on the North Shore, where if you were a merchant you must go with your dog-teams for supplies, and for every step of that cruel, cold journey you would be longing for a bridge to join the Manitoulin to the mainland. (It came in 1912.) When you got back you would serve your customers in your tightly-buttoned black suit, high collar and bow tie, having taken in your stride a journey which today would bring a battery of amazed television cameras whirring about you.

You could meet your friends at any of the three hotels, all named to make clear that Gore Bay was without any doubt an exceptionally fine harbour, Robert Porter's Ocean House, built in 1876, the Atlantic or the Pacific, and discuss the affairs of the day in a highly civilized atmosphere.

It took a pioneer's courage to run a store on the Island in the 1880's. Said a visitor from Newfoundland who came to investigate business conditions as he hurried back home: "You Manitoulin guys are freshwater Newfies."

Gore Bay was the headquarters on Manitoulin Island for timber. Railway ties, telegraph poles and paving timber were taken out in winter and provided employment for the men in the camps on the mainland. The other three stores monopolized the timber business and guarded it jealously from intruders. After months of vainly trying to break this monopoly Charles resorted to bluff. He had large notices printed stating that he would "contract with anyone for any quantity of timber and would pay cash for it when it was on the beach." These notices he sent to every post office in the neighbourhood of Gore Bay with the request that they be posted. They indicated that an unknown newcomer had managed to make his way into the timber market and aroused so much curiosity that timber representatives came to call on him. Then he admitted that he had been bluffing and eventually charmed them into giving him some business.

"I think there probably never was a business so demoralizing as the tie, pole and post timber business," he wrote in his diary. "Stealing timber after being stamped and culled was prevalent. I have known settlers block up holes and pile ties with short ends sawn off straight (which was no tie) and have it counted."

He also noted that some large firms sold burned ties as though they were green and passed off culls as good ties.

Induced by the fact that they could buy land for fifty cents an acre, settlers were coming in at a great rate. They were at once

Charles' customers and the agents from whom he bought the timber which he sold to the big companies. In an atmosphere of chicanerie and double dealing he held strongly to two principles. One was that straight dealing always paid, the other that customers must be protected even if such protection meant a quarrel with a big company.

He dealt in grain and furs. He sold beef carcases and dressed hogs for the Algoma Mills where five hundred men were employed. The supplies had to be taken by team forty miles over the ice and sometimes he had to take great risks. On one occasion he learned that a number of railway camps were about to close unexpectedly early and, as their closure would mean loss of business, he decided to go across with two sleighs loaded with meats, even though the ice was considered unsafe. After peddling his meat for a week he started back home and on the way he became lost in a snowstorm. He was alone, there were no landmarks, he was enveloped in thick haze and, to complete his misery, he found that in his haste to leave for home he had left his lunch behind. His rugged physique and doggedness saw him through.

In order to meet competition he devised novel ways of attracting customers. Never was he satisfied to sit back and wait for business to come. He neither drank nor gambled. His hobby was his work and he preferred to work alone. Sometimes he got business because he was the only dealer who could buy for cash. Thrift and diligence paid off; within three years he had the finest store building and the largest retail business on the Island. The more money he made the more austere were his living habits, the more stringent his economies and the harder he worked. But he did buy for the first time some "really good furniture" for his home.

CHAPTER FOUR

A Crippling Fire

A conversation took place in 1885 which made another sweeping change in Charles Woodward's life. While on a business visit to Sault Ste. Marie he met an old friend, Captain Robinson of SS *Frances Smith.*

"I have some information which may interest you," said the Captain. "The Canadian Pacific is about to build a branch line from Algoma Mills to the Soo. I'd judge that will mean good opportunities for an ambitious young man."

Robinson went on to say that CPR representatives had been investigating a small town called Thessalon, midway between Algoma and Sault Ste. Marie, which they considered a good place for another store. Charles made an immediate decision. On the way home he disembarked at Thessalon, quietly rented a building and made arrangements to commence business there.

He had a friend —to whom in his memoirs he gives the name of 'Si' — who wanted, but could not afford, to be married, and who seemed a reliable, clever young man. Si jumped at the opportunity of running the Thessalon store under Charles' direction at a salary of $900 per annum plus a share of the profits. The timing was exactly right. When the expansion which Captain Robinson had predicted came about, the Thessalon store was open and ready for business. In the first six months a profit of $4000 was made and sales continued steadily to grow. Now Si was able to marry and thereafter "he was not nearly so attentive to business." Not only was he constantly away travelling about the country but he indulged himself in all kinds of extravagances which could not possibly have

26

been afforded on his salary in less than two years. Periodically Charles visited the Thessalon store. In the spring of 1887, instead of an expected profit of at least $25,000, he found liabilities of $30,000. Charles' judgment of people whether as partners or managers had again been at fault. It seemed that he was a man who worked better alone. He dismissed Si and decided not to replace him.

The Thessalon store represented a considerable investment and was substantially larger than the other. Disaster could only be averted by selling the business at Gore Bay and moving with his family to Thessalon.

The Woodwards had been Islanders for almost twelve years and at first the comparative sophistication of the Mainland was alarming to Elizabeth. Charles kept telling himself: "You'll never get rich at Gore Bay" and was sure that destiny was drawing him on.

Thessalon was an old town. It appeared on maps as early as 1670 and in the war of 1812, Canadian settlers and Indians had helped the British capture two American armed schooners there. It was incorporated in 1887, the year of the Woodwards' arrival, and like Gore Bay was a lumber centre. Its position on the north channel of Lake Huron made it a busy harbour. Boats went every day to Sault Ste. Marie; numerous steamers and sailing ships plied from Georgian Bay ports and those on the North Shore as well as Buffalo and Toronto. When the projected CPR branchline from Algoma to the Soo was announced, Thessalon's population increased and was now three times Gore Bay's. Ten miles to the west was Bruce Mines, before 1875 one of the most important mines in Canada. It was now closed but there existed a substantial town larger than Thessalon. The Methodist Church was a small, time-worn building south of Mr. McGillivray's blacksmith shop and there the Reverend James McAllister conducted revival meetings and operated a social centre.

Charles noted with no consternation at all that there were several well-established stores: J. B. Dobie's was the biggest, John Glanville drew business because he also had the telegraph office, W. Bennet operated a successful hardware store on Main and Huron and there were others. A new bridge, a new post office, another hotel, the Queen's, to compete with Thessalon House, another planing mill, a race track . . . these were some of the signs of progress which greeted Charles and Elizabeth as they took their first walk along the winding streets and by the canal.

The fourth Woodward Store was on the east side of Main Street on a site now occupied by the Town Hall. Next door was a livery stable. The family, Charles and Elizabeth, John 12, Margaret 11, May 6, Donald 5, Ann 4 and William 2 lived over the store. Peg and Percival were yet to come.

At Thessalon Charles had a taste of unpopularity. Si was a genial man who had given his customers abundant and sometimes unlimited credit. Charles immediately installed a policy of 'Cash only' to the vast indignation of many regular customers. He had to battle against bankrupt stocks, use every means in his power to reduce the very considerable debts which Si had left. With his usual tactics of dedication to the job Charles brought the Thessalon store into line. By 1890 he had a thriving business, was worth $30,000 and had won the respect of the townspeople to such an extent that he was offered and accepted an appointment as town magistrate.

Ontario at that time followed the British practice of having the majority of criminal cases tried in magistrates' courts. Magistrates were usually unpaid laymen but might impose fines or even terms of imprisonment.

"(Accepting the appointment) was a big mistake as I found out," wrote Charles. "You cannot dispense justice without giving offence to one party or another and there is always a lot of contrariness . . . As a magistrate I saw many different characters, some revengeful and mean who had no scruples."

Suddenly catastrophe struck again.

On a cold morning in April 1890, as Charles went to open his store according to custom at 7:15 a.m., he was greeted by a fearsome stench and a horrifying sight. The whole building had been gutted by fire and was still smouldering. Everything was destroyed except the safe and its contents. The cause of the fire was a mystery never solved. Charles was always first to arrive and the last to leave. The night before, he had put the store to bed with his usual meticulous care, leaving nothing to chance. What could have caused that conflagration? He himself had little doubt about its origin. He knew that he had made enemies — among the 'mean and

28

revengeful' characters who had come up for trial before him, and among others who were still paying off debts to him.

He had placed a sarcastic advertisement in the *Thessalon Advocate* of March 19, 1890, which ran as follows:

Depression of 1890

Business has got so demoralized it seems impossible to make a living and pay a hundred cents on the dollar. The only apparent way to make money now and do business is to buy all the goods you can whether you want them or not, and then sell them for what they will fetch, pay nothing for them or as little as you can, and then seek the indulgence of your creditors who will kindly let you off 10 or 15 cents on the dollar. Those who succeed in making the largest liability and burst with the smallest asset get the most credit by being smart and clever.

These abrasive remarks brought angry mutterings, especially from his creditors.

He had even incurred political enmity because, though himself a Liberal, he had taken a successful stand against Sir Oliver Mowat's Liberal Government over timber legislation which it had enacted and which seemed to Charles to favour American rather than Canadian interests. He had ample reason to believe that the fire was arson, not accident. It was a staggering blow, for he had only $2,000 insurance and faced a loss of possibly $15,000 in merchandise. But because of his cash policies he had no debts.

He and Elizabeth debated far into the night whether they should stay in Thessalon or make a fresh start elsewhere.

W. C. Woodward and sister Cora Lily (Peg) — 1890. He was 5, she 3. Peg later married architect Sholto Smith.

CHAPTER FIVE

Vancouver, 1891

Charles Woodward decided to seek elsewhere that fortune which he meant to have. He considered moving to the United States because of its proximity, warmer climate and economic advantages. Canadians were often departing across the border to find a higher standard of living. Indeed, during the long depression of the 1880's commercial union with the United States at times seemed inevitable. But he had no wish to change his nationality. His father was English and he, a loyal British subject. All his life he had lived with threats of Yankee intrusions and annexations. He would prefer to go west to the country which would later be designated Alberta or to British Columbia. The territory beyond the Rocky Mountains, little known to people in Ontario, fascinated and absorbed him. Moreover since 1886 there had been a regular transcontinental train service with the Pacific terminus established one year later at the new city of Vancouver. Advertisements proclaimed British Columbia to be 'the land of opportunity, a lovely country unequalled for its beauty and salubrity of climate.'

In the spring of 1891 Charles moved his family back to the farmhouse at Arthur and alone boarded a CPR train bound for the West. He sat up for three days and nights in a Colonist car with his carpet-bag close beside him. Though adversity had made him suspicious and niggardly, the courage of this man at thirty-nine, who had already sustained three economic disasters, whose wife was ill and pregnant and whose eight children ranged in age from one to sixteen years, setting out to seek his fortune in unknown places two thousand miles away, cannot but command respect.

"My great loss through this fire was very trying as I had worked very hard but I was in the prime of life and not easily discouraged," he wrote.

He stopped off first at Calgary where he was greeted by a blizzard, and then to Kamloops where the temperature was colder than at Thessalon. But he tramped around in the cold and biting wind and tried to assess the marketing potential of each of these towns. He went on to Port Moody, a growing city of British Columbia which was originally intended to be the western terminus of the CPR and therefore was bitterly opposed to the afterthought which resulted in the line being extended to Vancouver. At Port Moody an auction sale of town lots was being advertised, sidewalks were being laid and the streets graded with teams and scrapers. Thousands of feet of lumber had been deposited over plots bearing the names of purchasers who it was claimed were about to build houses or businesses there. All this excitement lasted only until the day of the land sale when in many cases the lumber was gathered up and the building operations halted.

Charles investigated New Westminster and was impressed. It was unique in combining the atmosphere of the early American West with that of early Victorian England. More important, it had an abundance of good agricultural land, a long navigable river and consequently cheap transportation to markets. Governor Seymour had once called New Westminster "the most respectable, manly and enterprising little community with which I was ever acquainted," and had made it British Columbia's capital city.

It happened that the first tramway from New Westminster to Vancouver was opened while Charles was exploring New Westminster and the ever curious Charles still clutching his carpet-bag was one of the single-track street-car line's first passengers. The journey through the forest took two hours. He remained in Vancouver and learned some facts that interested him. Though the city had been totally destroyed by fire only five years previously and every building razed, a new city had risen from its ashes almost the next day. Already by the census of April 5th it had a population of 13,800. Three large and famous steamers, the *Empress of India,* the *Empress of China* and the *Empress of Japan* had recently docked in Vancouver. What trade implications that event had! The Vancouver Illuminating Company on Abbott Street between Hastings Street and Pender Street with a capacity of three hundred lamps had given Vancouver its first electric power plant. A town tram system had been opened to public traffic over six miles of line only a few months before and was already about to be expanded.

Vancouver was encountering hostility, like any other ambitious upstart. The citizens of Victoria, jealous for their own businesses, threatened to boycott Eastern merchants if they appointed agents elsewhere in British Columbia and spread a story that Vancouver's port was unsafe for shipping, a rumour dispelled by the arrival of the Empress ships. The name 'Vancouver' was disliked as being possibly prejudicial to the prosperity of Vancouver Island and infuriating for Americans whose city of Vancouver, Washington, had been founded sixty years earlier. For several years the little settlement had been known as Gastown, after the river pilot "Gassy" Jack Deighton. Then it was renamed Granville in honour of Britain's Colonial Secretary and so remained until the city was incorporated. Then CPR General Manager, Sir William Van Horne, changed the name again.

"This eventually is destined to be a great city of Canada," he said. "We must see to it that it has a name that will designate its place on the map of Canada. Vancouver it shall be if I have the ultimate decision."

Charles feared that Vancouver might turn out to be another CPR boom town which would vanish in the wake of the railway like some of the communities in Manitoba which he had seen suddenly created by the railway and equally suddenly cease to be. But the city seemed to him to have a robustness, a willingness to disregard calamity and the bludgeonings of chance, a philosophy similar to his own. Victoria, which he also visited and investigated, and New Westminster had more sophistication and were socially more mature. But soon he decided that brash, unconventional Vancouver was the place for him. With its majestic setting amid the mountains and towering trees, with the oceans and the ships of the world at its doors, with a climate which kept it green the year round, how could it fail to fulfill Van Horne's prediction? Then and there Charles affirmed a faith in Vancouver which he never lost.

In an exuberant prophecy which was to fall somewhat short of the mark he declared in 1928 to C. J. Winkler: "In fifty years Vancouver will be the biggest city in Canada."

Before he left to return to Ontario, he took an option on two lots at the corner of Harris Street (now Georgia Street) and Westminster Avenue (now Main Street). Nearby Cordova Street was the principal business thoroughfare and though there were more fashionable areas, the cost of real estate there was much higher.

Westminster Avenue was the main thoroughfare to Westminster and built up for at least a half-mile around the site for his proposed store. A half block away over a small shop was the First Baptist Church with Vancouver's first Salvation Army hut next to it. A little way up the street could be seen the tower of the market-hall, and just beyond it, the tall trees and thick brush that bordered the road to the Royal City.

Nearby on the northeast corner of Gore Avenue stood St. James', Vancouver's first Anglican Church, which had been built by the City's earliest pioneers in a clearing in the forest. It was destroyed in the fire and rebuilt in 1887 on two acres of ground bought for $450. On Mount Pleasant, east of Westminster Avenue, were creeks where children went to spear salmon. Grass grew where the first Public Library and City Hall were built a few years later. The passing of a streetcar was an infrequent event, for this was still the era of carts, carriages and gigs. There was a big livery stable on the Avenue. Palmer's Hay and Feed Store did a thriving business.

On his return to Thessalon, Charles was faced with another grave problem. The health of his wife, patient uncomplaining Elizabeth, had been steadily deteriorating. She had lost weight, she tired easily and a racking cough never left her. Though she tried to conceal it an even more frightening symptom had appeared while he was away in Vancouver; she had been spitting blood. The diagnosis was a rapidly advancing case of tuberculosis.

There could be no thought of abandoning the plan to move to the West. The die was cast. Charles' purchase of the two lots on Main Street had taken most of his capital. He had to go back to them as quickly as possible, start building his store and fulfilling his destiny.

It was decided that he should leave immediately with their eight children. Elizabeth would follow as soon as she was well enough to travel. Jack, the eldest son, almost seventeen, was ever a strong

34

right arm for his parents. Because of his father's frequent absences from home and his mother's failing health, he was accustomed to looking after his younger brothers and sisters. The six-day train journey from Toronto to Vancouver in a Colonist car was a highly uncomfortable experience for the young Woodwards and but for Jack's cheerful ministrations would have been insupportable.

When the Woodwards arrived in Vancouver in the first week of January 1892 the city was at its most delightful. Every day was one of warm, bright sunshine. Charles lost no time. He rented a house for his family on Barnard Street near his store lot and immediately made arrangements for a loan of $7,000 at nine per cent interest. Before the end of the week work had begun on a building seventy feet deep and fifty-five feet wide. The lot was fifty-seven feet wide: two feet he left to be used jointly with whoever built on the adjoining lot.

"But those owners never agreed. Two feet of valuable ground were wasted with no revenue from it for over forty years," he grumbled.

Charles worked with the builders himself. He had the earth excavated from the foundations put into some of the hollows on Harris Street which he said "needed filling up and now had levelled down nicely." Then he presented the City with a bill for two hundred and eighty-seven large double loads of earth which the City declined to pay. Thanks to the co-operation of the weather the store was completed in less than two months and was opened on Saturday, March 1st.

"The takings were satisfactory," he recorded in his diary for that day.

One side of the floor was for boots and shoes, the other for groceries. Before long he added drygoods and men's wear which he had noted were not sold elsewhere in the neighbourhood.

His wife and the new baby Ruby Fay arrived from Ontario but he was too busy to notice how pale and thin they both were.

Since the store was only partially complete and an easy prey for a thief, Charles decided to sleep there until it was well enclosed and safe. On the night after the opening he was aroused by noises and was just in time to surprise two men trying to force the safe. One was so alarmed that he jumped through a plate glass window, the other, after threatening to blow out Charles' brains, also escaped.

35

*C.Woodward's at Westminster Avenue and Harris (Main and Georgia Streets)
— c. 1897. Charles worked with the builders himself to have his first store
in Vancouver, opened on March 1, 1892, three months after his arrival in
the city.*

He was less concerned with the danger to himself than with the expense of replacing the window which was not insured.

From the first his was to be a working man's store with narrow aisles and no credit allowed. He wrestled with the problem of credit for a month but eventually resolved to abide by his principle of cash only. His chief hope of meeting competition was to sell more cheaply than his competitors, the practice he had followed religiously at Manitowaning, Gore Bay and Thessalon. It was to remain his guiding rule.

His first years in Vancouver were fraught with difficulties. He was operating on the proverbial shoestring. Mortgage payments had to be met, merchandise and fixtures bought. On top of these expenses he had heavy bills from doctors for his wife, his eldest daughter Margaret and the new baby, Ruby, all of whom were victims of the dread illness, the scourge of those times, consumption.

In August 1892 loyal, loving Elizabeth, who had stood by him in every catastrophe, died followed two weeks later by the baby. Sixteen-year-old Margaret lasted only a few months before she too succumbed.

The real estate boom which had promised unbounded prosperity for Vancouver came to an abrupt end. Logging orders were cancelled, construction halted. A financial crisis depressed the United States. A devastating flood of the Fraser River, equal in ferocity to the flood which Charles had encountered in Manitoba in 1882, compounded the misery of the early 1890's in British Columbia. It was not surprising that once again Charles found himself unable to meet his debts and anxious to persuade the Eastern wholesale houses from whom he bought to settle for fifty cents on the dollar "in three-six-nine and twelve months with a Chattel Mortgage on my merchandise as security."

His was one of many small Vancouver stores forced by the times into bankruptcy and he must have been one of the few who, years later, repaid the other fifty cents with interest. He claimed that the interest amounted to more than the principal.

"In those days," he wrote, "my pride was often hit, almost more than I could bear sometimes, but I fought doggedly on. I had a family to provide for."

He had, indeed. There were still six children at home, none of

37

whom was older than eleven, and he had no wife to care for them. Jack, his eldest son on whom all had leaned so heavily, was at College two thousand miles away. No wonder the Woodwards learned to be self-reliant.

Since he hated paying rent he bought a lot cheaply in the Mount Pleasant district at 401 Fifth Avenue, and contracted for a small house to be built on it. When it was finished he mortgaged it for little more than he paid for the property. Every day except Sunday he opened the store at 7.30 a.m., lunched in it and kept it open until 7.00 p.m. or later. He had no help except on Saturdays when eleven-year-old Donald lent a hand.

To reach his new home Charles had to cross the Avenue Bridge, a narrow, trestle bridge over False Creek where the Canadian National Railway Depot now stands. One night he was accosted by a man who ran at him and tried to overpower him. Charles, who was not lacking in courage, lashed out with his fists, hitting his adversary several times in the face. Luckily he managed to attract the attention of Mr. Bailey, one of his customers who lived at the other end of the bridge and came to his assistance. The foot-pad turned and fled.

That encounter led to a similar one shortly afterwards which was less successful. When he left the store at the end of the day he was sometimes carrying $100 or more and was always uneasy until he reached his house. He decided to carry a revolver. On this occasion the night was dark and rainy: close behind him he could hear someone sloshing through the mud on the opposite side of the street. The more he hurried the nearer the footsteps sounded. He became convinced that they belonged to the robber who had attacked him previously. Suddenly a man ran across and stopped in front of him. Charles drew the revolver, shot at him and he dropped.

"He was up without touching the ground," remarked Charles with a rare flash of humour, "and he started to run, yelling 'Murder, murder!' He jumped over a high fence into the yard of a friend, Mr. Towler who was an alderman of the City. I had not enough sense to go home about my business but followed him into Mr. Towler's house to render any assistance I could and explain the reason I was shooting at him."

Charles' victim turned out to be one of his near neighbours who

38

had been seeing a lady friend home and was running to get out of
the rain. He was not injured but nevertheless took Charles to the
Police Court next day where he was fined fifteen dollars for firing
off a gun within city limits.

On January 9, 1958, Barry Mather of the Vancouver Sun re-
counted the shooting incident and elicited the following letter from
a reader:

Bradner, B.C.

Dear Sir:

It was with great interest that I read your column tonight,
as our Dad was the William Towler mentioned in Mr. Woodward's records. At that time we were living at 136 Dufferin
St., now 2nd Avenue East, and I remember hearing a voice
pleading with my dad to let him come in. He was yelling that
he was shot. Soon afterwards another man was at the door,
but the first man was afraid that Mr. Woodward was coming
to finish the job. However, when both men got a look at each
other, they knew that they were neighbours.

My half-brother was reporter for the "World" paper at that
time so that may account for the news getting in the paper.
It was exciting while it lasted. Yes, Woodward's Store and
Vancouver have come a long way since those days, or rather
since that night. And thinking of the past brought to my mind
again the changes we saw in that part of Vancouver — even
in the years we lived there.

Gone are the two slaughter houses. Beg pardon, abattoir
sounds better, but the flavour was awful in those days —
especially when the tide was low.

The dog pound was across the street — road, rather — so
it was handy for the pound-keeper to get dog food on "killing
days". Naturally the dogs objected to their surroundings and
let the countryside know it. One night someone took some of
the boards off at the back, so the pound-keeper would have
to go and round them up the next day.

I have looked through some clippings, but I cannot find the
years that my dad was Alderman. I am sure I heard him say
more than once that it was in the days when it was counted
an honour to be elected — no pay then. My dad died in 1917
in his 75th year.

And as I sit in the easy chair and read again your column,
I can see that man coming home, past Thorneview Apts. They

39

were not built then. Down he goes — up and off at top speed and into our house.

Vancouver Casket Company's premises are on one of the lots my dad owned. Our house was on the next one west, while the third lot was Terminal City Poultry Yards. I doubt that any of the buildings are standing today, although a few years ago our old house was still there. Houses were well built in those days.

Well I have been back to 1895, so now I had better get to 1958 and read the rest of the paper, but it has been a treat to know that my dad had a part in Vancouver's affairs.

Sincerely,
(signed) Mrs. Fenwick Fatkin
(Charlotte Towler)

Since handbills were cheaper than newspaper advertising, Charles hired boys to stand at the school gates, and give out printed sheets describing items such as: "Good strong boots for boys or girls for seventy-five cents to one dollar per pair," or "Boys' caps fifteen cents." School books were offered at cut prices.

The litter on the school-grounds did not make Woodward's popular with the school janitors. Whenever he could obtain samples at low prices he passed the saving on to his customers. A Christie hat bought in this way and sold for $1.50, when the going price was $3.50, aroused great indignation among his competitors. In Eastern Canada The Boys' Own Annual cost $1.75, a reel of Coates' thread five cents. In the West they retailed respectively for $2.25 and ten cents. Charles sold both items at the Eastern price. As he saw it in his earliest merchandising efforts, to sell for less was good advertising.

A job lot of miscellaneous silks brought him into the piece-goods business. Since at this time most families had sewing machines and made their own clothes or had a seamstress come in and sew by the day, this was a shrewd purchase. Its success led him to buy from a warehouse $1,000 worth of furs, muffs, collarettes, capes, neckpieces and trimmings of different widths which the warehouseman resurrected from a huge pile of discarded furpieces.

"They were a little off style and I discovered later that some of the wonderful furs were goatskin," he said, "but they looked very nice. What the eye does not perceive the heart never grieves about."

Such items were usually confined to the carriage trade and had not been sold before in the working man's neighborhood where Charles lived and operated. But he found that fashionable ladies were by no means averse to shopping at Woodward's if they could get a bargain, even though deliveries were made by lowly hand-cart. He derived a malicious amusement when they asked him to put their purchases in a "high-class Ladies' store box" rather than a Woodward bag!

"Buy on the Avenue!" was the slogan of the merchants of Main Street or "The Avenue" as it was popularly called. Charles put out a catalogue and arranged with other stores to fill orders from it if he could not fill them from his own stock. His subsequent verdict on the catalogue business was "Leave it alone," but at this time the Main Street merchants used the phrase "Buy on the Avenue" to boost each other's business and found it a valuable tool for them all.

CHAPTER SIX

The Battle to Sell Drugs

The depression of the 1890's dragged on but Vancouver did not give in to it. St. Paul's Hospital was built, the corner of Christ Church Cathedral was laid with full masonic honours, a fine new Courthouse was opened and admired in September 1894 by Liberal Party leader Hon. Wilfrid Laurier and in October 1894 by Governor-General Lord Aberdeen. But unemployment was rife and many Vancouverites left for the Kootenays where mining was active.

Nor did Charles Woodward allow the hard times to diminish his enthusiasm or restrain his fertile imagination. Deadman's Island, now the winter quarters of the Royal Vancouver Yacht Club and the home of HMCS Discovery, was the scene of a bitter controversy and of Charles' first political battle. The Ludgate Lumber Company, a large firm from Eastern Canada with substantial capital, decided to build a lumber mill on Deadman's Island but met with heated opposition because some believed that such a mill would mar the beauty of Stanley Park. At a public meeting Charles, who favoured the commencement of any business which would give employment to 150 people, jumped on a table and expressed his views so vehemently that he was promptly elected chairman. To his disgust Ludgate eventually decided to build his mill in Seattle.

Charles attacked the Canadian Pacific Railway for its discrimination against the West in the assessment of freight rates.

He may have been the first man in British Columbia to commence agitation for shipment of prairie wheat to Europe via the port of Vancouver. He drafted resolutions on the subject to Premier of

British Columbia John Oliver, worried the Vancouver Board of Trade and again crossed swords with the CPR Company which was just as reluctant to ship through Western ports as it was to reduce Western freight rates. The fact that 309 ocean-going vessels entered Vancouver's harbour in 1895 offered strong support for Charles' arguments. He gave much credit to Hon. Harry Stevens, Member of Parliament for Vancouver, for awakening the East to the advantage of shipping grain through the port of Vancouver and to G. G. McGeer (Vancouver's Mayor in the 'Thirties) . . . Charles called McGeer "The bane of the railroads and the Eastern Interests" for obtaining a 20% reduction of freight rates and saving British Columbia twenty million dollars. Charles himself was an energetic pioneer in promoting both these thorny issues.

The reclaiming of False Creek was for him the most compelling issue of all. Every day he crossed Westminster Avenue Bridge on his way from his store to his home in Mount Pleasant and back across the shallow waters of Upper False Creek Flats. The only playground in Vancouver at that time was Stanley Park, at least five miles from the East End. This imaginative far-sighted man decided that the eastern part of False Creek could be drained and made into a park for the children of the East End and the western part could become manufacturing sites. Many years later the Upper False Creek Flats were filled in and became Thornton Park, the pleasant green area in front of the Canadian National Railway Station with wide busy Main Street beyond it. Almost one hundred years would pass before Charles' dream would be fully implemented. In 1895 the idea was almost an obsession with him. It was a complicated issue because the Federal Government which was Liberal owned the deep water part of the Creek and the Conservative Provincial Government owned the foreshore. A committee of five men was formed to press for the drainage of False Creek on behalf of the East Enders. Charles was its chairman but he claimed that the aldermen were using the matter as a political football. He decided he must run for the office of mayor. He was tactless and intolerably aggressive; after a while his friends persuaded him to withdraw his name in favour of Thomas Neelands, "who," said Charles, "turned out to be no better than any of his predecessors in regard to helping the East Enders secure the location of False Creek for a park."

43

Attracted by a way of making money which seemed to him far quicker than retailing and an activity which must become one of the chief industries of British Columbia, he seriously thought of switching his interests to fishing and even became a director of a cannery. But he quarrelled consistently with the other directors.

"Every annual meeting we had a big row," he said. "They certainly considered me a pest."

Perhaps, too, he remembered his other attempt to get rich quick, the disastrous entry into the cattle business in Manitoba in 1882. Fortunately for himself and for Vancouver he dropped the idea.

Jack, the eldest of the Woodward children, returned to his family in 1894. He had been apprenticed in the "Art, Trade and Business of a Pharmaceutical Chemist" to Horace Yeomans, a Mount Forest, Ontario druggist who had known him all his life. Yeomans had drawn up a Contract agreeing:

> . . . to pay John Woodward of Thessalon the sum of twenty-five dollars per annum for the first year and three months, fifty dollars for the second year and seventy-five dollars for the third year, making three years and three months, during which term the said Horace Yeomans will provide the said John Woodward with board and lodging . . . and the said Apprentice, his Master shall and will faithfully serve, his secrets keep and his lawful commands at all times readily obey.

Jack had served his apprenticeship, seen his family settled in Vancouver, returned to Ontario and obtained his degree at the Ontario College of Pharmacy. Now he came back to them, just nineteen and a qualified druggist.

Some description of Jack is provided in a letter written to W. C. Woodward by Jack's old playmate, Henry Anderson:

> Maggie and Jack were more to me than my own brothers and sisters. I remember how popular Jack was with the young people. They often remarked to me what a fine chap he was and they were right.
>
> Jack was anything but lazy and as money was scarce with him he worked with a farmer at Glenworth at all sorts of rough farm work 'till the College opened . . . He went to the Coast immediately after finishing College.

He was a serious loss to your family when he died, in more ways than one, especially acting as a moderating influence.

Great was the joy of the young motherless family on Mount Pleasant when cheerful, competent Jack returned to them. At last the children had someone in whom they could confide, to whom they could go for advice and help. What with his store and his civic concerns, their father had no time for small children with small problems. Charles was equally delighted. He had just the right spot for Jack in the store! In those lean years when he had had to sell everything saleable just to keep afloat he had disposed of his grocery business. He had sold it for $1,426, all of which had gone to his creditors. In the space once given to groceries he would set up a drug counter. It would be the finest drug business in Vancouver, a place where the best drugs could be purchased for the lowest prices.

Jack agreed to the idea readily and had himself listed in the Vancouver directory as John N. Woodward, Chemist and Druggist, 626 Westminster Avenue. Later he added the title Postmaster, East End Post Office.

A letter from Jack to Horace Yeomans, who had been not only his 'Master' and his mentor but his close friend gives such a good picture of Vancouver in 1894, of an early Woodward sales promotion (which closed Main Street for three hours) and of the current liquor problem, that the letter deserves quotation:

June 10th/94   624 Westminster Ave.,
                                       Vancouver, B.C.

To: H. E. Yeomans
    Mount Tolmie, Ont.

Dear Horace:
    Your welcome letter to hand and more welcome photograph. I am sorry I can't return the compliment but as soon as I get some more I shall remember you. I want to wait until I get a little fatter. I have not been improving as fast since I have come home so the doctor says I must go away again. Well, when I am here I can't help but do some work, but I am going out on a farm for a few days, then I am going on an excursion up into the mountains and through the interior valleys of British Columbia for a month or two.

We have put in a couple of soda fountains, one for each store. But here we advertised a free drink of soda-water to all customers, and Saturday was a scorching hot day. On the last day of school I went around to every school and gave a ticket to each youngster. Well, I bought six hundred pounds of nice white candy from the factory here and had oblong bags made which over we pasted a small Union Jack. We filled all these and I and four of the clerks worked untill nearly 2.0 clock in the morning, from 4 in the afternoon at it. Well we had a pile in the window 3 ft. high and the next day public exam closed at 12 and we were to give the candies away at 2.

Well the children began to arrive shortly after 12. At 1 they nearly blocked the street and at half past they got so thick that we had to start and distribute. Well it took me and one other nearly two hours to get them distributed with the jamming and crowding as space was small or they would have prigged them. Well it closed the street for three hours and the people came from all over to see the crowd.

Well I never tried it since with children for after getting their package they still held around and the little ones getting crushed or crying. I had to pull over a dozen out of the crowd to sit behind me till it was over. Some of their parents came to and the larger boys would steal the tickets from the little ones. It was a costly ad but a good one as the City talked of it for days and they brought it up in the school-board and had a resolution not to allow it again using the school for an advertisement.

Another time I scrambled $22.00 worth of gum but it was to advertise the gum too.

The Yukon trade which has boomed this spring has dropped away over half and has affected us some. They have taken off some of the steamers. I tell you this Vancouver is a busy port with the shipping. It has now the largest tonnage north of Frisco. The Line to Seattle to Victoria to Frisco, China and Japan, and to Australia, and five or six Lines to the north. There have been ten River Steamboats and one coal barge besides hundreds of smaller crafts built here this winter or in course of construction.

Vancouver I think grew 5000 this last year. There will be 1 new bank building and over a dozen brick and stone business blocks with most of them containing 2 stores or offices each. These blocks were from $10,000 to $150,000 each and over

200 dwellings. Business property has advanced 30% and rents too.

Well I must close with kind regards for all

Yours forever
J. N. Woodward

P.S.

I was sorry to hear of the fine (for selling liquor). It was a horrible trick to inform. Here we can sell gallons if we like or by the glass bottle or barrell. But I never sell any unless they say its for sickness. We have sold larger quantities to people going north maybe a gallon but its used or wanted for warmth or med. in winter as in half the outfits some is wanted but most go to the wholesale liquor stores who sell retail, Hudson Bay Co. and a couple of English agencies. Some think they can get it purer in the Drugstore. Some of the drugstores here sell it by the glass after 8 on Saturday and Sunday as saloons are supposed to close then (but lots don't. I have had them several times ring the night bell Saturday night coming home boozy and want drink but they don't now when they can't.)

Young Bradley is out here up Main Street. He has an uncle a doctor here. His sister is coming out too. He went into a lawyer's office here but he could have done that in Mt. Forest and live cheaper too but I hear he has gone surveying now.

The youngest son of Wallace on the town line is here and going in with Bob in the grocery line. That Doctor you wrote of is no great shakes and very little thought of. He got into some strange scrape in Victoria and I never heard particulars but he found it more congenial to leave there.

J.N.W.

Neither his father nor he at first realized the extent of the fight that lay ahead of them in establishing their drug business.

Charles had a stroke of luck when he heard of a man operating a drug business who wanted to sell his stock and fixtures and was not demanding an unmanageable down payment.

"I got a splendid deal," said Charles.

He intended the drug department to be a 'trade-puller'. By cutting prices on prescriptions and patent medicines he attracted customers to his store to the benefit of his other three departments, clothing, piece goods and boots and shoes.

"From that time I began to go ahead," he said.

Almost immediately the wrath of the established drug stores descended upon him. The two Vancouver wholesale drug companies refused to sell to him, the Provincial Pharmaceutical Organization ostracized him, engaged detectives to spy on his sources of drug supplies and determined to run him out of business. The Battle of the Drugs was the longest, fiercest and most significant fight in which he was engaged but he was ever a fighter. He thrived on such controversy.

Where was he to go for drugs? That was the problem. At first he obtained them from a friend who had a wholesale grocery business in Toronto. This source was soon detected and closed by threats to cut off the friend's supplies, too. Then Charles used the T. Eaton Company and The Robert Simpson Company in Toronto, hoping that the magnitude of these large department stores would cloak the relatively small purchases he was making. Later, he started two drug stores a short distance outside the city in the names of two men who were secretly his employees. They were instructed to drive into Vancouver, pick up what they wanted for their own stores (Charles' orders were also covertly included), and then have the Woodward supplies delivered by Express under the very eyes of the Association detectives.

The Woodwards encountered equally strenuous opposition from the doctors of Vancouver almost all of whom at that time told their patients where to have their prescriptions filled.

"One cannot afford to take chances with cheap drugs," was their view.

The quality of Charles' drugs was the best procurable. He sold them for less because low prices were his form of advertising and his basic policy. There were no holds barred in this fight. A doctor who was especially vehement in his enmity towards Woodward's telephoned the store one day because he had made a mistake in a prescription and marked it "to be taken internally" though one of the ingredients was poison. The doctor naturally was perturbed and anxious to have the prescription returned.

"Not so," said Charles to the assistant who had taken the call. "I will take charge of that prescription and if he behaves himself I will not use it against him.

"Ever after the doctor was meek and friendly whenever we met."

These troubles ended only when legislation was enacted against maintained prices and made it an actionable matter if restraint were put upon legitimate trade.

He had had similar trouble with the boot and shoe stores whose owners had circulated handbills urging boot and shoe wholesalers not to sell to any store not directly confined to the boot and shoe business. However, they did not present nearly such a formidable opposition as the Pharmaceutical Association which was organized across Canada and a closed combine with considerable influence.

Meanwhile Woodward's business grew. At last the upswing had come for which Charles had waited so long. It was enhanced by another lucky break far more significant, the discovery of gold in the Klondike, "the galvanic shock that brought Vancouver back to roaring life," as Alan Morley calls it in his book "Vancouver – From Milltown to Metropolis."

Morley goes on to quote Dr. Margaret Ormsby, British Columbia's official historian: "Every hotel and lodging house were filled to capacity . . . tents were pitched in every waterfront lot . . . Everyone from tea merchant to huckster prospered. Contracts were let for new mansions in the West End and for new business blocks in the heart of the City. Vancouver had started its climb back to prosperity."

Though often the victim of shattering misfortunes, at least twice Charles was exceptionally lucky in the timing of his ventures. He had started his Thessalon store just as the CPR announced its intention of building a railway to Sault Ste. Marie. He began to operate in Vancouver in a time of depression and became established when a fantastic Gold Rush burst upon the world.

Exceptionally rich gravel was discovered on remote Bonanza Creek, in a district of the Yukon called Klondike towards the end of 1896. At first the discovery was kept quiet. Then in the spring of 1897 came the news that two million dollars' worth of gold had already been panned. Vessels of every sort were hastily commissioned and adventurers from all over the world hurried to the Yukon Territory. Young and old, strong and weak, educated and illiterate, they streamed into Vancouver, Victoria and Seattle to equip themselves for their search for a fortune.

Charles lost no time. He rushed around buying every line he

could find of hardware, snowshoes, sleighs, clothes, dog harnesses. He acquired $10,000 of equipment mostly on credit.

"I had everything except the dogs and I knew where they could be procured," he said.

His experience on Manitoulin Island as an Indian trader fitted him to handle the Klondike trade better than most of his competitors. He knew that some miners would want the best and that others would not be able to afford it. He decided to provide for both types of customer but when his advice was asked he recommended purchase of the top quality.

"Freight rates are no higher for better class goods and you will be gambling with your lives in a cold, barren land," he told them and he spoke with experience of such conditions.

A public meeting was held to discuss means of procuring for Vancouver as much of the Gold Rush trade as possible. Charles was given a great ovation when he suggested raising $200,000 by forming a company and issuing shares or even by making a levy on every resident in the city "in order to charter ships that were lying idle in Great Britain." His advice went unheeded.

"We did not get the ships until the Canadian Pacific Railway put them on later, after the Klondike trade had petered out," he said. Seattle and Victoria secured the cream of it, though Vancouver prospered too.

While Charles Woodward was busily providing miners with supplies for their journey to the Yukon, a young English settler named Charles Edgar Wynn-Johnson was equally busy building the first wharf at Skagway, Alaska, for unloading those supplies. The two Charleses did not know each other at that time and no two men could have been less similar in background, looks or personality. In the years ahead they were to be connected by marriage and Wynn-Johnson would have much bearing on the Woodward story.

CHAPTER SEVEN

A New Store and a Big Gamble

Largely as a result of the Klondike Gold Rush, Vancouver's financial position was now reputed to be on a sound financial basis. Charles was renting the three stores adjoining his own and the name WOODWARD'S appears in big bold print in the 1897 Vancouver Directory with its new enlarged address: 622-624-626 Westminster Avenue.

Charles leased the house on Mount Pleasant in 1898 to help pay the mortgage and the family lived over the Store, as they had done in Manitowaning and, for a time, in Gore Bay.

The living quarters were cramped and uncomfortable for a family of seven. May, Donald, Ann and William were teenagers, Peg was 11, Percival 8. John, 23, was druggist, his father's right-hand man and the devoted guardian of his young brothers and sisters. They did not return to Mount Pleasant until Charles had sold the store on Westminster Avenue and paid off the balance of the mortgage.

It was typical of Charles to make this economy when times were so much better. He had become known and respected. The following article appeared in an 1898 issue of the *Vancouver Province:*

Woodward Stores

The rapid growth of the East end of the city is accountable for the many stores now located on Westminster Avenue. The above establishment now occupies a very distinguished position inasmuch as it compares favourably with any other in any part of the city and as a department store is unique.

51

The many departments are complete in themselves and consist of dry goods (very latest novelties and most desirable class of goods are kept): a boot and shoe department where the style is perfect and the fit is guaranteed in every line: and a drugstore department with Post Office presided over by a first-class druggist. Each separate department has an experienced manager with able assistants and the success of the business is mainly due to their efforts.

These flattering remarks appear as an editorial and not as a paid advertisement!

With the coming of the new century economic conditions in Canada improved rapidly. But for Charles Woodward the first few years of the 1900's were filled with frustration and misfortune.

On the 24th of May, 1900, even as the young city was celebrating the birthday of the old Queen, Jack, the eldest son, died at the age of twenty-five. The marks of the terrible illness which had already claimed the lives of his mother and two of his sisters had been evident for some time. He was unwilling to give in to it or even to recognize it, yet there were the unmistakable signs . . . the cough, the weight loss, the blood spitting. Charles had a bond with this son which he was never able to achieve with any other of his children. He respected him, depended on him, even sought his advice. His death was a shattering blow.

The store continued to increase its business. Charles' two eldest children were working for him, May as a book-keeper, Donald as a sales clerk. William, who had hero-worshipped his eldest brother and had repeatedly told his father with characteristic outspokenness that Jack should be sent away for treatment, whatever the cost to the business, was so upset at his death that he decided to strike out for himself. Soon after his sixteenth birthday he left school and joined the staff of the Royal Bank of Canada first at its East End branch, then in the Kootenays.

Major Matthews, former Vancouver City archivist, reminisced:

"Charles used to wear a long apron of white cotton held up by a tape around his neck, with another tape holding it round his waist and.I remember him walking up and down in front of the store with a water can, sprinkling water on the vegetables in a long box in front of the windows."

Another memory comes from J. B. Giffen, then manager of R. G. Dun, the Mercantile Agency (later Dun and Bradstreet), whose business it was to give financial rating to commercial establishments:

"The store was all in confusion, things scattered about in a regular junk heap, and he was busy with customers. But to my great surprise, when I told him who I was, he was interested in me, and my purpose; a thing not usual in such an establishment. As soon as he had served his customers, he took me back to his office; it wasn't a real office, but a sort of desk with papers scattered all around, stuck on nails. He explained to me his position very carefully; he got a rating of about five or ten thousand dollars, and I remember him making a striking statement. It was: 'I'm not going to be satisfied until it is a million dollars'."

J. E. Bird, his lawyer, had suggested to him more than once that he should combine with other similar businesses and that such an amalgamation would be to the advantage of them all. He hesitated because he knew that working with others on equal terms often led him into trouble. However, he knew the advice was sound and agreed to join a small group of merchants. Two of his new partners owned a jewellery business, another operated an exclusive Boot and Shoe store, a fourth dealt in fine china. Charles who had more experience than the others in the management of a large store was elected General Manager. It is doubtful if he would have served in any other capacity. He knew that they considered themselves his social superiors and took pride in his own unpretentiousness.

Choice of location for the store was the first point of contention. A site on Hastings Street no further east than Cambie would be the least expensive and in his view was placed in the area most likely to develop.

"Any further east than Cambie Street, until you reach Carrall Street, was practically no better than a country road; there were one or two old frame buildings on these two blocks, a couple of cemetery stone-cutting works, a blacksmith shop and a wooden sidewalk on one side only and no streetcars nearer than Cordova Street."

Charles tried to acquire the corner on which the Flack Building now stands but failed because his store on Westminster Avenue, which he offered in part payment, still carried a mortgage. Hearing that the northwest corner of Hastings and Abbott Streets, one block farther down from the Flack Building, was on the market and about to be sold, he rushed over to the agent and secured an option on it for $25,000 with a down payment of $500.

He had no authority from his colleagues to do this and knew that they would oppose this location. They did. They had hoped to buy or rent a large store in the centre of the city.

"There was a big row at once," said Charles almost gleefully.

He offered to take the lot and pay for it himself if his partners would release him from the combination, but as they were unwilling to do so, the deal was confirmed. It was certainly a bargain. Yet the partners' misgivings were understandable. In that part of Hastings Street real estate was not considered valuable. Moreover, at one corner of the lot was a deep hollow, a swamp eight feet below the elevation of the sidewalk, wherein grew huge yellow skunk cabbages and bull-frogs abounded. The wooden sidewalk was built on stilts on a level with the street. Across the road was a cistern for use by fire fighters.

"People forgot," said Charles, "that the hollow saved a lot of excavating and reduced expenses and the drain which was put in by the City took care of the swamp."

On September 12, 1902 the Company was incorporated as Woodward Department Stores Ltd., a loan for $79,000 obtained from Canada Permanent Loan Company of Toronto and construction commenced.

Charles' first Vancouver store had been built in less than three months. The building of his second Vancouver store took over a year, principally because of hostility from the Labour Unions. The contract had been awarded to the firm which had presented the lowest tender but this firm had an "anti-labour" reputation. Immediately Charles was condemned and criticized by Vancouver's two Labour papers.

"Why would a man with a store on Main Street in the heart of the workingman's area employ a contractor who uses non-union workers?" the editors demanded.

The contractor was made to suffer every kind of inconvenience and delay. His supply of stone for the foundation was cut off and could be obtained only by fetching it from across the border in a scow. He had equal difficulty procuring fixtures to display the merchandise.

At last after months of bickering Charles sought an interview with the executive of the Labour party. He pointed out that he had always shown himself a friend of Labour by keeping prices down, that the next lowest tender for his store had been $7,000 higher, that though he had lost his Labour customers he was doing the largest business he had ever done because of the patronage of anti-union supporters, that the quarrel was not of his seeking. He presented his books for the executive to study. His courage and forthrightness brought a change of union policy and the building of his store was allowed to continue unimpeded.

It was an ambitious project. "When the building began to take shape and the citizens saw the size of it they were amazed, for there was no building of the same size here," recorded Charles with such reverence for his achievement that his language seems almost Biblical.

At last on November 4, 1903, the Store was opened. It was a wooden frame building with a basement and covered the full size of the 66 by 132 feet lot. There were no concrete or steel buildings in Vancouver at that time. Steps were avoided by making the ground floor on a slant with the street and one doorway was placed as close as possible to Cordova Street to catch the Cordova trade. In the centre of the Store, from the ground floor up to and including the third floor, there was an opening with a rail around it. Customers enjoyed the novelty of leaning over the bannisters and watching what was going on below. Advertisements stated that "business is being conducted on a strictly cash basis, no credit whatever being given."

November was a quiet month and Charles tried by every means to attract customers. He managed to have loop lights strung across Hastings Street (there were no such lights on Cordova). He had a four-piece orchestra play in the store on Saturday nights. He boasted that Woodward's had the largest stock in town, though its magnitude was soon to lead to serious dissension among the partners.

First building on Woodward's present site at 101 West Hastings Street, Vancouver, 1909. It was open for business on November 24th, 1903.

56

Vancouver continued to grow in size and stature. The city had contributed a contingent of men to the South African war and had received amid great excitement and enthusiasm a visit from Their Royal Highnesses the Duke and Duchess of Cornwall and York, later to become King George V and Queen Mary. The start of a separate university for British Columbia had come with the creation of the Vancouver College of McGill University. Population had swept from 20,000 in 1898 to 41,000 in 1904.

In December business improved and sales totalled $50,000. The British Columbia Electric Railway Company agreed, in response to a petition and in spite of strenuous opposition from the Cordova Street merchants, to operate a street-car service on Hastings Street from Main to Cambie.

Charles' hunch that Cordova Street as Vancouver's main retail and business thoroughfare had had its day began to come true. Several notable pioneer firms decided to move away. Among them were the corner store at No. 102 Cordova occupied by George E. Trorey, watchmaker, Messrs. Johnston and Kerfoot, clothiers, at 104 - 106 and the Thompson Stationery Company, printers, bookbinders and stationers at 108. All three followed the trend to Hastings Street as the importance of that street grew. But the Metropole Hotel remained on Abbott Street for many years. It was recognized as a high-class stopping place for visitors and travellers and at its bar and rotunda men of importance met and conferred. The Palace Clothing House and the B.C. Supply Company at 110 and 112 Cordova respectively which outfitted and equipped men journeying to the North resisted any idea of leaving Cordova Street. So did Andy Tyson's Central Fish Market, and McLennan McFeely and Company whose dealings in picks, shovels, gold pans, sleighs and tinsmithing were so successful that Mc. and Mc. grew to become one of the largest establishments in the province. Fred Ackers' Tobacco store and shoe-shine counter with the Vancouver Reading Room upstairs and Shafer's Cafeteria, the first in British Columbia and perhaps the first in Canada were soon to be absorbed by Woodward's Department Store. Miss Carrie Smith did not even consider for a moment moving her elegant Millinery establishment from No. 132 Cordova Street where it had always been, next door to the Master Tailors.

Grocery Department, 1904.

CHAPTER EIGHT

Friction Among the Directors

When the new year 1904 dawned Charles Woodward still had a forest of troubles ahead of him.

From the first, relations between him and his partners had been marked by suspicion and jealousy. Hostility came to a head at the customary stock-taking in mid-January when a loss of $7,000 to $8,000 in less than three months' operation was revealed. Accusations of "padding stock" and "hiding the true state of affairs" were hurled about. An accountant was hired to take a second audit. Charles opposed this move because he thought he knew exactly how the loss had been incurred.

"We have about $60,000 locked up in unsaleable merchandise," he told his partners, "$40,000 in diamonds and jewellery, another $20,000 in crockery, whereas the goods I brought with me from Westminster Avenue are staple, everyday lines. Drygoods, Boots and Shoes, Drugs, Groceries, Stationery, Clothing, Wallpaper, Rugs and Furniture are in popular demand and can be sold every day of the week. Jewellery and Crockery are slow-selling. The salespeople in those departments have little to do yet you retain their help."

His remarks led to more charges and counter-charges. In February Charles insisted on reducing the salaries of all managers including himself from $100 to $75 per month. Even more unpopular was his refusal to accept delivery of large consignments of merchandise which at the height of their troubles suddenly arrived from Eastern Canada, the United States and England. There was a freight bill of $3,000 and invoices for some $50,000.

General Office, 1913. W. C. Woodward is shown at the right. His first position with his father's store was that of bookkeeper.

Charles would not allow these goods to leave the Canadian Pacific Railway warehouse.

"We should not take into stock goods which we cannot pay for," he said. "We should let the shippers know the state of our affairs and give them the opportunity of disposing of their merchandise elsewhere if they consider our account unsafe."

This decision which left the store short of many needed lines was strongly opposed by the other directors. But the goods remained in the C.P.R. warehouse.

The financial position of the Company and its internal dissensions became so serious that its affairs were put into the hands of a Receiver or Financial Manager. J. Helliwell, of Clarkson, Cross and Helliwell, a firm of accountants, was appointed and charged a fee of $5,000, an amount which was hotly but unsuccessfully contested by General Manager Charles Woodward. Helliwell produced a statement showing the Woodward Company with assets of $199,500 and liabilities of $89,000, stating that the delay in entering the new building and consequent loss of several weeks' valuable business had resulted in the present overstocked position and recommending that an extension of credit be sought from trade creditors and the Bank of British North America, to whom payments would be made at three, six, nine, twelve and fifteen months intervals with interest at six per cent. That recommendation had a familiar ring!

Shareholders, said Helliwell, had agreed to postpone their own claims of $34,000 until the claims of the trade creditors and of the Bank had been satisfied.

Though Charles was in agreement with most of this advice, he could not bring himself to stomach that fee of $5,000 nor to accept the fact that the Receiver was virtually in control of his business. Before long Helliwell joined his list of favourite enemies and he stipulated that "when everything was settled with the creditors Helliwell was to resign and leave the Woodward Company."

A fiery directors' meeting was held on May 12, 1904 at which much criticism was directed at the General Manager.

Cicero Davidson, whose jewellery firm was one of the strongest units in the combine and who was Secretary-Treasurer of the Company, launched the attack.

"The Manager should concern himself more with the departments and customers," he said.

"He should devote his time to the welfare of the Company instead of sweeping the floors," added George Healy.

J. Edward Bird, solicitor for the Company, also made disapproving reference to the Manager's insistence on sweeping the floors and working in the basement.

"Someone else should be able to do such work," he said.

R. G. Buchanan, Manager of House Furnishings, favoured a direct approach.

"I move that an outside party be appointed Manager," he declared. "It would cause less friction." He demanded with considerable vehemence that the balance of his own salary be paid forthwith.

Only John Little who had come with Charles from the Westminster Avenue store and remained his lifelong friend spoke in his defence.

Charles had no intention of resigning. He decided that somehow he must find a way of buying enough of his partners' shares to give him control of the Company. By a stroke of luck he sold the Woodward block on Westminster Avenue for cash. After paying the balance of the mortgage he had enough money left to buy out the Davidson brothers and another director, T. B. Hyndman. The two directors who operated the Crockery Department sold their shares to Charles in return for an equity in his house, some life insurance and all the crockery merchandise.

"Thus I was rid at a great loss of the original directors and could start again," he said in his diary.

Charles was fifty-two and almost penniless. His chief assets were a well-located store, loaded with debts, and unbounded confidence in himself and in the future, amply justified as events were to prove. He had told J. B. Giffen:

"I am not going to be satisfied until I have reached a million dollars."

Within the next eight years he was to attain that goal and, perhaps even more important, a reputation with Dun and Bradstreet and with his customers as a sound and honest merchant.

Helliwell engaged in private deals behind Charles' back and was a subversive influence in many ways. To Charles' fury he appeared to have no thought of relinquishing his position as receiver.

In July 1904 Charles put out a circular in which he stated that disagreements and friction between the directors had been the cause of the troubles and the reason for the Company's having to seek favours from its creditors. He was now, he said, the heaviest creditor and stockholder as well as managing director. He owned 75,000 of the 84,420 shares and would not ask for one cent of the money owed to him until all the creditors and the Bank had been paid up. The business was very prosperous and had a splendid future. He sought Mr. Helliwell's immediate withdrawal from the position he occupied though he would retain his services as auditor. He did not wish his remarks to be construed as a reflection on the Davidson Brothers.

Soon after the publication of this circular Helliwell unwillingly resigned.

The Bank of British North America had watched Charles' affairs closely, had immediately checked him for the smallest overdraft and often complained that he was paying off his creditors faster than the Bank.

"What is a Bank for if you cannot use it at a pinch?" demanded Charles angrily after one particularly hectic confrontation. Next morning he called on Mr. Crosby, Supervisor of the Royal Bank of Canada at the corner of Hastings and Homer Streets, said that he wished to change his bank account and sought a loan of $25,000. Crosby examined the Store's books, formed a favourable impression of its potential and recommended the loan at a modest six per cent interest. This generous treatment led to an association between Woodward's and the Royal Bank which still exists. Woodward's is the Royal Bank's oldest customer in Vancouver.

Alan Morley in his vivid story "Vancouver: From Milltown to Metropolis" entitles the chapter describing the first years of the Twentieth Century "The Golden Years". Though Charles was as shrewd, daring and diligent as ever, Woodward Stores would not have prospered so greatly or so rapidly if Vancouver had not been going ahead at full boom pace. "The City," says Morley, "was built up solid to English Bay." He gives an impressive account of wide roads and tall buildings, new Post Office, new Opera House,

Men's Wear Department, 1910.

64

new Theatre, the Orpheum, new Stock Exchange; of sky-rocketing assessments, bank clearings and building permits; of business enterprises expanding almost as soon as they had been launched. Morley's chapter ends with the words, "Oh, it was a wonderful, wonderful time!"

Charles made the most of it. He was now in complete charge and unhampered by the whims or wishes of directors or receiver. The extension notes were paid regularly and punctually, but it was no easy matter to find the money. He was operating on such a slender margin that on one occasion he had to hold up the sales clerks' wages for one day to meet the payments on the notes. He had sunk everything he owned into his store.

He and his family had continued to reside over the old store on Westminster Avenue even after the business had been moved to Hastings Street. Now that building had been sold. Nor could they return to the house in Mount Pleasant because it too had been sold to buy the shares and procure the withdrawal from the Company of the Crockery Manager. Somehow or other Charles managed to rent a house at 1240 Pender Street and this remained the family home for many years.

The family in 1906 was much reduced in size. Jack, Margaret and Ruby, the two oldest and the youngest, had died. Ann had gone to Winnipeg to train as a nurse . . . there was no Nurses' School in Vancouver at that time . . . and while there had met Arthur Sanders, a young banker who had fallen in love with her. They were married in Vancouver and had then gone to live in St. Thomas, Ontario, where Arthur's family lived and where he entered his father's business. They were a happy couple but Ann was to die before she was thirty.

Cora Lilley, now the youngest daughter and known as 'Peg' because she disliked her given names, was also married. Her husband was Sholto Smith, an architect with the firm of Smith and Goodfellow. They had a house at 2216 West 14th Avenue, some way out of town at that time. In 1912 Sholto opened his own office at 303 West Hastings, doubtless hoping for some business from the Woodwards, but it never came his way.

William, still working for the Royal Bank, had been transferred to its branch in Havana. Only May, Donald and Percival were at

Ladies' Dress Department, 1910.

66

home. May, the eldest daughter, had relinquished her job as book-keeper in her father's firm and become a teacher at Seymour School. She was 26, had seen her younger sisters marry before her but bore no resentment. She was a gentle, loving woman whose later deeds of charity were outstanding.

Like many other great men, Charles usually put his work ahead of his family. In his lengthy reminiscences his first wife, without whose trust and support he could never have survived, received only two brief mentions. Of his children only Jack is mentioned by name. Donald had been his oldest surviving son for some years but there was no close bond between him and his father. Donald was too pugnacious, too assertive, too much like the old man. He had been a salesman with the store since 1900. In 1906 he became Secretary-Treasurer. He did not enjoy working for his father and was always looking for a way out of the business. Before long he found it.

In 1907 Charles' two younger sons joined the Company. Twenty-two-year-old William returned from Havana to become a book-keeper, seventeen-year-old Percy left school and started full-time work as a salesman. Charles would have been astonished if he had known that both these sons would far eclipse his own achievements and be among the most distinguished British Columbians of their era. William had managed to pack as much adventure into his six years away from home as most bankers achieve in a lifetime. After a spell with the Royal Bank at Nelson, Grand Forks and the Lardeau, he managed to get himself transferred across the border to Republic, a tough cowboy town in Washington, where he heard shots fired in anger for the first time. Then he was moved to the Royal Bank in Cuba where he arrived just in time to witness the revolution against Estrada Palma's rule. Palma, the first President of Cuba, had not kept his election promises and some insurrectionists determined to oust him. On his twenty-first birthday William was a goggle-eyed spectator at a South American-style revolution with its peculiar mixture of tragedy and comedy.

A few months later he abandoned the shelter of his banker's job and went to work for a firm of Cuban stock-brokers. It was an unsuccessful venture and he soon lost every cent of his savings. He found himself thinking more and more about Vancouver. Pictures

W. C. Woodward, member of Argonaut Junior Rugby Club. He and his brother,
P. A. Woodward, were keen sportsmen, specializing in soccer, rugby and boxing.

68

of his boyhood kept coming into his mind's eye . . . chasing the wobbly old street-cars over the planked streets of the East end, selling newspapers on the wharf to the miners who would toss him a dollar as they roared off to the Yukon, catching salmon in the creeks that ran from his home in Mount Pleasant down to False Creek, digging for clams at the foot of Abbott Street, skating and sliding on the big pond near his father's new store on Hastings Street. He felt homesick for Vancouver. Cuba with its extremes of vast wealth and total poverty, its unending sunshine and spurious glamour no longer appealed. He wrote to his father. Charles was delighted. He had just the spot for him in the store!

No young man was ever happier to leave school and begin work in a store than the youngest member of the family, Percival Woodward. The excitement of merchandising was bred in his bones as in his father's. He had the same short sturdy build as his brothers but a different temperament. William was extroverted, open-handed and liked to be liked. Percival kept his own counsel, was suspicious of other men and their motives, demanded efficient performance, spurned popularity. At school neither brother was more than an adequate student, both boxed and played football with determination and courage.

A photograph of the Argonaut Junior Rugby Club, Junior Football Champions of British Columbia for the 1901 season, shows as its smallest member, W. Woodward who sits with legs crossed in the front row and looks out at the viewer with massive resolution. There are several names in that picture that were to become well-known in British Columbia in the years to come: among them Campbell Sweeny, C. Brydone-Jack, R. Brydone-Jack, A. E. Jukes and Lyall Fraser.

Percival's best game was soccer. One of his earliest subsequent donations was $150,000 to the Royal Jubilee Hospital, Victoria, because that hospital had treated him for a bloody nose, an injury he sustained playing soccer for Vancouver High School against Victoria. This donation he said was a belated "thank-you". He knew every inch of the new store. After school and on Saturdays he had fetched and carried for the builders while it was going up and had even dug with them. He was to become a great merchant who changed the buying habits of much of Western Canada.

Towards the end of that same eventful year that intrepid young Englishman Charlie Wynn-Johnson came back from Alaska to British Columbia and in 1908 made a purchase which was to have far-reaching effects on the Woodwards even on many still unborn. It was the purchase of Alkali Lake Ranch. After building his wharf at Skagway and unloading mountains of supplies for the miners, Wynn-Johnson caught the fever for gold himself and went over the Chilcotin Pass in search of it. He had no success but some spectacular adventures. Then with Stewart Sheldon, a big-game hunter from New York, he roamed the Stewart River country in search of moose and bear for museum pieces. At last he decided that it was time to settle down; he already had two daughters and Mabel, his wife, was pregnant again. When he saw the 30,000-acre ranch set among the hills and valleys of the Cariboo country, he fell in love with it.

H. W. Bowe of New Westminster had started Alkali Lake Ranch in 1860 and stocked it with 500 head of heifers driven there from Oregon. Wynn-Johnson bought it from his son and made it one of the most famous ranches in British Columbia.

CHAPTER NINE

The First One-Price Sale

The $25,000 loan and the new association with the Royal Bank set Charles' mind at rest.

"I felt more free now," he said. "I plodded along, worked hard early and late."

Bank Manager Crosby having made his assessment never at any time requested payment in full or in part or bothered Charles in any way. In his 1905 report to Head Office this shrewd observer wrote:

"Woodward's are now doing a good trade for spot cash, meeting their obligations and the future of the concern is assured."

Charles met the two conditions upon which the loan depended, that he should personally endorse it and that he should assign $30,000 of Fire Insurance to the Bank. Both stipulations he considered fair.

By the time he was joined by William and Percival he had paid all his extension creditors, had settled the mortgage on the store and repaid his fellow directors. Then he liquidated the bank loan.

"My business was now jumping ahead faster than I could take care of it," he wrote in his Reminiscences.

Charles was unswerving in his policy of pumping profits back into the store. He put in new furnaces, renovated the building from basement to roof and added two storeys. The property immediately west of Woodward's on Hastings Street was owned by an Englishman who would not sell "at any price". This same lot Charles had tried to persuade his partners to buy in 1904 when it could have been purchased for $32,000. He had even taken an option on it

Delivery trucks. In 1913 Woodward's had twelve horse-drawn delivery trucks. The horses were sold in 1919 and automobiles used thereafter.

72

which he was forced to relinquish. Nine years later Woodward's obtained this lot for $350,000 and were pleased to get it for that price. Meanwhile Charles lamented that he was confined to 66 x 132 feet with basement and six storeys.

A new stable was built for the delivery horses at the corner of Hamilton Street. Hitherto they had been kept in the alley behind the Travellers' Hotel. In the days of the old store on Main Street merchandise had been delivered by wooden hand-cart manipulated after school by youngest son Percival.

Charles remained in his office almost every night until 10 o'clock. When commenting on the business habits of some of his competitors who took life more easily and indulged themselves with family life or hobbies, he said: "I stuck to my business and possibly had as much fun and enjoyment as any of them."

This remark was true because his work was his hobby. He even admitted that he was going to extremes and ran the risk of ruining his health.

"I was a strong man and hardy or I never could have pulled through," he said.

The advent of his sons into the business was a great relief to him though he did not let them know it. He kept them on a short rein by the simple method of keeping them short of money. It had taken Charles over thirty years to achieve financial stability and he was determined that no children of his would have any easy road to riches.

Vancouver continued to grow by leaps and bounds. There was a substantial and continuing boom in real estate. In 1908 there were 228 miles of city streets. Next year the new Granville Street bridge was opened, a swing structure "which," says Eric Nicol in his delightful book 'Vancouver', "was engineered to provide exquisite frustration to almost half a century of Vancouver motorists."

The Dominion Trust Building, consisting of fourteen storeys and advertised according to Nicol, as "the tallest building in the British Empire and the finest edifice in Canada" was completed in 1910. Henry Birks' store, the Lost Lagoon, the Stanley Park Causeway . . . the list of Vancouver landmarks completed during those flourishing years of 1907-1912 is impressive. The city's population increased from 60,000 in 1907 to 129,000 in 1912.

One day in the spring of 1910, Charles learned that McTavish, a wholesale drygoods merchant on Homer Street who had been in business as long as himself, had decided to retire and had not been able to sell his merchandise en bloc. He had been left with a quantity of small wares and planned a special sale to clean them out. With his infallible scent for a bargain, Charles was on the scene on the day of the sale at least one hour before anyone else. He nosed around and carefully examined what was to be sold. Set out in boxes and baskets on tables was a profusion of braids, braces, bootlaces, fans, beads, hatpins, garters, tapemeasures, ladies' side supporters and waist distenders and many other items known in those days as "smallwares".

"How do you plan to dispose of these small items, Mr. Mc-Tavish?" he asked. They had known each other for ten years but he invariably called his business associates "Mr.".

"Everything will be sold by the table," replied McTavish. "Each table will go for $35. You'll find some pretty good buys."

There were indeed good buys. As Charles went around making rapid mental calculations, he found that most of the tables contained merchandise worth at least $100 and the table itself was included in the purchase price.

He bought heavily.

He and his assistants had to transport the purchase back to Woodward's and then found that the stockrooms would not hold such an immense quantity. McTavish's smallwares had to be stored in every corner and passageway. Charles kept bumping into them as he went about the store and being reminded of his reckless buy. The thought that perhaps he had made a mistake occurred to him and was promptly dismissed. He advertised a sale and tried to unload some of them but it was not successful. His customers were not inclined to stock up on smallwares but preferred to buy them as they were needed. At the end of the sale he was still left with a large assortment of McTavish's items.

The manager of the drygoods department did not help the unhappy situation. Charles describes him as a "very firey (sic) red-headed man," but does not name him.

"What do you want to buy all this rubbish for, Mr. Woodward?" he demanded, not bothering to conceal his exasperation.

74

"I can't move in my department without falling over the stuff."

"Well, we have them," replied Charles. "It is my mistake and we must make the best of it. You will have to help dispose of them. It's no use fussing around any more."

Then suddenly Charles thought of the very principle which had attracted his own interest . . . a one-price sale and a bargain at that. He decided to put twelve assorted articles in shoe-boxes. They would be five-cent articles and he would price each box at 25 cents. He would call the sale 25-cent Day, and he would have one such day each month until he had cleared out every last one of Mc-Tavish's smallwares.

This was the beginning of Woodward's one-price sale days. Later the day was re-christened 45¢ Day, in 1919 it became 95¢ Day. The idea was successful beyond his wildest dreams. Some years later he wrote in his diary:

"Can you imagine our store waiting on 150,000 customers in one day, at a time when the population of the Province of British Columbia was 700,000?"

Ninety-five Cent Day became known all over the North American continent. The big day was preceded by a one-page advertisement set out in tiny print and doing no more than list values offered, in splendid defiance of high pressure tactics. Again and again Woodward's was asked to reveal the secret of its one-price sale. There was no secret. The whole magic of this sale lay in values which were really worth pursuing. The one-price sale days were discontinued in 1941 owing to the shortage of merchandise. When they were resumed after the Second World War, it was evident that Vancouver people had not forgotten them. As $1.49 Days they became as popular as ever.

"Give the public the best in values and you will win and hold their loyalty, however bad times become," said Charles.

Nevertheless he realized that sometimes customers did not appreciate the values they were getting and it was no use being naive about this fact.

"One year," he related, "I bought 350 pairs of men's boots at a little under $4 a pair and put them on sale at $5 so as to give the public the benefit of my good buy. At that time money was plentiful and people liked to spend. My competitors were selling practically the same article at a much higher price and men would not buy our boots because they were too cheap. Later we put the same boots on sale at almost double the price and sold them quickly. Price does not always govern the value of the article."

He told the story of a man who went to London to buy a silk hat for one guinea. The shopkeeper had none at this price but showed him some silk hats at a lower price. The customer declined: he was determined that the hat must cost a guinea, neither more nor less. So the shopkeeper called out to his assistant:

"Open the shipment that has just arrived and see if it contains any silk hats."

Of course, one was found, just the same hat as had been previously shown at a lower price. The customer was satisfied with his bargain.

But the story bothered Charles.

"Would you call this dishonest on the part of the merchant who had tried to be fair and square with the purchaser?" he asked.

The acquisition of a house on Pender Street in Vancouver's exclusive West End was an unexpected move. Charles who had always lived as near to his business as he possibly could now elected to live 1½ miles away from it. His previous dwellings had been in the working man's part of the town. Now he was invading a close-knit social unit with very definite ideas about the desirability as neighbours of "people in trade".

The deWolfs, the Maitlands and the Morgans were his immediate neighbours. Across the street was the imposing mansion of Major-General J. T. Twigg and his brother Samuel. Few were invited to visit the Twiggs, certainly not the Woodwards, but Ruth Wynn-Johnson, Samuel Twigg's granddaughter, sometimes came down from her father's ranch at Alkali Lake in distant Cariboo and stayed with her grandfather, only a few houses away from the home of the man she was going to marry.

Every day at exactly twenty minutes to eight, Charles and his three sons, Donald, William and Percival, would leave their house, always by the back door which led on to Melville Street, and walk to the store. Donald was a reluctant merchant ever seeking an escape from his father's iron control. William was becoming more and more enamoured of the business. He had a fondness for all sorts and conditions of men and he met a great variety in the store both among customers and staff. Percival found merchandising a fascinating study of which he never tired.

In 1909 Donald at last found Woodward's Store more than he could bear and left its employ. He tried several enterprises of his own without success and then his father sent him to California to look into the prospect of buying land there, either as an investment or Charles' own retirement purposes. Donald enjoyed the climate and the friendly people and decided to remain permanently. William was appointed to succeed him as Secretary-Treasurer.

Business was good and real estate went on booming. A front foot on Hastings Street, which in 1886 could have been bought for $8, in 1911 cost $4,000. These years of success have been less fully recorded than the years of trial and trouble. There is ample evidence that the store was always packed. People told one another "you can always buy it cheaper at Woodward's" and though money was plentiful in Vancouver, who could resist a bargain? The fleet of delivery wagons grew to twelve. A mail order department was added and immediately boomed. There were twenty departments and Charles admitted that sometimes he had more business than he could handle, especially as space was limited and he could see no way of expanding.

He was easily worth a million dollars, had $100,000 of it in cash in the bank and owed not a cent to anyone. After so many years of struggle and loans and mortgages he was satisfied.

He was 60 and decided to retire. There was now a second Mrs. Woodward, a lady of whom little is known. Only one reference to her is to be found in Charles' Reminiscences, a parenthesis: "(I had married again in 1909.)" A Minute Book shows her given names as Alice Farrow.

So he had a partner with whom to enjoy his prosperity. He had been working as hard as ever. For the first time in his life he had health problems and felt he was losing his grip. His sons William, 27, and Percival, 24, were able and ambitious with plenty of drive. They wanted nothing more than to see their domineering old father away from the business and to be free to try out their own ideas. They received the news of his retirement with delight but an incredulity which proved to be well-founded.

CHAPTER TEN

The Self-Service Experiment

Charles had been making regular buying trips to Europe and had become fond of rural England. He decided to settle in Kent where he had the offer of a thousand acres of good farmland for 20,000 pounds. At a directors' meeting held on February 12, 1912, the faithful John Little, who had worked for him in the Main Street store and ever since, moved a vote of thanks to him "for his many kindnesses" and wished him and Mrs. Woodward "a bon voyage." A motion was passed by which the Company would pay him a rental based on a property value of $300,000 since he personally owned the Store building.

Little, Manager of the Drug Department, right-hand man and invariable deputy in Charles' absence, was elected President. It is probable that the mantle of leadership did not sit easily on the shoulders of this modest, unassuming man. Few believed that Charles really intended to retire, certainly not John Little who knew him so well. Moreover, he made no move to relinquish his equity control of the Company.

With mounting misgivings and an ever-diminishing enthusiasm Charles accompanied by his wife set out for England in the spring of 1912. Even before they left Vancouver he who had never known illness became ill. They pushed on as far as Seattle and there called a halt. Charles moaned and groaned in an inexpensive hotel.

"Why go to England, 6,000 miles away?" he demanded of his wife, placid Alice. "Why not go to Los Angeles where Donald says the weather is warm and the people friendly?"

Immediately he felt better. Before long, recovered and full of energy as ever, he was calling on every real estate agent in and around Los Angeles, shaking his head over the land prices which he designated as "exorbitant."

At last he made a good buy direct from the owner —

. . . ("we had cash and should obtain full benefit from it.")

He bought fifty-six acres for $48,000 at Rivera, ten miles from Los Angeles City. He spent another $50,000 renovating, putting in fruit trees and a rose hedge 1100 feet long on the boulevard in front of the ranch house. He who had been born and raised on a farm showed the Yankees that he was no 'greeny', that he could plough, harrow, cultivate, harness horses, in fact do any practical farm work as well as any of his neighbors. He dispelled a current theory that walnuts from the time they leafed to the time of harvesting required no water, by noticing that two rows of walnut trees growing at the lower part of a slight grade where irrigation water always gravitated, had a larger leaf and were a deeper green.

Gradually his ranching activities began to pall. What was happening at the Store, he asked himself a dozen times a day? Could mild old Little really manage those managers? Some of them were as cunning as monkeys. Could Little stop them from overbuying? Would Billy with that ridiculous lavishness of his give the Store away? Would they all remember that the place must be kept spotlessly clean?

The records show Little in the Chair at a Directors' Meeting held on August 30, 1912 and at another on March 11, 1913. That was the end of his brief reign. Officers elected for the year 1913/1914 were once again:

Charles Woodward	President
John W. Little	Vice-President
William C. Woodward	Secretary-Treasurer

Charles' Reminiscences suggest that he lived in California in happy retirement until the outbreak of the First World War in August 1914, when he returned to the Store in order to allow his sons to enlist. But in this matter his memory deceived him. The truth is he could not keep away. Again and again he went through the motions of retiring only to rush back "to fuss some more," as Mac Reynolds expresses it in his brilliant article published in

MacLeans Magazine on the Woodward Stores. This was the first of several brief, temporary withdrawals. However, for some years his address remained "Rivera, Cal."

Though William and Percival volunteered for military service as soon as War was declared, it was not until 1916 that Billy was accepted, for they were engaged in an occupation essential to the War effort. Percival's poor eyesight would never permit him to go on active service.

At the February 1915 Directors' Meeting John Little retired as Vice-President and Percival Woodward was appointed to replace him. William remained Secretary-Treasurer but retained his seniority. An increase in the share capital of the Company was authorized by the addition of 109,763 shares at a nominal value of one dollar each "to be paid out of profits." Of these shares 33,000 were allotted to John Little, 29,000 to William and 26,000 to Percival. Charles divided the remaining shares among other old employees "who had stood by him and still had to work for a living."

This was the beginning of a profit-sharing policy which was to be greatly developed by his sons and grandson. Two of the smallest allotments went to Charles' daughters, May and Peg, who received 180 and 20 shares respectively. The account of the meeting ended with the words: ". . . some nice speaches was made regretting Mr. Little's retirement."

A final motion was passed "that Miss Blaike be appointed auditor for the coming year and that she be paid five dollars for services rendered."

In spite of its wealth the Woodward Company remained unsophisticated.

When his father moved to California William went to live at Glencoe Lodge in the West End of Vancouver. A high-spirited cheerful young man with a great love of life and people, he was delighted to have his father's ever-watchful eye and inevitable question applied to every project: "Is it good for the Store?" — at least temporarily removed. His friends, of whom Billy Woodward, popular young man about town, had a vast number, were equally pleased. There was a noticeable increase in the store's social events, such as picnics and concerts. In August 1916 his application to enlist was accepted and he spent the next three years with the First Canadian Heavy Battery in France and with the Army of Occupation in Germany. He was a courageous but unenthusiastic soldier who found warfare dull and disagreeable.

One month after Billy's departure, Percival wrote a letter to his father:

Dear Sir:

I wish to tender my resignation as a director and Vice-President of the Woodward Department Stores to take effect Sept. 15, 1916.

P. A. Woodward

John Little was of course pushed back into Vice-Presidential harness. Billy was a Director of the Company even while absent on war service but Percival was not. It is probable that his resignation was prompted by one of his frequent disagreements with his father. Percival too had a wide circle of friends but his nickname "Puggy" indicates the pugnacity which marked almost all his relationships. He too retired and returned more than once. His name did not reappear on the list of Woodward Directors until February 1918 and then he was not listed as Vice-President.

"In the last days of 1912," writes Alan Morley, "the world was plunged into an economic depression and the Vancouver boom came to what the Board of Trade euphemistically called 'a pause'. It was more than that, it was a dead halt that lasted all through 1913 and 1914."

Charles Woodward back from his brief retirement addressed his directors in March, 1914:

"Gentlemen," he said, "this is a year in which it will pay us to be very careful, as things are in a very critical condition throughout Canada."

They were indeed. To the citizens of 1914, the total war which came five months later was something new. Many remembered the South African Campaign and other skirmishes involving for the most part small professional armies and barely touching the life and the economy of the nation. The implications of the First World War at first were hard to assess. The immediate reaction was that it must be over in two or three months.

81

"There was not enough money in the whole world to protract it longer," said the economists.

All the eligible young men flocked to the colours convinced that if they did not get to the front in a month they would never see action. There were bands and glamour and marching and many who thought it was all rather a lark. Only after the gas attack at St. Julien in April 1915 and the first shocking wave of Canadian casualties, did people realize the extent of the horror and was the temper of Canada stirred.

Meanwhile in Vancouver business tried to go on as usual. Throughout the war years there was little development in the city except as dictated by contracts directly connected with the War. Alfred Wallace's shipyard on the North Shore built and outfitted six auxiliary powered schooners, known as the "Mabel Brown" type and a number of steel freighters. The machine-shops drew off an army of workers. The war years were the only years on record when the sound of hammer and drill was absent from the Store. Fortunately the new building on Hastings Street which Charles had tried to persuade his fellow-directors to buy for $32,000 in 1904 had been converted to provide much-needed extra shopping space. The price the Company had had to pay, $350,000, still irked him but the acquisition of this 86-foot lot immediately adjacent had already justified itself.

In time of war the merchant has a role no less important than the soldier's and has to cope with frustrations often as severe. He must overcome problems of communications, delivery, shortages and soaring costs and he knows that without adequate food and clothing, morale will slump. At first the war intensified the economic depression. Vancouver was far from world markets and throughout the war years there was no civilian shipping.

The Woodwards who had been reared in the hard school of adversity were in no way daunted. They rolled up their sleeves and proceeded to give vigorous support to Canada's war effort. The difficulties were immense. In 1915 nine departments, almost half the total number, operated at a loss. In 1916, a motion was passed that "owing to the serious depreciation of rentals and values in real estate in Vancouver over the last three years $100,000 be written off the Company's Real Estate." In 1917 the Dominion

War Tax levied on the Store was over $12,000 and though the usual 7% dividend was declared, a clause was added that it was to be paid only when the Company could do so without borrowing from the Bank.

At last to a weary world in November 1918 came the end of the war that was to have lasted three months. In Victory Square, where little more than thirty years before dense fir forests had been cut down by pioneers to make the old Vancouver Courthouse, a cenotaph was built to do honour to the memory of 62,000 Canadians who had given their lives. The spirits of free people all over the world soared. Business boomed. Vancouver, destined by nature and geography to be a great city, resumed its strenuous growth.

Puggy Woodward returned to the Store in 1918, his quarrel with it mended; Billy, who had served with the Army of Occupation, in mid-1919. Five years earlier these two young men had successfully managed the Company without the presence of their father's overpowering personality. Now, aged 28 and 33 respectively, they had had in addition the maturing experience of the War years. Their impact on the Store was strong and immediate. They were to prove themselves more outstanding merchants even than their father. Their personalities were different but complementary. Billy liked to be liked, could make the humblest member of the staff feel important, and exuded immense charm. Puggy never courted approval or popularity. He had an eagle eye for any deficiency or misdemeanour, drove others as hard as he drove himself and had a scalding tongue. He was Merchandise Manager in charge of operations. Billy was Vice-President and in his father's absence in charge of the Store.

From time to time Charles, to his sons' relief, went to his ranch in California. On one occasion Puggy seized the opportunity to try out an idea which he had been turning over in his mind for months. Horses and wagons for delivery were gradually giving place to motor vans. This expense and other rising costs were pushing up the price of merchandise. He believed that nothing mattered more to customers than the ability to buy the best for less. Why not let them *serve themselves?* Why not, in certain departments such as Food, cut out free delivery, minimize the sales staff and pass the savings to the customers?

The Grocery Department at that time was twenty-five hundred square feet. Taking advantage of his father's absence, he removed the counters, replaced them with kitchen tables which he had loaded with groceries, reduced prices by fifteen percent and started Woodward's Self-Service Groceteria. Even the word "Groceteria" was then almost unknown.

The results of the experiment were electrifying. On the first day the crowds were so large that they could hardly be handled. The head butcher who had been sceptical of the innovation was so overwhelmed that when the last of his customers had departed, he got roaring drunk. There was no meat on the second day but the crowds were larger still. Charles rushed back from California as soon as heard the news and Puggy had a stormy hour with him. Large crowds were all very well, he said, but only if the customers were satisfied and the Store profited. Was this the case? He doubted it and continued to raise every objection he could think of.

"Are you going to let dishonest people wander round filling their shopping bags with our groceries without paying for them?" he demanded.

"We're making them check their bags and parcels at the desk before they start to shop," replied Puggy who had already anticipated this problem.

"So we will seem to distrust our customers, the very people who provide our living. They'll walk out and never return," retorted Charles.

Some customers did take offence when asked to check their bags but when they realized the reason for the rule and the impartiality with which it was applied, they soon came back.

Charles was never generous in his praise where his sons were concerned, and though he eventually accepted it, he sought to belittle Puggy's bold and imaginative move. He claimed that he had been about to start such a system himself. However, he could not deny its success. Woodward's "Groceteria" had come to stay. Customers who had been used to buying their groceries over the counter with free delivery proved beyond doubt that they preferred to buy them at a reduced price, select them and carry them home themselves.

Charles ended his account of the experiment with this comment:

"There were 17 drivers paid off with one week's pay in lieu of notice. We had 20 horses and had to get rid of them and we had 17 wagons and two autos. We did not require the wagons either and sold them and I estimated there was an annual saving of about $40,000. The autos we kept.

"You will understand the risk we ran of wrecking our business as we had nothing to go by. The whole thing was planned in the dark, it was under severe criticism both from within and from our customers."

He did not mention that he had been one of the severest critics and that 28-year-old Puggy was the hero of the story. Billy tried to find jobs for the laid-off drivers and as times were good was successful. Rather sadly he went over the list of the horses: Trixie, Pilot, Roly, Buster, Queen, Chum, Jim, Maud, Daisy, Dan, Prince, Flo, Kate, Sam, Tracy, Mack, Ben, Tom, Jerry. On the books they were listed as an asset of $4,135 but he was more concerned that they should go to good homes where they would be well treated.

In the summer of 1920, Billy Woodward, recently demobilized and still finding it hard to settle down to civilian life, went on a fateful holiday with his friend and brother-officer Clare Underhill, with whom he had served in the Artillery. Underhill had been invited by the Wynn-Johnsons to visit them and as their ranch at Alkali Lake was a place of vast and continual hospitality, he knew that one guest more or less would make no difference and suggested that Billy go with him. So the two young men went up through the Fraser Canyon along a road at that time as tortuous and precipitous as any highway in British Columbia. The ranch lay in a valley forty miles south of Williams Lake.

There was some excitement among the Wynn-Johnson family because eldest daughter Ruth had just come back from Europe to her parents whom she had not seen for five years.

Billy fell immediately and deeply in love with her and remained so for the next thirty-six years.

On the ranch where she grew up Ruth had acquired a fondness for cattle, horses and life on the range which she never lost and which was transmitted to her children.

"At the age of 13," she once told a reporter, "I became impossible so my parents sent me to finishing school in Paris. It was run by a retired Swiss missionary called de Rougemont whose four daughters taught us music, literature and the arts. We toured museums daily. I stayed there so long that eventually I was delegated to take over some of the lectures. The summers we would spend in Switzerland and the outbreak of the First World War found me at Neuchâtel.

"My parents thought the Continent was no longer safe but could not bring me home since passages for civilians were almost impossible to obtain. So I went to live with an aunt, Sidney Kenworthy, my mother's sister, in Wales."

In 1916 they moved to Dublin where Ruth's mother, née Mabel Twigg, had two more sisters and a great number of relatives. The Twiggs were an ancient and distinguished Irish family. Ancestor John Twigg's commission with the Rifle Brigade and the Royal Ulster Regiment had been sponsored by Field Marshall the Marquess of Wellington and Colonel the Earl of Westmeath. Members of the Twigg family had also pioneered in British Columbia and made a notable contribution to it. Major-General Despard Twigg, brother of Samuel Knox Twigg, Ruth's grandfather, had served as Deputy-Speaker of the Provincial Legislature and as Attorney-General.

Ruth worked at the Soldiers' Central Club in Dublin. She took singing lessons from Miss Agatha Irelande and sang in concerts for the troops. She became a member of V.A.D. Detachment 76 in the County of Belfast. She witnessed the Easter Revolution in 1916 when the general post-office and other parts of Dublin were seized and the city paralyzed for a week by street-fighting. It was an abortive revolution doomed to failure from the start. She felt some sympathy with the Sinn Fein revolutionaries, some indignation at the broken promises and betrayals which had spurred them on and at the prolonged succession of executions and deportations which followed. Her scrapbook contained photographs of several of the men who were executed . . . William and Patrick Pearse, James Connolly, Thomas Clarke, Thomas McDonagh, Eamonn Ceannt, Joseph Plunkett, Edward Daly.

Ruth spent the last year of the War in England working as third cook at Waverley Abbey Hospital, Farnham, Surrey, a beautiful country house turned into a hospital. She stayed there for six months only; she had to pay to work there. Then she returned to Ireland and became a volunteer at the Ulster Volunteer Force Hospital in Belfast. It had been set up for the casualties of the expected rebellion against Home Rule but when the First World War was declared, the hospital was turned over to the Red Cross.

As soon as the Armistice had been declared, Ruth returned to Canada. She had left a rather hoydenish schoolgirl, more at home rounding up cattle than making polite conversation in a drawing-room. She returned a lovely young woman, composed, serene, as free from affectation as the Cariboo hills she loved so well. Nothing had spoiled her, not the Dublin high society nor the soldiers whom she had nursed, many of whom fell in love with her on sight. Much of her early childhood had been coloured by her adventurous father's escapades in Alaska and remote parts of British Columbia. She knew how to do without comforts and could talk to cowboy, Indian or statesman on equal terms.

She was twenty-three, tall and compact . . . a little taller than Billy . . . with blue, laughing eyes and a mouth forever curved in a smile which reflected her love of life and humanity. Many men had wanted to court her and even now, a forester from Williams Lake . . . "a most undesirable chap," her father called him . . . was making feverish advances.

Billy was thirty-five, a gay bachelor who had been close to marriage many times but had always steered away at the crucial moment. Though their backgrounds were very different, he and Ruth had much in common, especially a candour, an honesty and a simplicity which in spite of the great wealth and high honours which life was to bestow upon them, they never lost. Ruth returned his love in full measure. The forester was heard of no more: and the couple were married at Alkali Lake the autumn of 1921.

Charles Woodward did not attend but wrote to Ruth as follows:

October 13, 1921

To: Miss Ruth Johnson
Alkali Lake, B.C.
Dear Madam:

Both Mrs. Woodward and myself sincerely regret that we are unable to attend your wedding. I hope the explanation I have given your father will be accepted by your kind self.

We also enclose you a small check of one hundred dollars as a help to start the pot boiling. If you and Bill should decide to visit us this fall or winter which would be a great pleasure to us down here this check is payable here at face value and no bank exchange or loss to you.

One thing more I wish to point out to you is that I have drawen it in your maiden name and should you neglect to endorse it before the 26th it will be forgery for you to endorse it after the 26th. Don't take any chances with Bill he might have you arrested.

With best wishes and kindest regards from us both,

We are yours sincerely,

Mr. and Mrs. C. Woodward

Younger brother Puggy had already been married for seven years. Marion, his wife, also wrote to Ruth:

. . . When I phoned Billy to congratulate him he sounded most awfully happy. Billy has had an ideal for a long time and from what he said this morning his choice leaves nothing to be desired . . .

Marion was right. He could not have made a better choice or had a happier marriage.

CHAPTER ELEVEN

Charles Woodward, M.L.A.

By 1924 Charles Woodward had his million dollars and many more besides. Partly through his immense diligence and more than a touch of genius, partly through the almost irresistible prosperity of the 1903-1912 period, he had attained his goal and at the same time founded a business which had become an institution in Vancouver. But he did not enjoy spending his money and the stories of his parsimony are legion. He did not really enjoy his family. He considered that the boys had too many ideas of their own and resented their innovations. Because life had never indulged him, he had no intention of indulging his children. Yet as the Store grew he could not avert their prosperity though he could and did seek to minimize it.

In his quest for a new challenge he turned to politics. He had always taken an interest in civic affairs and considered that unless one kept a watchful eye on the bureaucrats, they could handicap a businessman in some unexpected way before he knew what was happening. He loved Vancouver and believed wholeheartedly in its greatness. Its Mayors and Aldermen were recipients of his frequent letters, brief, often misspelled, always to the point. Here are some extracts, just as he wrote them, which show the wide range of his concern:

> To His Worship the Mayor and Aldermen:
> "As convenor of the Board of Trade Committee selected to meet your honourable council I wish to discuss ways and means of securing the upper end of False Creek and other foreshores of the city . . ." (June 17, 1899)

89

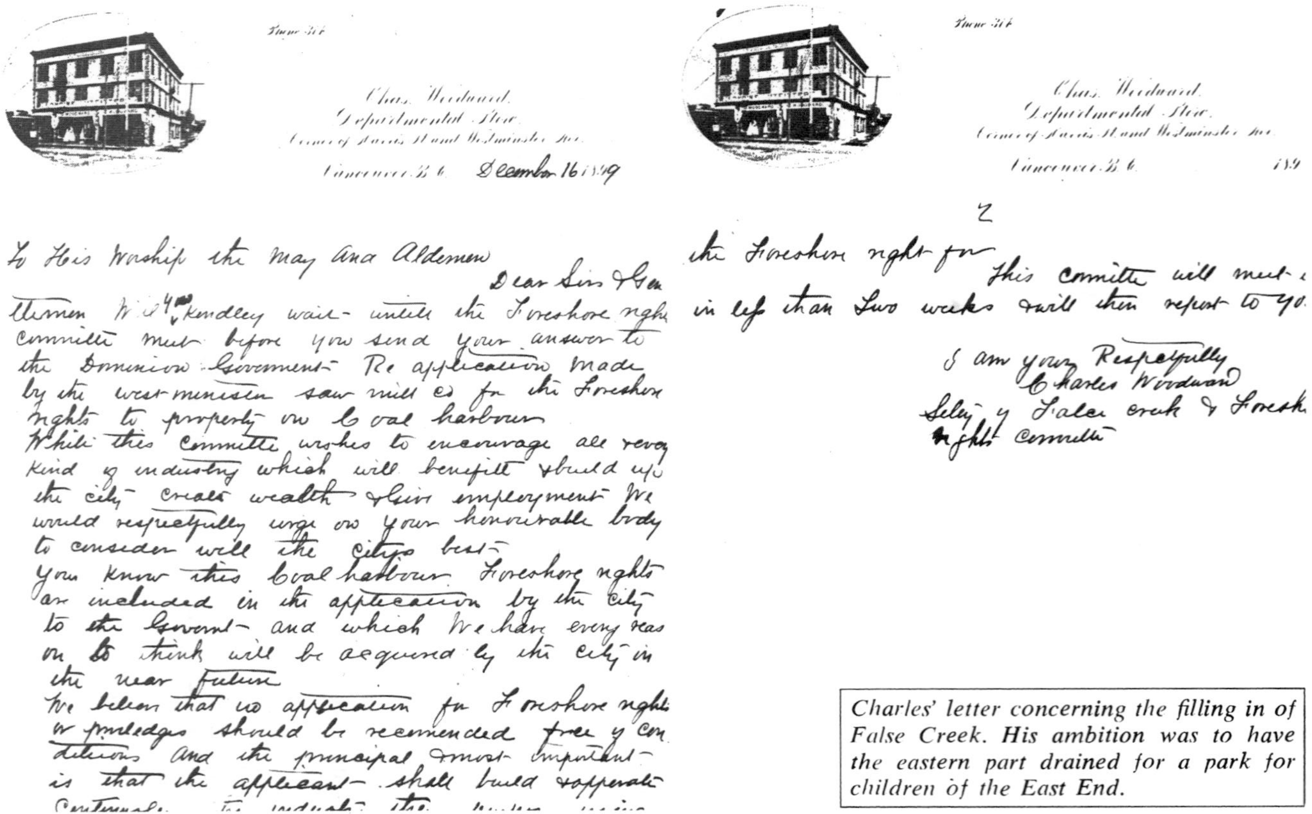

Phone 314

Chas. Woodward.
Departmental Store.
Corner of Harris St. and Westminster Ave.

Vancouver, B.C. December 16 1899

To His Worship the Mayor and Aldermen

Dear Sirs & Gentlemen Will you kindley wait until the Foreshore rights Committee meet before you send your answer to the Dominion Government Re application made by the West minister saw mill Co for the Foreshore rights to property on Coal harbour
While this Committee wishes to encourage all every kind of industry which will benefitt & build up the city create wealth & give employment We would respectfully urge on your honourable body to consider well the citys best
You know this Coal harbour Foreshore rights are included in the application by the city to the Government and which We have every reason to think will be acquired by the city in the near future
We believe that no application for Foreshore rights or privileges should be recommended free of conditions And the principal & most important is that the applicant shall build & operate continually ... industry ... ...

Phone 314

Chas. Woodward.
Departmental Store.
Corner of Harris St. and Westminster Ave.

Vancouver, B.C. 189

2

the Foreshore right for This Committee will meet in less than two weeks & will then report to you

I am yours Respectfully
Charles Woodward
Secty of False creek & Foreshore rights Committee

Charles' letter concerning the filling in of False Creek. His ambition was to have the eastern part drained for a park for children of the East End.

As your Honourable Body contemplate amending the City Charter would you Honourable Gentlemen have any objections to meeting a committee of citizens on this very important subject?" (November 13, 1899)

The only thing I wish to know is what the amendments are and how it will affect the charter and citizens in general." (November 15, 1899)

I was instructed by the Committee to write your honourable body for any information and the use of all papers or maps showing the boundaries of Old Granville Townsite previous to the building of the C.P.R. into the City. This Committee is under the impression that the C.P.R. is encroaching on the City's rights and lands by filling up the foreshore and the ends of Carrall, Abbott and Cambie Streets." (Jan. 29, 1900)

Where their is a difference of opinion between the electors and the Mayor and Aldermen comprising the Council of the City. A petition signed by fifteen percent of the qualified Electors who have their names on the voters list shall compell the whole council to resign their seats at the Civic Board." (undated)

(He does not quote his authority for this last statement but clearly the aldermen took it seriously.)

In the general election of 1924, when in his 72nd year, he ran for office as Liberal M.L.A. for Vancouver. He was widely known as the workingman's friend whose merchandising policies kept prices low and whose integrity was unquestioned. He headed the polls.

Almost immediately he tangled with the Minister of Lands, Thomas Dufferin Pattullo, tough politician who had been Lands Minister in the Brewster Cabinet as well as in the present Oliver administration and who resented the criticism of this elderly newcomer to the political scene. The two men remained at loggerheads throughout the four years of Charles' political life.

On September 6, only a few weeks after his election, Charles wrote to the Premier:

91

The Honourable John Oliver
Parliament Bldg.
Victoria, B.C.
Dear Sir:

I notice in "The Sun" of this morning, that the matter of Dr. McDonald which you were anxious to have kept quiet, has been given to the press and also an interview by Mr. Pattullo saying that he is determined to sell that piece of land on the Water Shed.

I think Mr. Pattullo is acting very foolish in selling that land and furthermore at this present time when people are very much opposed to it, to come out and declare, as he foolishly does, that he intends to do what he thinks, when the Liberal members elect of this City are opposed to it. In doing this very thing he is only weakening himself in the eyes of the public and making very little of the members elect.

I think and feel very strongly on this question and if it comes to a question of Mr. Pattullo or the City of Vancouver, I am going to take a stand, irrespective of what the other members do, to back up Vancouver in their claims.

Last night, before parting, I suggested to Mr. Pattullo that he and the Members get together for a conference, but he refused to entertain this. Now, if Mr. Pattullo thinks to ride rough shod over the City of Vancouver he certainly is making one big mistake and it reflects on you and your Government to have a man who is so bullheaded against the wishes of the members . . ."

Charles was a strong supporter of the Pacific Great Eastern, as the British Columbia Railway was then called. Premier Oliver had assumed control of this railway reluctantly, calling it a "waif left on my doorstep, the illegitimate offspring of two unnatural parents, conceived in the sin of political necessity." Woodward, with his innate vision, saw the potential of the P.G.E. and repeatedly pressed for its completion to terminals in Prince George and North Vancouver.

He was unalterably opposed to what he scornfully called the "liquor element". The Government had been charged with accepting large contributions to its campaign funds from the brewers in return for permitting the price of beer to be increased. Officials

92

of the Liquor Board had also been accused of corruption. These charges were never substantiated but Charles gave his opinion in unmistakeable terms.

"The Liberal Party are loyal to you, Oliver," he said, "and feel the stigma of reported domination of the Liberal Party by liquor interests. The liquor element pretty well controls Vancouver."

He endorsed his remarks in a letter to the Premier:

> . . . I wish to point out to you very strongly that I do not think Mr. Odlum, Mr. Mcrae or myself who claim to be respectable men will be supporters of a government that undoubtedly will be called a whiskey government . . ."

The interests of Vancouver were always first in his loyalties.

> I wish to say to the Hon. Minister (Pattullo): Step light when you are in Vancouver. Consult all Vancouver members about everything within Vancouver borders. Don't presume just because we have no cabinet representation that we, members for Vancouver, will let you roughride us. Profit by experience. It will save you a lot of trouble in the future.

Three years later he was battling with Pattullo as fiercely as ever. "Charles Woodward, Vancouver member, ripped the Department of T. D. Pattullo, Minister of Lands, from stem to gudgeon," reported the *Vancouver Province*.

The speech criticized at length the raw deal by that minister in granting the Campbell River franchise and concessions to a new company, after promising to respect the claims of a pioneer B.C. firm which did extensive work on the proposition before the war. Too many school students were employed in the Lands Department, he said, to decide on homestead matters of which they knew nothing.

'I think the Honourable Minister's judgment is bad,' added Mr. Woodward, 'in dealing with homesteaders living on the land. I have had dozens of letters complaining of conditions. If all these bad conditions exist, why is there not some system of investigating them?' (*Vancouver Province*, February 10, 1927)

Nor did he spare the Premier. Oliver was, like himself, a man with a farming background, little education and a reputation for

93

total honesty. In many ways Charles respected him but he was highly critical of the 1927 Speech from the Throne.

> I do not think the premier could have been himself when he drafted it and I do not think he could have taken his cabinet into his confidence. Nothing is said about that octopus the P.G.E. and nothing about getting a market for B.C.'s fruit industry. If you or I handled our own business as the government has handled the P.G.E., Mr. Speaker, we would be placed in an insane asylum. We should not drop the P.G.E. Make no mistake about it. We should finish that road.

The elimination of succession duties for estates under $25,000, the protection of families from company promoters and shady prospectors, the purchase of railway ties manufactured by settlers along the P.G.E. instead of buying ties from Alberta . . . in clear, strong phrases this man whose formal schooling had ended at fourteen, ranged over the problems of the day and directed the keen searchlight of his mind upon deficiencies and incompetence wherever he found them.

Towards the end of that year 1927, the executive of the Young Liberals Association met and composed a letter to the Premier:

> We know that there are influences in the party which would like the elimination of Oliver from leadership and from public life. You have made enemies by your honesty . . . Vancouver must have cabinet representation in the person of Mr. Charles Woodward as your chief cabinet caucus and house supporter. You should retain leadership on condition that Woodward accept the portfolio of finance.

It was a notable tribute for Young Liberals to pay a man of seventy-five.

The letter went unheeded, Charles' proposals were disregarded. The next year Oliver's government went crashing to defeat.

Meanwhile the Store grew and grew. On March 8, 1925, Billy announced a huge new addition to Woodward's Limited, which already comprised a main floor and five storeys.

"When completed," he said, "the store will occupy the whole frontage from Hastings to Cordova Streets along Abbott. There will be a clear space on each floor, without partitions, of approximately 300 feet in which the already overcrowded departments will find room to develop and give increased service to the public.

"The old Metropole Hotel which has stood at the corner of Cordova and Abbott since I was a boy will have to go, but in its place will rise a fine addition in keeping with our present buildings."

He went on to say that the lane between Hastings and Cordova would be closed but another outlet for traffic would be provided on Cordova on the site of Pat Burns' Meat Store. This old landmark would also have to be demolished to provide a lane entrance as required by law.

The Hardware Department which could then be reached only from Cordova Street or by a stair from the Hastings Street entrance would be linked on the same floor space with the other departments. Later the Cordova Street annex which had been opened two years previously would be built up to the height of the other parts of the Store.

"The completed building will be the last word in fireproof construction with automatic sprinkling throughout. Messrs. Carter-Halls, Aldinger to whom the contract has been awarded have undertaken to finish it in six months.

"It's Vancouver's own fault," he added, twinkling at the reporters, "if the city has to lose two of its old landmarks. People come swarming to us everyday in such throngs that we are constantly outgrowing our premises. We love to serve them but we have to do something about our overcrowded departments."

Then he concluded: "My brother Mr. P. A. Woodward and I are making this announcement on behalf of our father Mr. Charles Woodward, M.L.A., who is in California."

Billy would have been in trouble if he had forgotten that last sentence! Charles Woodward was indeed still President. Only death would pry him from control of the Store which he had fought so hard to build but as each year went by, the impact of the strong, intelligent and driving characters of his two sons made itself more and more keenly felt. This addition, the largest of any so far, was their brainchild. They had to push, wheedle and cajole to get the old man to agree to it.

"So much money, so much money," he kept repeating, shaking his head, but he was deeply involved on the local political scene

Woodward's Annual Staff Picnic. W. C. Woodward, its originator, is shown in the front row — fifth from left.

Woodward's Annual Staff Picnic, Alberta Beach, 1928. The picnic was attended by customers, relatives of staff members and staff.

and so let the boys have their way. He could never get it into his head that the "boys" were in their middle and late thirties.

Billy and Puggy were vastly dissimilar in personality and perhaps for this reason made a fine team. Though Billy was the financial expert he was equally concerned with the welfare of the staff. A department store clerk has a trying, difficult job. Constant exposure to the general public whose demands however unreasonable or inconsiderate must be met with unfailing courtesy, requires exceptional patience and tolerance. Billy had the confidence of staff members at every level. He had a knack of appearing just at the moment when a salesperson had almost reached the end of endurance and saying something kindly or funny or understanding. He made frequent journeys through the Store and his trail could be observed by the looks and smiles of the men and women to whom he had spoken.

Billy was not merely popular. He was loved. He thought of the staff as a family, spending hours each day listening to their problems. The annual picnic, attended by all staff and as many of their relatives as Union Steamship *Princess Royal* would hold, was his concept and his delight.

In April 1924 his profile was one of a series of sketches appearing in the *Vancouver Province* called "Men About Town" and describing "Persons filling Interesting Jobs."

He beams out of the picture, stocky and confident, with the same thick, close cropped moustache as his father, holding "one of the prides and joys of his existence his two-year-old daughter Sidney Elizabeth." He is described as a pioneer of Vancouver, a keen sportsman having been a member of the Argonaut Football Club, the Rowing Club and the Jericho Golf Club, a shrewd financier and a member of the Board of Trade, already marked for the presidency.

Puggy stayed in the background. He trained the managers, understood and foresaw with astonishing intuition the buying habits of the public, introduced vision and imagination into a line of work often bereft of such qualities and allied them with sound judgment and bold action. He was respected by all, liked by only a few, and he preferred it to be that way.

One time Billy had a brush with Vancouver's underworld.

At 8:00 a.m. on Sunday, January 5, 1924, three men dressed in overalls and carrying sacks climbed by means of a rope on to the fire escape, nine feet from the ground, on the Cordova Street side of the store. They were not observed for the streets were empty and the curtains of most houses drawn. The men made their way to the fifth floor, bored a one-inch hole in the door, pressed the inside bar releasing the catch and entered. They chose this time of day because they knew that the three night-watchmen would have just gone off duty and been replaced by one lone watchman who would be in sole charge of the building for the day.

Thomas Brown, the watchman, according to custom made an immediate round of inspection. When he reached the fifth floor he was pounced upon, struck several times on the head with the butt of a revolver, tied up and deposited unconscious in a corner while the robbers attacked the safe. They used a mattress obtained from the Furniture Department to deaden the sound of their explosives, and after four attempts managed to blow the front off the safe. Then they helped themselves to its contents, some $500 or $600, and turned their attention to the vault which held the whole of Saturday's "take."

Thomas Brown who had awakened by now received further ill-treatment. He was warned that if he watched them too closely his life would be in danger.

Suddenly the robbers heard the ringing of a gong.

It happened that one of the managers wanted to enter the Store that Sunday morning and rang the bell on the Hastings Street door at 11:15 a.m. The pressing of the button caused large gongs located on each floor to clang and be heard by the watchman in whatever part of the building he might be. When the manager received no answer despite repeated ringings he telephoned Billy Woodward.

Billy was on the scene within ten minutes and using his own key to gain entrance rushed to the fifth floor, where he found the wreckage of the safe, the equipment left behind by the burglars and the trussed-up Thomas Brown. They had taken Brown's keys, let themselves out by a side door and escaped.

A similar attempt had been made one month before to rob the

safe of the Fraser Valley Dairies, and Police Chief Daniel Leatherdale, suspecting that these were the same robbers, put every available detective and officer on the case. Thomas Brown suffered bruises and shock but was back at work within two weeks. The robbers were caught.

That same summer Billy had another experience with gangsters. He was working in his office when a letter was delivered to him by special messenger.

"Unless you give us $4,000 in cash," said the note which was badly written on an ordinary piece of writing paper, "your home will be blown up. You are to send this money by messenger to the post office where a man wearing a rose in his buttonhole and carrying his cap in his hand will receive it. If you notify the police your family will suffer."

The two men who thought up this plot were poorly-trained amateurs and the police had no difficulty in picking them up at the post office that same day.

Woodward's famous Beacon Tower, model of the Eiffel Tower, 75 feet high with a searchlight 48 inches in diameter, built on the roof of the Store in 1927. For many years a landmark to Vancouver people returning home.

CHAPTER TWELVE

The Fight Against Price-Fixing

One of Puggy's brightest ideas was the declaration against comparative prices. One day in 1927, as he was making his daily round checking other stores and ensuring that Woodward's was not being undersold, he spotted in a competitor's window an Axminster rug with a showcard stating: "$69.50, reduced from $85.00."

He knew that this particular rug had been on sale for $69.50 for several months. He knew that a great many shoppers would be similarly aware. Customers were not unintelligent and they disliked being fooled or lied to. This not uncommon practice of making misstatements in advertising was in Puggy's view bad merchandising and his opinion was shared by his brother.

On June 5, 1927, Woodward's newspaper advertisement carried this editorial:

Comparative Prices

By demonstration of results, we know the shopping public of Vancouver respond to honest endeavour.

It is very gratifying for us to know we can do business without using *fictitious regular prices* to bring in our customers. When making a special reduction consistent with quality of merchandise *Our Aim* is to sell better merchandise for less money than our competitors, and when we use the word *"Special"* it covers all the price reductions any competitor could make in using comparative figures. Value for value your money goes further here.

As old Charles read the strong statement he was reminded of some of the fiery editorials he had used when making his way in

Manitowaning. He had pulled no punches then and he was glad the "boys" were equally ready to speak their minds.

Woodward's has not used comparatives prices in its advertising since that day. Its stringent advertising policies probably have had an impact on Consumer Department legislation and control. British Columbia later revised its Trade Practices Act and condemned "a representation that a specific price benefit or advantage existed if it did not" and "the use in any oral or written representation of exaggeration, innuendo or ambiguity" as a "deceptive act or practice".

That same year, 1927, Puggy had another brainwave in the field of advertising. He had a giant tower built on the roof of the Store. It stood seventy-five feet high, held a searchlight forty-eight inches in diameter and threw out a two-million candlepower beam which revolved six times each minute and spread its rays far over the Lower Mainland across to Vancouver Island. For many years the Beacon Tower was a landmark to the people of Vancouver. Because it was exactly similar to the type of beacon in use at the Vancouver Airport, orders came from Ottawa during the War to remove this brilliantly imaginative advertisement. A sixteen foot "W" was substituted.

Charles' long-standing battle with the drug companies, his sturdy resistance to their attempts to stifle competition by fixing minimum prices, the cunning methods he used to outwit the drug combine, have already been related. Puggy now became the leading combatant in continuing his father's fight. Sometimes he had to pay more for drugs than he could sell them for but, much as such an extravagance hurt, it seemed worthwhile. Indeed it was the only way in which he could keep the drug department going and at the same time maintain the principle of the free trading of merchandise which was such an integral part of the Woodward philosophy. Only when the Dominion Government passed the Canadian Combines Act was Woodward's able to buy drugs through regular channels.

The battle went on. In 1926 the druggist formed a new combination known as the Proprietary Articles Trade Association which became extremely powerful. Almost all the druggists in Canada had to join it in order to stay in business. Woodward's, of course, refused to be part of the P.A.T.A., had its supplies cut off for a year and a half and to obtain drugs had to resort to costly unorthodox methods, such as buying from corner drug stores at fixed high prices and selling at a loss, as had been practised by Charles thirty years earlier. At last the Dominion Government took action under the Combines Act and broke up the Proprietary Articles Trade Association.

In 1938 yet a third attempt was made to fix retail prices. At the instigation of the B.C. Retail Merchants' Association, provincial legislation was passed in 1938 known as Bill 89, the Commodities Retail Sales Act, by which any store selling certain items for less than the price fixed by the wholesaler or producer could be fined $500.

Woodward's answer was a full page advertisement in the newspapers. Under banner headlines it proclaimed:

> *Another combination started to force the consumer to pay more for his household commodities.*
>
> The effect of this legislation is to increase the cost to the consumer of very many commodities by 5 per cent to 20 per cent.
>
> The Act gives wholesalers and producers the right to fix retail prices which are the minimum prices at which any commodity may be sold.
>
> Checking over the list of prices set by manufacturers and jobbers in conjunction with the Retail Merchants Association . . . we find a hundred or more items in this list which will have to be marked up from 5 per cent to 20 per cent higher. In fact one Eastern Manufacturer here has set a price 25 per cent higher in the West than in the East. If this bill is allowed to stand, people in the East will buy some of their necessities much cheaper than we can sell them in the West. This act not only adds to your cost of living but puts a premium on the more or less inefficient merchant who wishes to get a long profit.

In an astonishingly prophetic vein the editorial concluded:

> *As a consumer this is your fight as well as ours. This is just the beginning of price fixing under government supervision increasing the cost to the consumer.*

103

When you try to legislate or restrict the free trading of merchandise you build up a costly army of officials who add tremendously to the cost of handling. This Bill No. 89, passed at the last Session, should be rescinded; *we advise the consumers to form into leagues and petition the local members to have this Act rescinded.*

We feel that this is very vital and affects every person in the Province of British Columbia. This Province is naturally a province of Primary Products. Anything that adds to our cost of living lessens our chance of producing at a price to meet competition in the world's market, in which 65 per cent to 70 per cent of British Columbia's business is carried on. There is only one way to control business, and that is by honest competition which has survived for a thousand years or more, and legislative action can not change human nature. This is undoubtedly but the beginning of a comprehensive scheme engineered by certain interests, to exact from the public the highest possible prices on the everyday necessities of life, and if permitted to spread to include the grocery, hardware and other trades, will set back business forty years, and nullify the results of years of earnest effort in the economic marketing and distribution of goods which has saved our customers thousands of dollars in substantially reduced prices, at the same time netting us a satisfactory return on money invested. Along this line the Dominion Government report of 1926 stated that: The distributor who pioneers and devises more efficient means of distributing goods, increases his business by reducing his prices and so passes on part of his economies to the consuming public. If other distributors are to maintain their position, they must effect similar economies or persuade the public that they offer greater service and that the greater service is desirable.

Not by any antiquated methods of boycott or law can manufacturers hope to achieve their object, but by evolving more efficient, economic and progressive means of merchandising that will accrue to the benefit of the customer, can they hope for favor with the buying public.

Woodward Stores Ltd.

Saving the customer money was the nub of the whole matter. There were many points on which the three Woodwards, Charles,

104

Billy and Puggy disagreed, but on this principle they were in total concurrence: *Merchandise as efficiently as possible and pass the savings on to the consumer.*

The year 1926 was a fantastic one in Vancouver. Speculative interest changed from real estate to stocks and bonds. Wild financial adventuring, which was to end in panic and collapse three years later, was rampant. The prosperity of the city can be seen from this one statistic: bank clearings which in 1892 had totalled $8,000,000 in 1926 exceeded $888,000,000. For the next three years the city continued to expand. The municipalities of Point Grey and South Vancouver were amalgamated into it. A fine road was built up Grouse Mountain with a chalet at the top of it by means of which one of the most impressive views in the world was brought within easy reach and attracted thousands of tourists. The long projected Burrard Bridge was completed. So was the Second Narrows Bridge linking the mainland with the North Shore of Burrard Inlet. An air base at Sea Island was commenced. The employment index rose to unprecedented heights and sales of every commodity or gadgetry soared.

The Vancouver Board of Trade report for 1926 showed a population of 160,000, 240 miles of graded streets, a mineral wealth for British Columbia of $62,250,000. When Charles first arrived in the city these figures had been, respectively, 13,800, 38 miles and $472,442. The 1926 President of the Board of Trade, Melville Dollar, after commenting in his annual report on the excellence of Vancouver's Art Gallery, the University ("a showplace"), a thriving port, drydock and ever expanding store buildings (Woodward's success was particularly noted), concluded his report with these words:

In Point Grey alone the number of houses built amounted to 1,113 with a value of $4,446,000. This is an exceedingly encouraging sign showing that people are contented and happy, satisfied to invest in the community in which they live.

Woodward's served five million customers in 1924; by 1928 that number had grown to more than nine million. A sixth storey had been added to its building and the main block on Cordova Street extended westward to consolidate in a massive structure with the detached stores put up a few years previously. This expansion costing little more than $400,000 was modest when the prosperity of the city and the buoyancy of the economy were taken into consideration. Charles who was at times an impetuous gambler could also be at times prudent and cautious.

"This store has always paid cash for all its merchandise and fixtures," he stated in one of his editorial-type advertisements. "It is a home institution, owns all the premises it occupies and is not encumbered with mortgages."

The fixtures, moreover, were simple. He had watched with suspicion and scepticism the elaborately magnificent structures which had tempted many of the merchant princes of the North American continent and he had consistently avoided embellishment which was not functional.

When towards the end of 1929 came the crash which brought financial disaster to countless homes and businesses all over the continent, Woodward's not only weathered the storm but found that the principles and policies on which it had been founded were practically depression-proof.

CHAPTER THIRTEEN

Wynn-Johnson of Alkali Lake

The ranch at Alkali Lake which Charlie Wynn-Johnson, Billy's father-in-law, had bought in 1908 had by the mid-1920's become one of the best-known properties in British Columbia. This ranch had a powerful influence on the lives of the Woodwards. It was here that Billy first met and wooed his adored Ruth. Alkali Lake remained an abiding love for Ruth, her sisters and her children and became an indispensable part of the Woodward story.

Charles Edgar Wynn-Johnson was a remarkable man. His father, R. Byron Johnson, a London solicitor, had travelled in his youth all over Europe, had joined the rush to the Cariboo goldfields of British Columbia in 1862 where he had remained for several years and had even found time to write a book about his adventures there, as exciting as any novel, called "Very Far West Indeed". The family lived at Richmond on the banks of the Thames. Charlie and brother Dick had to start the day with a plunge into the river, summer or winter, sometimes with the ice running. Their father scorned the conventional public school and university education which he had had himself and sent his sons instead to a small boarding school at Guisnes in the Pas de Calais called Britannia House, a "fighting school of the old type" Byron called it, where it was strictly forbidden to talk English from breakfast to evening meal and where students fought each other every day at every spare moment. Then the brothers attended a day school at Twickenham where all activities were subordinated to rowing. After a final year at Nevenheim College, Heidelberg, Charlie studied Civil Engineering at the Crystal Palace of Practical Engineering and at the same

107

Charles Wynn-Johnson in 1908, the year he bought Alkali Lake Ranch. His daughter Ruth married W. C. Woodward in 1921.

time took night courses in chemistry and electricity at King's College, London. In the 1880's this was an unusual programme of studies for a "gentleman's" son.

Before he was eighteen Charlie was earning his living. Aged twenty he found himself working in an office in Euston Square, London, as secretary of several companies which operated light railways serving as feeders to the main trunk railroad lines. He considered his life to be deadly dull and suddenly decided to follow in his father's footsteps to British Columbia which had often been described to him as "one of the roughest, wildest countries on the face of the earth." The practical schooling he had received, his strong physique and his restless temperament equipped him well to cope with life in the wilds of Canada.

That same year, 1891, he was sheepfarming on Lasqueti, a tiny island a few miles off the east coast of Vancouver Island.

When he acquired Alkali Lake Ranch he was thirty-seven. His roving nature had taken him to the Yukon, Alaska, the Stewart River and other remote parts of the Northwest Pacific Coast. His marriage to Mabel Twigg was happy for them both. Though she had been brought up in comfort and luxury, she had a pioneer spirit as indomitable as her husband's and she followed him happily wherever fate took them.

Together they built Alkali Lake into one of the leading ranches in the country. On its hills and valleys Charlie eventually ran a herd of pure-bred Herefords numbering some three thousand head — a great contribution to the development of livestock in British Columbia. Former city archivist Major Matthews described his visit there in 1910: "I tied up the horses, walked through a luxurious garden of flowers and vegetables and mounted on the broad verandah of a sort of manor house . . ."

"Alkali Lake," reported Harry Marriott in his book 'Cariboo Cowboy', "was owned by the very fine family named Wynn-Johnson who had the respect of that whole area. They sure were real people."

Two extracts from Wynn-Johnson's diary show that he possessed a philosophy which made Alkali Lake much more than just a prosperous cattle company. One of these notes set out his religious faith.

How many of us have a real conception of the meaning of religion? Not many! Some of us even think that it is not a matter which should be mentioned as if it were a matter of weakness should we really think on those lines . . .

Religion is the the basis of good government. After all it is not a very complicated question and is all contained in the commandments. The question of how we are to worship God is largely one for our own selves, and many of us do not even go to church . . .

The perfect religion which most appeals to God and agrees with His teachings through Christ must mean worship. Charity in thought and deed, and chastity. The one millenium will come through, when all sects and separate creeds are embodied in one true religion, based solely on Christ's teachings.Wars will not occur because nations will be bound by the same consciousness as that of the individual.

Another entry in his diary outlined his plan to start at Alkali Lake a school colony for young men. Education in remote parts of British Columbia was then as now a formidable problem. These were the principles on which he decided that Alkali Lake Ranch School should be run:

A School Colony

A school Colony for lads between 14 and 18, to be recruited from families unable to maintain and start them in life.

The school to be non-denominational but general; religious education to be encouraged though not compulsion, i.e., lectures to be given inculcating a spirit of Christianity, honesty, industry and charity. Talks on the lines of those given by Mr. Cameron of the Ford Company.

One building to be lecture room and chapel and social hall.

The main course to be livestock farming, agriculture and all contributing trades. Carpentry, blacksmithing, mechanics and every other form of work. Complete shops.

Prizes to be constantly offered to create competition in efficiency. Stables and livestock sheds.

Pure bred Hereford herd to be kept and improved for shows. Work on ranch to be done by students. All labour to be paid for moderately, so much to be given for pocket money and balance to be given at end of time and invested as earned so as to earn interest.

A tribune to be established of which principal shall be president. To consist of six teachers and six students to be elected. The president to have casting vote, and right to veto under certain circumstances. An employment bureau to be maintained so as to obtain positions for those who graduate.

No politics. Common sense to be one of the mottoes.

Any teachers encouraging class prejudices or preaching communism to be replaced.

Later it may be wise to institute apprenticeships in trades not allied to farming, such as plumbing, bricklaying, etc.

Much depends upon the selection of a Principal who can govern without giving the impression of government. One who can institute friendly competition in all things that really matter.

To include cooking as some students will help in the kitchen and Hall.

By 1930 Billy and Ruth had three young children, Elizabeth, Charles and Mary Twigg. Life for Ruth was always happiest on a ranch and especially at Alkali, the home of her youth and the repository of her dearest memories. It was not surprising that she would elect to spend as much holiday time as could possibly be contrived at her parents' home in the Cariboo. Though Billy's upbringing had been exclusively urban he was quick to see the advantages of such an influence as Alkali Lake Ranch in the lives of his young family. Being a Woodward he was equally quick to realize that there was a potentially profitable source of supply for Woodward's Meat Department. His father-in-law was pleased to let him build a summer home on the ranch; and so it was that on his third birthday Charles, future Chairman of the Board, gravely surveyed the world from the back of a large brown mare named Flash.

Coming to the ranch for the summer holidays was the highlight of the year for all the young Woodwards but especially for young Charles. He rode the range with his aunt, Paddy Harris (later Mrs. Harold Cripps), Ruth's younger sister who knew as much about ranching as any cowboy. He watched the roping, branding and breaking in, saw the beef drives, round-up trips and night herding, the tons of alfalfa put up, the calves wrestled. He listened spellbound to the yarns of the cowboys and Aunt Paddy's children,

111

Mary Mabel and Jimmy, were his companions. History was repeating itself. Sixty years earlier his uncle John had spent the happiest part of his short life playing with his cousin Henry Anderson and young Cull Woodward on his grandfather's farm in Arthur, Ontario.

The Billy Woodwards were usually accompanied by Mabel Light, later Mabel Lloyd and affectionately known to all Woodwards as "Nanny". In 1975 Mrs. Lloyd celebrated the 50th anniversary of her service with the Woodwards. During the Second World War she married and returned to live in England. After she became a widow, she rejoined the family as housekeeper and companion to Ruth. At this writing she occupies a cottage on Woodwynn Farm.

In 1929 Billy Woodward was elected President of the Board of Trade. A perceptive journalist described him thus:

"His personality is as direct as his work. He is a man who acts quickly and surely, speaks directly, attack problems with a vigour and clarity of thought that are a tonic to see. He is completely unselfconscious, very human and entirely individual in everything he says, does or thinks."

Though he was the son of a rich man and vice-president of a thriving business, he had been familiar with poverty and privation. His father had seen to it that he had earned every dollar he received. As the years went on and Charles became more and more niggardly, cautious and cantankerous, Billy found his father's unyielding control of the Company hard to accept. Surely a man of seventy-seven, worth millions and with well-trained successors, should be ready to hand over the reins, he reflected.

The resentment was mutual.

"Of course we all like our sons," Charles wrote to his old friend C. J. Winkler in 1930, "but I have not the same affection for my sons as I have for my daughters."

He added with growing bitterness: "The people we meet today are only passing acquaintances. We don't make friends with them or they with us."

But it was Charles who had changed, not the people. Great wealth had brought in its wake suspicion and loneliness.

On October 29, 1929, the New York Stock Market broke. Prime securities tumbled like ninepins. Savings of a lifetime were wiped out overnight. Canadian markets simultaneously began to collapse.

112

The Great Depression, the worst in history, had began. Charles, with his sons Billy and Puggy, and office manager Silas Folkins met in private conclave.

It was a grim meeting. There had been a severe fire in the Store the previous June 7 and the fire insurance companies had proposed a settlement which Charles considered inadequate. Furthermore, there was the matter of the proposed garage. In view of the Stock Market disaster should they go ahead? The building of a garage on Cordova Street with parking space for the continually increasing number of customers' cars, with service station and a pedestrian tunnel connecting it with the Food Department across the street, had been under consideration for some time. The sons were convinced that such an addition was indispensable. Their father was uncertain.

Nothing like the Stock Market Crash had ever happened even within Charles' long lifetime.

"Perhaps we had better wait awhile," he said.

"Father," said Billy, "whatever happens on the Stock Market, people will have to buy groceries and household supplies. The tighter their finances the more likely they are to come to us, and more and more of our customers will own cars, no matter what. It is the way of the future. Not even a stock market collapse can stop it."

"Our firm is in as strong a financial position as any in the country," added Puggy. "You have often said so yourself."

"And," said Billy, "we have been conservative in our expansions. As you know, I have sometimes thought, too conservative. The only thing wrong with the plan is the garage might be too small."

Charles smiled grimly. In his opinion Billy would have had the building ten storeys high by now if matters had been left to him. But this time he gave in to his sons and at the next Directors' meeting he brought to their attention "the necessity of building a garage on Cordova Street for parking purposes and the better accommodation of customers while shopping."

After "considerable discussion" it was moved by W. C. Woodward, seconded by E. Hall that the garage be built that year.

Depression or no, it was opened on Saturday, October 18, 1930, preceded by a typical Woodward Advertisement.

113

First a lengthy statement summarized the Store's small beginnings to the "very high position it now occupies in the confidence of its customers and patrons". A eulogy on Vancouver followed. It was Canada's third largest city, had a harbour unsurpassed on the Pacific Coast, was destined to be the largest city in Canada. Its markets included China, Japan, Australia, New Zealand and all the South American countries as well as Canadian hinterland. Woodward's had the largest groceteria, the highest commercial rating, paid all its dividends to people who worked in the Store and were Vancouver residents.

After full and thorough descriptions of the Ramp Garage ("almost the entire material has been purchased in British Columbia"), the Gasoline, Oil and Tire Service, the Elevator, the Beacon Light "shining for all", the Underground Subway and the System responsible for such rapid growth, the editorial ended with these words:

> Our garage is the largest, we think, on the Pacific Coast; we know it is the largest in Canada, it will accommodate over 500 cars at one time — equal to two miles of cars.
>
> This garage, we believe, is the most up-to-date with its conveniences and appliances anywhere. Furthermore, this garage is built for the accommodation of our customers and patrons of the store.
>
> Some people express wonder at such a large place and ask, "Why spend so much money for this accommodation," They think a smaller place might have done. Possibly it would today, but we build for the future — what is big enough today is not large enough for tomorrow. Building this garage at the present time served two purposes — one was for the accommodation of our customers and the other was to help out the unemployment.
>
> We averaged 120 workmen per day for nearly six months in the construction of this one unit of our original building programme, and the entire building when completed will cost over $500,000, land included. This is not given to you in a braggadocio way. These are facts and history is always founded on facts. It goes to prove the wonderful possibilities of the City of Vancouver, where we have had the wonderful co-operation and the good will of our friends and patrons, these, combined with honest toil, show what can be accomplished. We thank you for your assistance and good will.

114

CHAPTER FOURTEEN

The Great Depression

The opening of the garage at that time was indeed a bold decision. In spite of U.S. President Hoover's optimistic predictions, the depression on the North American continent was becoming more and more severe. A cabinet committee in the United States had been appointed to formulate measures for the relief of rampant unemployment and had set high tariffs to shut out Canadian goods. In Canada the depression was just as bad as in the rest of the world. In fact, as Barry Broadfoot points out in "Ten Lost Years",

> Even the weather turned against us. The drought was destroying the West — the $1.60 a bushel price of 1929 (of wheat) skidded to 38 cents in 2½ years.

Broadfoot calls the Depression "the most traumatic period in our nation's history, the most debilitating, the most devastating, the most horrendous."

At this time, whenever Charles was in Vancouver, he lived in a big square house on Marine Crescent, a quiet attractive district of old houses and spacious gardens. His two daughters, May Fisher and Peg Smith, kept house for him and fussed over him in a manner that he enjoyed.

Since John Woodward's death in 1900, May had been his eldest child. She remembered the stores at Manitowaning, Gore Bay and Thessalon, had run the family home on Pender Street, had been a bookkeeper in the Main Street Store before she decided, on one of the rare occasions when she opposed her father, to become a teacher. In 1908 when she was 27, she had married Frederick

115

Fisher who worked for Canadian Fairbanks. He had no very elevated job and the young couple lived modestly and happily on Thurlow Street. They had no children and when her father asked her to look after him she was glad for she was by then a widow.

Peg's marriage to Sholto Smith had ended in divorce. Billy, who had never liked his brother-in-law, was not surprised at this outcome and encouraged her to join her father and sister on Marine Crescent. Peg's children, Phyllis and Jock, lived there too until Phyllis married and Jock grew up and moved away.

Every Sunday, after Sunday school, Billy's children — Elizabeth, Chunky and Mary Twigg, would be escorted across the park from their own house on Balsam Street nearby, to visit Charles. They would walk with trepidation down the long, dark, somewhat alarming corridor to the big room in which their grandfather, also somewhat alarming, would be seated by the fireplace, his back to them, his bald head showing at one end of his easy chair, his laced boots protruding at the other. One naked globe would be burning in the middle of the ceiling.

After a lengthy survey Charles would give each of the children five cents and a packet of tiny candies known as "hundreds and thousands". Sometimes, because he had a perverse streak, he would withhold this treat from one or the other and give no reason. Then he would tell them to be on their way, apparently as glad as they the visit was over.

On one occasion Twigg, too young to feel the awe which her grandfather inspired in the others and irresistibly tempted by his shining pate illuminated by the single globe, collected a mouthful of spittle, tiptoed to his armchair and carefully began to anoint him. Perhaps she thought her effort would restore some hair. Always unpredictable Charles seemed to enjoy the experience.

His sons never lost their awe of him. When he came to Christmas dinner with them, even when they were middle-aged, there would be frantic gargling and peppermint chewing to conceal the fact that they had had a drink or two before he arrived. Certainly there would be none until he had left. Restraint and uneasy formality marked the Christmas parties when grandfather was there.

"Charles had no car, one suit and one bag, and no porter ever carried it," wrote journalist Mac Reynolds.

116

One of his few extravagances was to go to the Beacon Theatre on Hastings Street where he could see a Vaudeville show for ten cents. Sometimes he liked to take his nine-year-old granddaughter Elizabeth with him, though the entertainment was, in today's parlance, "mature".

In 1935, when he was eighty-three, he visited his relatives at Arthur and Mount Forest and saw again the Ontario farms where he had been born and raised. He gave lavish presents to his sister Hannah and his brother Cull, nineteen years younger than himself and former playfellow of his own son, John. How long ago those days seemed and how little real contentment his success had brought him!

His eighty-fourth birthday he celebrated at his desk in the Edmonton store. When asked by some brash youngster why he bothered with the discomforts of travel when he had so many experienced and able assistants, he replied: "Don't fool yourself, young man. I like to know what's going on for myself."

In the Vancouver store he kept his eye on the business by opening all the mail himself. He would slit each envelope so as to use the back of it for scrap paper. Then he would walk around to the various departments, never using the elevators, would fix each manager with a direct look, say "Good morning, Squire" and hand him his mail. The manager would feel the uselessness of trying to hide anything from that penetrating scrutiny.

Once when he returned from a trip and found no one to meet him, he walked from the Canadian Pacific Railway Station along Cordova Street to the Store, let himself in with his key and went to sleep in a display bed in the Furniture Department where he was discovered by an amazed night watchman.

His integrity was unassailable. A fiercely anti-government letter that he wrote in 1928 to the editor of a local paper ended his career as M.L.A.

"I warned him," said the editor. "I told him: 'That's a nice piece of news but it will put you out.' He looked me in the eye and replied: 'I just want them to know where I stand.'"

He could be generous especially where money was not concerned. A department manager sued the Store for wrongful dismissal and lost; later Charles rehired him. Sometimes he displayed a sardonic sense of humour, as for instance when a charity collector mustered the courage to acknowledge his fifty-dollar gift by telling him:

"But Mr. Woodward! Mr. W. C. Woodward gave five hundred dollars to this cause!"

"Ah!" replied Charles, "but he has a rich father."

His love for Vancouver was deep and genuine. In 1932 when the Second Narrows Bridge went out he offered to put up $30,000 to keep the link with the North Shore.

As the Depression deepened and its impact on the lives of the Canadian people increased, salary cuts became more and more widespread. At the University of Toronto in 1933 reductions in academic pay ranged up to 35%. Even lecturers who earned but $1,000 a year were knocked by 5%. Other universities across the country were forced to make pay cuts just as severe. So were the major banks and businesses. Salary cuts were accepted without protest on the grounds that a reduced wage was better than no job.

Wage levels were depressed almost beyond belief. Twenty to twenty-five dollars a week was good pay in Vancouver in the Thirties and a man earning such a wage was luckier than most. A family on relief received ten dollars a month. Junior teachers earned thirty dollars a month, waitresses four dollars a week.

These appalling conditions led Charles to one of the most regretted events of his life. In 1933 Woodward salaries were cut by 10% for staff earning less than $30.00 a week, by 15% for staff earning more than $30.00. This decision was induced by a belief that the Depression showed no signs of lessening, indeed quite the contrary, and by a conviction that the Store could thus avoid laying off staff. Wasn't there already a vast army of unemployed, he argued? Hadn't he saved the Company from liquidation in 1904 by reducing all the managers' salaries including his own to $75.00 a month?

In spite of the Depression Woodward's basic low-priced, honest value policy and reputation for fair dealing brought a steady advance in sales and profits. Charles believed that nobody would benefit if this trend were to be reversed. The sea of financial distress in which the Store existed and continued to thrive made him more cautious than ever.

Its swift, spectacular growth, however, had attracted the attention of the Parliamentary Mass Buying Committee sitting in Ottawa. Charles, the friend of the workingman, the promoter of profit-sharing by making his staff members shareholders, was accused of making unjustified salary slashes.

Billy had never approved the wage cut. What his father had done in 1904, what other businesses were now doing, he declared, was irrelevant. Woodward salaries should go only in one direction — up. Before long the reduction in wages was restored. But the damage was done, the newspapers seized on the incident and the good name of the Company suffered.

Charles, an honest and courageous man, the enemy of corruption, who by his vision and his enterprise had added greatly to the prosperity of British Columbia and Alberta, never fully recovered from the blow to his pride.

"I sometimes like to think I have contributed something to Vancouver," he said to a reporter later. "You know, reducing the cost of living and giving people good service is supposed to help any community."

When he died in 1937 the people of Vancouver showed that they thought so, too. On a hot June afternoon many hundreds of them came to St. Andrews-Wesley Church which he himself had formally opened four years previously and where he had worshipped twice each Sunday since. Representatives were there of the Province, the City, the Pioneer Association, the local Council of Women and of countless business organizations. Men and women from all walks of life crowded into the large church filling every seat. The pallbearers were his friends and associates, the young department managers who, led by his sons and grandson, would bring Woodward Stores to heights which even he had never envisaged . . . Bill Mann, Tom McBride, David Blackburn, George Duncan, W. T. Ells, Bill Sinclair and, from the Edmonton Store, John Ferguson.

"I doubt if the life of any individual in this community was more significant in the development of Vancouver than Mr. Woodward's," said Dr. Willard Brewing in paying his tribute. "I never met a man in whom success was so mingled with sheer simplicity."

That same month, June of 1937, an impoverished 42-year-old

Charles Woodward, founder of the Woodward Stores, c. 1925.

Canadian named Roy Thomson purchased a small remote radio station in Northern Ontario and started to build an enormous fortune. His career and character bore an astonishing similarity to Charles Woodward's. The two men had been born within fifty miles of each other, left school at the age of 14, were the sons of poor men and made little or no money until they were middle-aged. Both were ingenuous, had an unassuming manner which belied their forcefulness, were frank and looked frank even when they were not. Both were business gamblers, went broke more than once, were confident in adversity, were non-drinkers, loved money but hated spending it. Both had political leanings and were widowed for much of their unusually long lives. Both were totally honest and believed that all parties to a deal must be happy with it.

CHAPTER FIFTEEN

Billy Goes to Ottawa

The new President, William Culham Woodward, was also a man of sheer simplicity. In vision, vigour and integrity he matched his father and he had much greater ebullience. Unlike Charles, Billy had had to serve a thirty-year apprenticeship before taking the reins and at times this apprenticeship had been irksome. Though he admired and respected his father, the unyielding control which he had exercised right to the end of his life led to frequent disagreements.

During those thirty years the new President had travelled widely, had amassed a huge number of friends and had held appointments in a variety of different organizations in British Columbia and beyond. These were advantages Charles had never enjoyed. Apart from four years as a political stormy petrel his total interest had been contained by the Store.

Billy was a charter member of the Board of the Bank of Canada. This government-owned central bank established in March, 1935, had seven directors. He was unanimously elected representative for Western Canada. He had served as President of Vancouver's Board of Trade, was a life governor of the General Hospital, founder and patron of the Little Theatre, member of the Vancouver Welfare Association, Honorary Lieutenant-Colonel of the 15th Field Regiment R.C.A., director of many companies, and of the Royal Bank as well as the Bank of Canada.

These appointments gave him a wide contact with men and affairs at many levels and in many spheres and would play a part in the Store's tremendous growth which was to follow.

Billy had another incomparable asset. Puggy was now Vice-President and in sole charge of merchandising. Billy was unexcelled in public relations and an excellent financier; it is doubtful if there was a more brilliant merchandiser on the American continent than his brother. Between the two of them to what new heights could they not take their Store! And indeed they did achieve a most remarkable expansion.

The year before his father's death Billy had been in England, France, the U.S.A. and many countries of South America. Great Britain and Canada were the best countries he had visited, he declared on his return. In London he had witnessed the great procession of Jews protesting the persecution of Jews in Germany and had formed ominous conclusions of what was going on in Europe.

In 1937, as if to vindicate Mayor Gerry McGeer, who had built his much criticized million-dollar City Hall and a fountain at the entrance to Stanley Park during the Depression, there was at long last a visible upturn in the economy. Another bridge over Burrard Inlet, the Lions' Gate Bridge, was authorized by the Federal Government. Vancouver, much scarred by those lean years, nevertheless had survived them.

Before 1937 was over Woodward's had completed the largest expansion it had experienced for many years. The Store was increased to eight floors; the Lower Main Floor and sub-basement were extended to Cordova Street. An auditorium large enough to seat one thousand persons was presented to the staff in memory of Charles but was not completed for another eighteen months. It was to be used for recreation and for meals served at cost price.

In the Spring of 1938 the Provincial Government decided that it was time the Depression ended. It withdrew relief from unemployed men who had come to Vancouver from the Prairies, it reduced loans to the municipalities and made begging illegal. But sixteen hundred men who still considered themselves to be living at starvation level staged a "sit-in" at the Post Office, Georgia Hotel and at the Art Gallery. They were evacuated only when the police threw tear gas bombs amongst them. In revenge they tore through the streets breaking windows at David Spencer's and Woodward's Department Stores. Billy surveyed the shattered glass with tears, not for his windows but for the unemployed men's plight.

A few week's previously he had attended a reunion of former students of his two old schools, Strathcona School and the East End School on Cordova Street (in his young days called Oppenheimer Street). Angelo Branca, known as 'Kid', Alex McKelvie, Harry B. McKelvie, Walter and Russell Jordan, George Fitch, Brenton Brown, Jack Barker, Jack McMillan, George Millar, Frank Parsons and some forty others had been at the dinner. Later these reunions were attended by 300 or more. They elected Billy chairman. The East End was his part of the city and always would be. He had sympathy and understanding for those men who had broken his windows.

One year later, in March 1939, Germany occupied the whole of Czecho-Slovakia and Britain at last abandoned her policy of appeasement. During the Thirties Germany had withdrawn from the League of Nations, had broken the Treaty of Versailles by building a huge peacetime army and by remilitarizing the Rhineland, had annexed Austria and seized the Sudetenland. Each blatant act of aggression was accompanied by promises that Germany's "just claims were now completely satisfied" and each of Hitler's savage attacks was met with solemn protests from other European powers but with no retaliatory action. The occupation of Bohemia and Moravia, however, convinced Britain that she had been hoodwinked. She at once guaranteed Poland, German's next intended victim, against aggression. War between England and Germany became a virtual certainty.

Billy had great admiration for the British people. High on the list of people he admired was their monarch George VI, the modest man who, in spite of a pronounced stammer and much innate shyness, had unexpectedly to assume the throne after his brother Edward VIII abdicated and who set throughout the war years an outstanding example of courage, self-sacrifice and devotion. King George and Queen Elizabeth's visit to Vancouver the previous May with its opportunity to meet them had increased Billy's admiration. His loyalty could not be increased for it was total.

A surprise Nazi-Soviet friendship pact enabled Germany to launch its invasion of Poland on September 1, 1939. Two days later Great Britain and France declared war.

The people of England prepared themselves for war of a type

and on a scale never before experienced. They expected that bombs would rain down from the skies, that their cities would be set on fire, that normal living conditions would be utterly and immediately disrupted.

Nothing of the sort happened. Hitler, perhaps hoping to negotiate a peace after his conquest of Poland, took almost no action against the British or French. Canadians scarcely were aware that they were at war. This was the period of what was to be called the 'Phony War'. In the midst of it Billy was suddenly invited to join the War Supply Board. He was to be one of a number of "dollar-a-year" men, all of whom were asked to lend their business and administrative talents to the Canadian Government without pay.

Canada contributed to the winning of the Second World War by providing not only some 730,000 Canadians for the Armed Forces but also a vast supply of ships, aeroplanes, guns and munitions. This part of the Canadian War effort meant the creation of a whole new industrial front.

Vancouver was well satisfied to have W. C. Woodward as its representative in work so vital. Local newspapers carried such headlines as "Coast Businessmen hail Woodward's appointment to War Supply Board as ideal choice". Billy himself had no hesitation in accepting the challenge. He was 54, vigorous, confident, experienced. He insisted that his services should be gratuitous and refused to accept even the expense money which the Government offered its "dollar-a-year" men.

On December 14, 1939, 500 members of Woodward's staff crowded into the Canadian National Railway Station to see him off. They sang "The Gang's All Here", "For They Are Jolly Good Fellows" and "Auld Lang Syne". Bill Sinclair, the senior department manager, gave him a framed Illuminated Address. Catherine Bernard, manageress of the Wool Department, presented Ruth Woodward with a bouquet of longstemmed roses. Though the War was still 'phony' and casualties were minimal, some of the crowd wept as if they realized the imminence of the savage fury about to be unleashed.

From the platform of the train, Billy made a short speech:

"I'm glad to have this chance," he said. "In the last war I was commissioned as a Lieutenant with the First Canadian Heavy

125

Battery in 1916 and I returned three years later with the same rank, which is the easiest way of demonstrating what a good officer I was. Now I shall be serving in an area I know something about. My brother Mr. 'P. A.' will be as good a General Manager as Woodward's could possibly have."

They cheered him and cheered him as the train took him away to his duties. Ruth ever indispensable to him went with him.

Billy's new boss was Clarence Decatur Howe, an American-born engineer, a driving, indomitable man who was to be a leading figure in Canadian politics for the next twenty years. Already he had had an astonishing career. As a graduate engineer from the University of Boston he had come to teach civil engineering at Dalhousie University. Then he formed a business of his own in Port Arthur, designing and building grain elevators. Several of Vancouver's grain terminals were constructed by his firm. In 1935 he was elected M.P. for Port Arthur. In Parliament his career was meteoric. So successful was his direction of the new Department of Transport that his appointment to organize the all-important wartime Department of Munitions and Supply was an almost automatic choice.

Howe could be rude, presumptuous, arrogant and bullying but Billy liked him at once. In spite of their differences of background and personality the approval was mutual and Howe decided immediately that he would have this retail merchant from British Columbia as his right-hand man.

Another dollar-a-year man whom Howe marked for promotion as soon as the Department was set up was E. P. Taylor, President of Canadian Breweries and much involved Toronto businessman. Taylor was as modest and unassuming as Howe was brash. The Honourable Gordon Scott, former Provincial Treasurer of Quebec, was Howe's financial adviser and a third key man.

Howe, Woodward, Taylor and Scott were to share an experience as hazardous as any serviceman's and in it one of them would lose his life.

Though Ruth missed her children sorely she found the Ottawa scene interesting and frequently sat in the Members' Gallery of the House of Parliament to hear the debates. She was a fascinated spectator on January 25, 1940, the date of the famous session

126

W. C. Woodward leaves for Ottawa, December 1939, where he worked in the Dept. of Munitions and Supply as Hon. C. D. Howe's Executive Assistant.

127

when crafty Mackenzie King resenting opposition attacks on the 'scandalous apathy of Canada's war effort' on the spur of the moment dissolved parliament. This bold move, denounced by his opponents as political trickery, secured for the Liberal Government a greatly increased majority.

Billy proved a loyal subordinate. When some of his rich, distinguished colleagues were obstreperous and hard to handle, he took them to task, declaring: "Dollar-a-year men who offer their services to government must become public servants amenable to team discipline. They can't be free to blow off like any other private citizen."

There was ample criticism of the Department from all sides, even before it was set up: "The advice of Members of Parliament should be sought," shouted George Cruikshank, M.P. for Fraser Valley, "rather than some of these dollar-a-year men who couldn't be elected poundkeeper."

The Province newspaper severely rebuked Howe for saying that B.C. shipyards were filled to capacity whereas only eight cargo ships were presently under contract to be built in British Columbia.

"The installation of steam generating equipment in the Winnipeg Chemical plant has led to government overspending by $200,000," charged M.P. Ralph Maybank.

"I wonder how much Maybank knows about cordite," remarked Billy to the newsmen.

Such criticisms Ruth collected and pasted in the Woodward scrapbook, even the few personal attacks such as the letter from a disgruntled Communist who wrote anonymously to him:

"The people of your own province of B.C. tell me that you are only a fourflusher and not even loyal to the natives of the province in which you and your father made your livelihood. People in B.C. cannot make a living. Rabble and riffraff are in control."

Billy took a positive approach to all the problems. He encouraged the owners of small machine-shops by promising that, as soon as the Department had been organized, every industrial plant no matter how small would be used to expand war production.

"Already B.C. occupies third position in the Dominion in production," he said. "Shipyards in Vancouver and Victoria will soon be working 24-hour shifts for a long time to come" . . . He added:

128

"Mr. Howe has been under considerable fire in the House of Commons but he can take it." These promises were kept.

Early in April, 1940 the Department of Munitions and Supply was inaugurated with the Honourable C. D. Howe as its Minister and with a sizable group of administrators, consultants and technicians. Edward Taylor was Director-General of Munitions Production. Billy was Chairman of the Executive Committee and Director-General of the War Supply Board. One of his first appointments to the Board was J. P. D. Malkin, an old friend and business associate who had been Vice-President of W. H. Malkin Ltd. This large Vancouver firm of wholesale grocers had been recently acquired by Western Grocers and Philip Malkin was in virtual retirement. He became Director of Purchases, a position which his experience and ability enabled him to fill admirably.

Hardly had the new Department been established and Mackenzie King's majority government returned at the March 26 election, when Hitler struck. In quick succession Denmark, Norway, Belgium and Holland were overwhelmed by the mighty German War machine. By mid-June France lay prostrate before it.

CHAPTER SIXTEEN

The War Years (1)

Meanwhile under Puggy's forceful leadership the Store went on with its business, determined competently to serve the people and meet the difficulties of wartime operation. As anticipated from the 1914-1918 experience there were enormous difficulties of supply and shortage to be surmounted.

Puggy did not encourage his managers or key men to join the Armed Forces. He believed that they would make the most useful contribution to victory by staying with the job they knew and he did not underestimate the importance of that job. In the First World War an unending flow of reinforcements had been needed to re-place the great stream of casualties which occurred almost from the start. But in the Second World War this was not the case. It was to be years before Canadian casualties would occur on any large scale. So he sternly told his men that though the soldier's uniform was more glamorous than the storeman's smock, the store-man's work was no less important.

The first of Woodward's war efforts came from the Mail Order Department with the inauguration of Overseas Food Parcels.

There had been a service to enable customers to buy by mail since the Store began to operate in Vancouver. When Charles bought his first horse and buggy in 1896, it was used to travel around the countryside putting the Store sign high up in the trees. The Mail Order Department began to serve customers and spread Woodward's reputation for service all over British Columbia and beyond.

Mac Reynolds in an article published in the *Saturday Evening*

Post in 1952 reported some of the stories told by Charles Flanders, Mail Order manager for twenty-nine years:

> Mounties would order six months' supplies on one day's notice before leaving for the Arctic and usually find Woodward's had the supplies loaded on the boat before it sailed. Homesteaders would ask Woodward's Mail Order Department to buy headstones and to place the headstones on graves for them and Woodward's would do this. And then one morning the Mail Order manager would open his mail and find a gift of venison from a satisfied customer or perhaps a steelhead wrapped in ferns.

The Mail Order manager became father-confessor by correspondence to lonely up-country customers whom he seldom met. Once he was summoned to the side of an old lady who had collapsed on the street outside the Store with a heart attack. She asked to be carried to the Mail Order Department where she handed Flanders a purse containing three thousand dollars. Would he divide it among her three children? Would he see that they didn't spend it recklessly? Then she died, quite confident that her requests would receive Woodward service.

Sometimes the department was less efficient, as in the case of the plumber who sent in an order for a two-inch nipple and received a rubber attachment for a baby bottle with a note. "We regret this is the longest nipple we carry."

Woodward's was the originator of the Mail Order Food Parcel. When the war was less than one month old the suggestion was made, comical when one reads it in retrospect, that there would be in Great Britain "a shortage of certain luxury food lines" and that these might be provided by mail from Canada since parcels could still be sent weighing up to twenty pounds.

As the anticipated shortage of certain "luxury foodlines" became a desperate need of basic necessities, so did the idea of food parcels grow. Orders flocked in for them to be sent to England from all parts of the United States and every province of Canada, from Australia, New Zealand and the Pacific Islands. In October 1940 fifty thousand parcels were despatched from Woodward's. All through the autumn of 1941, when England and the nations of the

131

P. A. Woodward, Vice-President of Woodward Stores, a brilliant merchandiser whose genius made a major contribution to the firm's success.

Commonwealth gallantly waged war alone on behalf of civilization, all food parcels were supplied at cost. Many were lost at sea but Woodward's held the only insurance policy issued on such parcels.

The genius of Puggy Woodward was now unfettered. No longer did he have to contend with his father's domination and interference in every trifling matter. Even Billy who could be stubborn at times was off the scene. This Store which he loved so well now was his to guide and direct as he thought best. As a lad of fourteen he had worked with the construction crew to dig its foundation; he had helped clean it before school and delivered parcels for it after school. He knew every corner and as he walked about, hat on head, his keen eyes glinting behind his rimless glasses, he missed no detail. The managers, many of whom he had himself carefully chosen, seeking in them vision and initiative rather than slavish obedience, he could now train in his own beliefs, which were an updated, more imaginative version of his father's and marked by an innate brilliance of concept.

He was a sad man. He had inherited Charles' thriftiness and suspicion, he lacked Billy's exuberance and love of life, he never liked to show his feelings. Since he was the youngest of the family there was always someone whose approval he must seek before he could implement his ideas. The least suggestion of laziness, incompetence or dishonesty he could not tolerate. He was a hard taskmaster. The tragic loss of his only son Douglas, who contracted cancer of the bone from a football injury and died in 1932 when only sixteen, embittered him further. He and Marion had no other children.

He was to find his great satisfaction in the widespread wisely-planned charities which were to make him one of British Columbia's most generous philanthropists.

The War did not touch Vancouver for more than two years. In fact a small boom developed. Thousands of men were employed in the shipyards, at the Boeing Aircraft plant on Sea Island and in the port which was setting new records monthly. The City for the first time in Canadian history became headquarters for Pacific Command and embraced all army establishments in British Columbia and the Yukon. The Burrard Drydock built and outfitted 109 wartime cargo vessels, more than one-third of Canada's ten-thousand-tonners. The new Vancouver Hotel which had been built jointly by the CNR and

1st Row: (left to right) V. Hoby, Men's Clothing, D; Ebert Howe, Mgr. Optical, R; S. Devlin, Mail Order Shipping, LE; M. Francis, Mgr. Lamps, Millinery, D; T. Dale, Grocery, LE; W. Hadfield, Bldgs, Supt., D; "Taffy" Jones, Delivery, LE; E. Hayes, Carpets, R; Ken Caine, Mgr. Engineers, R; F. Baldry, Maint. D; A. Elson, Mgr. Furn., R; T. Davis, Furn. Warehouse, D; J. Shillito, Furn. warehouse, D; 2nd Row: U, Appliances, LE; D. Blackburn, Dir. & Mgr. Draperies, D; A. J. Rowse, Office Mgr., D; H. Wood, Mgr. Oakridge Centre, R; T. Polson, Mgr. Bakery, LE; U; N. Gray, Furn., R; R. Binley, Div. Merch. Mgr. Sporting Goods, R; U; Wm. McBryde, Mgr. Cash office, R; J. McHugh, Mgr. Staples, LE; G. Hodgson, Furn., SE; T. Dack, Super. bakeries, R; 3rd Row: F. Bradbrer, Mgr. Delivery, R; K. Beck, Mgr. Furn., Port Alberni, LE; H. Conroy, Men's Clothing, D; G. Kelly, Mgr. Watches and Clocks, R; U; U; H. Scarlett, Office Mgr., D; G. Rutledge, Grocery, R; Ted Fulcher, Mgr. Garage, LE; U; S. Olsen, Personnel, LE; W. Ince, Mgr. Drugs, LE; Back Row: S. Crimmin, Sales-Furn., D; R. Baldrey, Mgr. Food Floor, Oakridge, R; J. B. Drain, V.P., Appliances, R; T.R. Farrell, President, R; B. Boren, Supvr. Food Floors, Alta., SE; Alex Ross, Store Mgr., New West., SE; J. Cain, Mgr. Housewares, R; J. C. Haddock, V.P., Victoria, D; G. Rennie, Dir., Div. Merch. Mgr., Grocery, R; W. Lemon, Sales-Furn., LE; U; U.

SE - still employed   R - retired   D - deceased   LE - left employ   U - unidentified
Unless otherwise indicated, all Vancouver employees.

134

CPR just prior to the outbreak of war was continually filled to capacity. The old Hotel stood like a symbol of the past. Once it marked the ultimate in grandeur. Now it became a military headquarters and later a temporary answer to returning veterans' housing problems. It was torn down after the war because Vancouver had outgrown it.

Puggy saw to it that Woodward's supported Canada's war effort in every possible way, short of supplying manpower not then needed. The Store was used to promote the sale of Victory Loans: Woodward's and the Woodward family were the largest donors to the War Chest. Vancouver's Air Raid Precautions Unit organized by Mayor J. W. Cornett was aided by the sale of stirrup pumps, scoops and buckets at prices low enough to encourage the average householder to buy them. Servicemen were entertained at dances and parties held in the Charles Woodward Auditorium. A Reserve Army Unit, 50 strong, all Woodwardites and known as The Frontiersmen "W" Squadron paraded twice a week using the roof of Woodward's Garage for a parade ground.

The practice of price control was again rearing its ugly head and Woodward's opposed it as strenuously as ever. At a Directors' Meeting in December 1940 "recent Provincial legislation regarding Price Fixing was regretted and steps were proposed to deal with the situation." In wartime arbitrarily fixed minimum prices seemed to Puggy a measure likely to promote profiteering.

The steadily rising cost-of-living in wartime Canada was met at Woodward's by the initiation of a cost-of-living bonus at first of 5% then increased to 9% with in addition a special war wage of 5% for more senior staff. Charles' plan permitting a few staff members of exceptional promise and seniority to become shareholders in his company was greatly extended. Puggy not only permitted but encouraged staff members with over one year's service to buy shares. At the first three Directors' meetings held in 1940 the purchase by staff of 5170, 6550 and 4980 five-dollar shares respectively was authorized. No down payment was required and though the amount allowed was governed by the salary earned "special consideration was given to deserving individuals."

Many staff members took advantage of this benefit and at each annual meeting there was invariably a motion expressing "the great satisfaction felt by employees in being allowed to purchase stock." They had every reason to feel satisfaction. As the Company grew in financial stature and reached a point where Woodward shares had to be placed on the open market, they were split more than once and increased greatly in value.

During the War years no building programme was carried out at Woodward's in Vancouver. C. Woodward's in Edmonton, however, which had had small additions in 1932 and 1939 was bursting at the seams and in January 1940, a two-storey addition was announced. The work was to begin in April, would cost between $150,000 and $200,000, would make the Store a five-storey building and would take two years to complete. Billy came from Ottawa to make the announcement. He said:

"Our Company's record of steady growth here has more than justified the faith in Edmonton's future which was held by my father when he started business here. He was always sure that Edmonton would be a great commercial centre and he has been proved correct."

Before returning to Ottawa he attended a service at the little United Church where his father had worshipped when in Edmonton. Billy was a religious man with a fondness for small unpretentious churches. In Vancouver he frequently went to services at the chapel of St. George's School, the private school where Chunky was being educated. In Ottawa he worshipped at St. Barnabas.

"I cannot thank you enough for the glorious surprise and generous gift: thank God for your warm heart," its rector the Reverend Herbert Browne wrote to him on receiving one of many unexpected contributions.

Regrettably few top-flight businessmen, either then or now, could elicit such a 'letter to the editor' as this one, published after an address to the Tacoma Chamber of Commerce:

> Lt. Col. Woodward proprietor of a large retail store made a very good impression as a man, speaker, and a minister of the crown. In the dangerous place where destiny has now brought civilization he advised several steps . . . One of them, that of persistent prayer, will bring a smile to many faces, but may it not be that this outstanding leader speaks out of more searching wisdom, a more penetrating knowledge?

CHAPTER SEVENTEEN

Torpedoed Mid-Atlantic

Billy was now C. D. Howe's executive assistant. He liked and admired Howe more than ever though even in his letters to Ruth he always referred to him as "Mr. Howe" or "the Minister" and it is probable that the two men were never on a first-name basis.

In December 1940 Howe decided to go with his key men, E. P. Taylor, Gordon Scott and Billy to England to study at first hand that embattled country's needs and to learn from her methods.

Submarine warfare was at its height. Though Germany never succeeded in her attempt to cut supply lines across the Atlantic, her submarines were sinking millions of tons of shipping. Within the last few weeks the Canadian Pacific liner *Empress of Britain* and Canadian destroyers *Fraser* and *Margaree* had been torpedoed and sunk. Canadian destroyer *Saguenay* had just managed to limp to a British port.

"The week ending September 22 showed the highest rate of loss since the beginning of the war: twenty-seven ships of nearly 100,000 tons were sunk, many of them in a Halifax convoy. In October another Atlantic convoy was massacred by U-boats, twenty ships being sunk out of thirty-four." ('Their Finest Hour' by Winston Churchill)

There was no minimizing the dangers which were involved in a trans-Atlantic journey and which were accepted without hesitation by Howe and his "dollar-a-year" men.

On Thursday December 5 they boarded the liner *Western Prince* which had a passenger list of 70 including four women and a total complement of about 175 and sailed next day. Howe's diary for Friday December 13th read:

"Everyone is rather nervous having regard to the day and date! It is generally felt that if we are to be torpedoed this will be the day. Practically all the passengers finished the day in the smoking room and at 12 midnight everyone breathed a sigh of relief and left to go to bed."

The torpedo struck at 5:30 next morning. The ship reeled to the tremendous shock. Billy awoke, grabbed the lumberman's suit which Ruth had given him for just such an emergency, rushed on deck, found that the crew were starting to lower a lifeboat, returned to his cabin to salvage a prize cigarette case and pencil, also gifts of his wife, and marvelled at the total absence of hysteria.

It was pitch dark and raining. A 70-mile an hour gale was blowing. The ship was rolling and pitching, the lifeboats crashing against her with each battering wave. There were two women and four babies among the 38 people in No. 2 Lifeboat to which Billy, E. P. Taylor and Gordon Scott had been assigned.

Western Prince had been hit towards the bow and was sinking rapidly. Captain Reed refused to leave the bridge. Second Officer R. F. White and the Captain's Steward Jimmy Franks elected to remain with him. As the lifeboats drifted away Reed sounded three blasts on the ship's whistle as a farewell gesture to his passengers and in defiance to the Nazis. White was picked up later after eight hours in the water but the Captain and Franks lost their lives.

Suddenly the submarine surfaced, top works and perimeter out of the water, empty deck awash, her crew taking photographs of the wreckage. She passed by, leaving the lifeboats to the grey dawn and the fury of the mounting gale. So high were the waves it seemed incredible that the lifeboat could climb them.

At 2:00 p.m. after eight fearful hours of rowing and baling, of being soaked with freezing water, of courage and concern for others and of all the wonderful qualities which men and women display in times of catastrophe, a small vessel was sighted coming towards them. It was a 5000-ton freighter *Baron Kinnaird* of Glasgow en route to Tampa, Florida, in ballast. Flares were fired, then somehow the lifeboats were alongside the rescue ship. Ignoring the nearness of an enemy submarine she proceeded to take the 160 survivors on board a ship which had accommodation for 40. In near hurricane conditions transfer from open boat to steamer was not easy.

Then tragedy struck again. Gordon Scott had not gone in the life-boat assigned to him but in another, equipped with a motor and filled mostly with crew. This lifeboat struck the side of the rescue-ship and capsized. Seven of the 26 men in it were crushed or drowned in the icy waters. Scott was one of them.

The women and babies in Lifeboat No. 2 were hauled aboard the *Baron Kinnaird* in a coal basket while the men scrambled up rope ladders.

"Woodward," recorded C. D. Howe, "was in good shape but Taylor had been very seasick and looked badly."

The Captain, a cheerful, dauntless Scot named Dewar, turned over his cabin to ten of the passengers including Howe, Taylor and Billy, and he did not sleep from then until the arrival in Glasgow four days later. The cabin had one bunk into which two people could crowd while the other eight slept on the floor. On account of the blackout the door might not be opened when the lights were turned on and with the door closed, the room was almost airless.

"Woodward," recorded Howe, "was elected Doorman, his job being to close the door when the lights were on and open it when the lights were off." Food for the trip was hardtack and canned beef.

Merchantships received strict instruction from the Admiralty not to go to the rescue of torpedoed ships but to leave that job to the Navy. Fortunately for the 160 survivors of *Western Prince* Captain Dewar and his officers held a meeting and elected to disregard that instruction. Fatal casualties amounted to six crewmen and 10 passengers.

Howe, E. P. Taylor and Billy stayed in England for almost a month. Some of his letters home deserve substantial quotation both for their content and their simple, graphic style. Here is his account of the torpedoing:

LETTER No. 1

The Dorchester Hotel,
Park Lane,
London, W. 1.
21st December, 1940

My Darling Ruth,

While the incidents are fresh in my mind, I would like to put them down on paper for the children to keep. You must

139

have had a frightful three or four days, and I think I possibly worried as much about you as I did about myself, if a selfish man can worry. Anyway, it was wonderful to get your cable.

The first four or five days of the voyage were uneventful, quite rough and cold, sixty-two passengers in all. The ship was comfortable but bitterly cold, no hot water for baths particularly, but beyond that no inconveniences. I surprised all my party by going on the wagon, so much so, that a Petition was got up to ask me to come off the wagon.

The evening before the torpedoing was Friday 13th, and a great number of passengers stayed up until after twelve o'clock. I went to bed fairly early. At six o'clock in the morning there was a tremendous thud, and I yelled to Gordon Scott who was in the next cabin, that we were "for it" and to get dressed. I had all my heavy clothing ready on the bed and I think I was into them in less than three minutes, then went in to see how Gordon Scott was getting on. He was quite dressed, but I asked him to put heavy clothing on. We proceeded to the boat deck, and on the way up we met a steward who informed me that all passengers were out of their cabins. It was eerie when the Captain blew the whistle to abandon ship.

It was bitterly cold on deck and a heavy sea was running, pitch black and no light on. Passengers and crew were wonderful. I saw not one case of hysteria or fright, although God knows most of us must have been damn frightened — I know I was. All this time the ship was well down by the bows. Taylor, Scott and myself were in No. 2 boat and Howe was in No. 3 boat. I asked a chap on deck if he had seen Howe, and he informed me that he was at his boat. As our boat by this time was quite full, and the women and babies had been put away, I said to Gordon "We had better get in" (Eddy Taylor had got in just before us). Gordon said "Go ahead". I stepped into the boat and thought he was following me, but unfortunately for him, he moved off to another boat which had a motor. The boat was lowered and we had several anxious minutes. No. 4 boat was being lowered on top of us and swinging over us, but after that was corrected we struck the water and shipped a heavy wave, which about a quarter filled the boat. As we were on the windward side, our boat was continually banging against the ship and there was a great deal of confusion trying to get the oars out several of which were broken.

Eventually we managed to get clear of the ship and drifted

140

off to leeward. Some bright lad by this time discovered the plug was out of the bottom of the boat, but this was not true. I kept checking very carefully if the water were coming up in the boat. The waves were so high that at times it was impossible to see our steamer. In about ten minutes there was a terrific explosion and a sheet of flame which was the last of our boat. The Hun had shot another torpedo into her.

We continued to float and drift around for eight hours, the sea getting larger all the time and a storm blowing up. Some idea of the height of the waves, if you can imagine it, were this extent — when our boat was on the crest of the wave, we could look down upon the deck of the rescue ship. We had a wonderful sailor keeping our boat head on to sea, but beyond him and myself, there was not a soul who had the slightest idea of how to handle it. One of the men insisted on putting up the sail. I told him that if he did it would be over my dead body and if he had any ideas that he could reach Iceland, England or Canada, or whatever place he thought he might get to, he was "all Wet". I also told them that if there was one boss in the ship that was the sailor steering the boat and everyone would take orders from him.

Unfortunately for Eddy Taylor, he had a zipper suit on and the zipper would not work. Poor Eddy arrived in the boat with a coat on and nothing else and I am afraid he was terribly cold. When I went on deck, I took all the rest of the woollen things in case some of the passengers might need them, also my cigarettes, but these soaked immediately.

Ten minutes after we left the ship, we were all horribly sea-sick. I managed to recover in about half an hour but the majority were miserable for the whole journey. My bad knee became frightfully cramped and absolutely numb, with no feeling in it. I was interested in getting the reaction of the people in our boat when we sighted the rescue ship. Nobody seemed the least bit excited. I think we all were perfectly sure we should be picked up, but how I do not know, as it was about two hundred miles south of Iceland where we were torpedoed. After a great deal of work we managed to get alongside our ship and immediately the women and the babies were hoisted up in a basket, and I had one anxious moment when I gripped the ladder in my hands, put my left weak leg on the step of the ladder and it immediately collapsed, leaving me swinging by my hands! I eventually dragged myself up.

141

Our rescue ship was only a nine knot boat and we immediately proceeded to race before the wind to the north. By this
time the sea was tremendous and the wind was roaring so that
you could not hear yourself. I asked the Captain to allow me
to go up on the Bridge with him, which he did, and at times
the seas were so high that when we were in a trough, all we
could see was green water on each side of us. It was a fearsome sight, but a grand one also. For twenty-four hours we
raced before the gale. I should think by this time we were well
north of the Orkney Islands, before we turned for Port. The
rest of the voyage was more or less uneventful, except that a
number of us realized the fearful danger we were in — two
hundred people in a ship with four life boats, accommodation
for forty, even if they could have been launched! I can assure
you the day before we reached Scotland, the most welcome
sight we saw were a couple of Destroyers. We had an added
bit of excitement seeing the Destroyers blowing up mines
which had been spread by the Hun a day or so before.

The Minister was wonderful throughout it all.

All my love, my dear. I am thinking of you constantly, and
the children.

Eddy Taylor and C. D. Howe send their felicitations.

Your loving husband,

LETTER No. 2

27th December, 1940

My Darling Ruth,

I spent Christmas with Sir Clive and Lady Bailleau at a
place about twenty miles from London. They have a beautiful
home and are delightful people. Christmas morning we went
to church in the King's Chapel, Windsor Great Park. It is a
very handsome small Church and the Parson was exceptionally
nice. We had dinner at the home of Lady Bailleau's father,
an Australian, about seventy-five years old, but hale and
hearty. He owns possibly one of the finest gardens in England.
It was a very old-fashioned Christmas. Eighteen of us sat
down to dinner, the Banks' and myself being the only strangers. In the afternoon quite a few young children came in,
the eldest was about five years old. They were mostly grandchildren of the Countess Jellicoe. Lady Jellicoe is a nice old
thing but a bit difficult to talk to. However, I got along very

well for a Canadian! Anyway, I was asked to make my home there while I was in England, which was not bad.

After ten minutes the old man and myself were calling each other Bill — not too bad, but he is the sort of chap you instinctively take to and if he likes you, makes no bones about telling you.

We are going to the Palace this week to leave our names, but the only person to be received (and who has been) is, naturally, the Minister. At least I will have written in the Book of books. They are all terribly kind here, and no one could humble the spirit of these wonderful people. Most of them must at one time or another have lived with death, but you see little signs of nervousness and they are taking it in their stride. They will never defeat these people if their leaders are right.

Your loving husband,

Billy enjoyed V.I.P.'s and did not hesitate to say so. During his month's stay in England he met a great number of them including Lord Beaverbrook, Lord Woolton, First Lord of the Admiralty A. B. Alexander, Generals McNaughton and Crerar, Lady Patricia Ramsay, Vincent Massey, Mr. Handly Page and, most frequently, Minister of Supply Sir Andrew Duncan. With these notables and many others he had to do business, determining to what extent and in what areas Canada should continue to supply the sinews of war. He was never obsequious nor overawed but able, as could his father and his son, to "shoot the breeze" on equal terms with any man.

LETTER No. 3

My Darling Ruth,
Continuing the Diary . . .

First, I cannot tell you how thrilled I was today to get your letter. If I had not been so tough I might have wept. Mrs. Howe said some very nice things about you in her letter to her husband. Of course, you acted just as I expected you to, though I think you flatter me much when you say that you think I would give my life for the Minister. I doubt it, and I hope to God I am never in the position of having to.

We arrived back just ten minutes after Fritz started last night, in the dark. The night before last we had been to a Reception given by the Second Division, and Taylor and I had to motor for two hours in pitch black. I must say our driver was a wonderful chap, he had cat's eyes, as nothing seemed to nonplus him.

We got home about eleven o'clock, but I am afraid there was terrific damage done and all to non-military places in London. I have never seen worse fires. Young Bill Howe and I went on the roof of the Hotel. When we got up there and saw it all, as I said, I could have wept. I doubt if there ever will be a deep enough Hell for Hitler and his gang. I loathe them. The harrowing thing about these raids is that one has a helpless feeling of not getting back at them, but these people can take it. This afternoon with the Minister, I attended a meeting at the Ministry of Supply and met Sir Andrew Duncan and other notables. It was very interesting and I must say C. D. handles himself damn well with these people. He is very diplomatic but he also is very firm and very correct in his dealings. I think they all have a great respect for him.

I shall read your letter peacefully again tonight and write you in a day or so.

Your loving husband,

I attended a meeting this morning of the Ministry of Aircraft Production, Lord Beaverbrook presided. He is certainly a histrionic old gentleman, with tremendous batteries of telephones, orders issuing, and all he needed to complete the resemblance to a busy American Executive, was to be biting off the end of a cigar.   January 4, 1941

Unfortunately, I have been unable to contact practically any of my friends in the City, as on Sunday the whole district of London was absolutely gutted. I should say the damage extends three-quarters of a mile square. There was never anything like it in France in the last war. All the firms we do business with have been absolutely wiped out.

(The above reference is to December 29, 1940, the worst night of the London blitz.)

I had an interesting experiment the other evening, when I stayed out all night chasing around different parts of London while it was being bombed up. I must say once more, these chaps who do their work night after night, also the women, are pretty wonderful. On Saturday night we had another fair-sized "Blitz". There were a number of fires and bombs around the Hotel.

144

In Piccadilly, some large car showrooms were demolished and eight people were killed. I don't think any of us have any idea of the amount of quiet suffering that goes on in the City. One hears of it casually but it shows very little openly. They certainly are not the people to whine . . .

Well, my sweet, I should think this will be the last letter I shall write, and the next time you will be seeing me in the flesh. I am going home with very mixed feelings, sometimes hating leaving and other times damn glad to get out of it, but I have an idea we will be coming back next summer.

January 13, 1941

CHAPTER EIGHTEEN

The War Years (2)

Billy came back from England on the battleship *King George V* and persuaded the captain to give him its ensign. This historic flag he presented to St. George's School in Vancouver. Two cheques for $1500 and $780 covering expenses allowed him by the Government for his trip to England he returned to Hon. J. L. Ilsley, the Minister of Finance.

In April, 1942 Billy terminated his duties in Ottawa and returned home. The needs of his family, of the Store and of many people who in one way or another depended on him, necessitated this move, even though he indicated that he would be willing to return to Ottawa at a later date or even be a representative of the Department in London. Two of the letters he received were especially valued. One was from Prime Minister Mackenzie King:

Ottawa, April 4, 1941

Lieutenant Colonel W. C. Woodward,
   Chateau Laurier,
      Ottawa, Ontario
My dear Colonel Woodward:
   I have been very sorry to learn from your letter of March the 28th that circumstances have obliged you, at least temporarily, to return to Vancouver.

My colleagues and I are most appreciative of the unselfish service which you have given in the promotion of Canada's war effort from the very inception of the activities of the War Supply Board up to the present time.

The large and important share which you had in the work

of organizing the War Supply Board, and in laying a solid foundation for the expansion of the production of munitions and supplies on a wartime basis, has helped to make possible the tremendous war programme in which Canada is now engaged.

The loyal and unfailing co-operation you have extended to my colleague, the Minister of Munitions and Supply, in the ordinary work of the department in Canada, and particularly during your recent visit to the United Kingdom, has been of great assistance to Mr. Howe himself and to the Government as a whole.

I should like, on behalf of the government to express our warmest thanks for the splendid service you have given to Canada. I need hardly assure you that your willingness to be of service on some future occasion will be kept in mind by my colleagues and myself.

With kindest personal regards to Mrs. Woodward and yourself.

(W. Mackenzie King)

The other letter came from C. D. Howe:

Office of the Minister of Munitions and Supply
Ottawa, Canada
March 29th, 1941

Dear Mr. Woodward:

I have your letter of March 28th suggesting that your services as Executive Assistant must be terminated at approximately the middle of April. I sincerely hope that this will not be necessary. You have contributed greatly to the work of this Department since its inception, and I am most reluctant to terminate your association wtih the Department.

. . . .

In the meantime, I cannot tell you how much I appreciate your work to date. Your public speaking in Western Canada during the past three weeks has been particularly helpful.

Yours truly,
C. D. Howe

On his return from Ottawa Billy was given an official civic reception and was at once inundated with requests to talk to meetings about his experiences in England. All such invitations he declined until he had spoken to the employees of Woodward Stores.

147

Eleven hundred of them crowded into the Auditorium one April evening after the Store was closed, gave him a tumultuous welcome home and a gold Honour Roll indicating that every member of the staff was making a monthly contribution to the War Savings Campaign. This one hundred per cent participation was unique. Billy congratulated them and spoke to them about lessons he had learned abroad:

"I was a careless citizen of Vancouver before I went to Ottawa," he said. "I criticized politicians, took for granted my church, our way of life, our freedom of speech. My experience has made me feel humble, humble because of my impressions of how the people of Britain are facing their attackers."

He arranged for Woodward's to subscribe one quarter of a million dollars without interest to the Government.

Puggy at once relinquished his position as General Manager and was not pleased to have to do so. Now once again he would be the younger brother and would have to submit to debate and discussion of his decisions. Again there would be fraternal disagreements.

Family rows among the Woodwards were frequent and furious, especially between the brothers and the sisters. Donald, next eldest to May, who had lived on his ranch in California with his wife Nina since 1911, was not implicated. His decision to cut himself off from his father's Store remained firm and he took no part in the battles that followed Charles' death. For battles there were, and of considerable dimensions. The founder's will seemed to have been drawn up in such a manner as to make dispute inevitable.

Ever since the meeting of December 30, 1937 of Woodward Holdings, the family company which Charles had set up five years earlier, brothers and sisters had barely been on speaking terms. The first motion, made at that meeting by Billy, was that his elder sister Mrs. F. W. Fisher should take the chair. But May stated that she was entitled to be chairman of the meeting by virtue of her office.

"I refuse to put the motion," she declared.

With this ominous pronouncement the meeting commenced and continued for two unhappy hours of protests and objections. Fifteen days later the President and Directors (Billy, Puggy and solicitor Kay Collins) received a letter in which May "irrevocably tendered her resignation as Director from the said Board."

148

Had Peg Smith been a director she would have resigned, too.

A large part of May's income was derived from the lease of the Abbott-Cordova corner of the Store which Charles had retained as his personal property and only leased to Woodward's Limited. The brothers, therefore, to whom had been left the control of the Store sometimes felt they had reason to charge their sisters with "interference" while the sisters often felt powerless to make decisions about their own money. Descended from Charles, they were all strong-minded people, even gentle May, and so the bickering continued.

In spite of her withdrawal from Woodward Holdings May Fisher was a rich woman and from her penthouse atop the Marine Building she continued to support with intelligence and thoroughness a wide variety of charities. Probably the most far-reaching of these was a gift in 1938 to the Cancer Control Agency of $50,000 to be used to start the B.C. Cancer Institute. The gift, she said, must remain anonymous until after her death, and so it did, until 1966. Wartime Vancouver provided many outlets for her generous instincts. It is a little-known fact that throughout the war years she provided servicemen with a place for recreation and cheap meals while on leave by privately paying the rent on the Georgia Dugout.

The war was still a long way from British Columbia. Though Japan was drawing closer to the Axis powers, Vancouverites could only share vicariously the tribulations of their sons and relatives overseas.

Puggy was soon back as General Manager of Woodward's for in August 1941 Billy was asked to accept the appointment of Lieutenant-Governor.

The Lieutenant-Governors of British Columbia have been remarkable in their devotion to duty but none can have been more dedicated than the new incumbent. The Crown's representative must recognize, encourage and support worthwhile causes and meritorious people. Now their number was greatly increased. To the claims of the local institutions and the visiting ambassadors must be added the Victory Loan Campaigns, the Investitures and more naval, military and airforce activities than can be enumerated Fortunately both Billy and Ruth were blessed with unusual energy and used it without stint in the service of British Columbia.

Approval was given at Cabinet Council on August 30, 1941 to Billy's appointment which was acclaimed even more enthusiastically than had been his appointment to the War Supply Board. This was the boy who had once sold papers to the gold miners roaring off to the Yukon! This was the young man who in 1907 had sat perched on an office stool, keeping the books of a small corner-store on Main Street! This was a man of the people! To a host of them in the city and all over the province he was "Billy", friend and neighbour. The *Vancouver Sun* editorialized:

"If a Gallup Poll were possible for this responsible position, Colonel Woodward would have been practically a hundred per cent choice."

On all fronts the War news was bad. German troops were advancing rapidly into the Ukraine and had almost completed the encirclement of Leningrad. The widespread demand for the Allies to launch a Second Front went, for good reasons, unheeded. Mackenzie King visiting restless Canadian troops in England had been roundly booed. The landing of Canadians on the almost uninhabited island of Spitzbergen "in order to destroy whatever might be of use to the Germans" had done nothing to satisfy the clamour for action.

Billy was sworn in as the sixteenth Lieutenant-Governor, Trustee and Keeper of the Great Seal of British Columbia, at a private ceremony with only Government Ministers and Officials in attendance. Chief Justice M. A. MacDonald administered the oath, A. D. M. Fairbairn, Permanent Government House secretary, read the Royal commission and appointment. Premier Pattullo, Minister of Finance Hon. John Hart and retiring Lieutenant-Governor Eric Hamber were the first to congratulate him. The Bible used for the occasion was presented to him and remained his treasured possession.

The date of his appointment was the second anniversary of the outbreak of war and his first public duty was to attend a Rededication ceremony. At City Hall he inspected the Vancouver Branch of the Corps of Commissionaires and other Imperial War veterans. He took their salute as they marched to church at St. Paul's.

Speaking to the assembly he said: "We dedicate ourselves anew to continue the struggle until the evil of Nazi tyranny is destroyed and

150

W. C. Woodward — Lieutenant-Governor of British Columbia.

the foul thing that is rampant in the world today is stamped out."

Ruth's first official act was the opening of a Victory Fair to provide another mobile canteen for overseas use, her second to launch a ten-thousand-ton steel cargo ship built at Burrard Dry Dock. The launching was a totally British Columbian effort. The ship was named *Fort St. James* after the original Hudson Bay Trading Post. Even the bottle of champagne smashed against her bows came from the Okanagan Valley.

Almost at once Billy found himself facing political troubles. Premier T. D. Pattullo, that same politician with whom fifteen years earlier Charles Woodward had tangled so fiercely and whom he had accused of "riding roughshod over the people of Vancouver," was losing popularity. Pattullo had been charged with putting his own political interests ahead of Canada's. In the election held on October 21 the Liberal Government, to its surprise, lost ten seats and was reduced to a minority position. Vancouver did not return a single Liberal. Even John Hart, Pattullo's closest friend, turned against him. His great contributions to British Columbia were disregarded.

In this political climate, Hon. R. L. Maitland, leader of the Conservative party, made a dramatic plea for the establishment of a Coalition Government. He believed that with twenty Liberal, thirteen Conservative and fourteen C.C.F. members, a stalemate had been reached, and that no party could win a majority. Though Harold Winch, leader of the C.C.F., called Maitland's proposal "opportunism", it was an act of statesmanship against his own political interest which provided British Columbia with good government for the duration of the War. When "Pat" Maitland died in 1946 the Province lost a great orator and a distinguished politician.

For six weeks the drama continued. There was an open break between the two former friends, Pattullo and Hart. At last, at a Liberal convention held on December 3, 1941, Hart was elected head of the Liberal Party, Pattullo resigned and Hart formed a Coalition Government with Maitland as Attorney-General.

To the new Lieutenant-Governor the world of politics was unfamiliar and distasteful. In his Speech from the Throne he made an urgent appeal to all to sink "party" for "war unity".

152

"One regime died and another was born without interruption of the King's business," wrote Bruce Hutchison. "Without violence, almost without argument, the will of the people was enforced."

On the day of the fateful week an event occurred of even greater magnitude than the formation of a new provincial government in British Columbia. The Japanese attacked without warning the U.S. Naval base at Pearl Harbour, inflicting on the U.S. Navy over two thousand fatal casualties, totally destroying three battleships and damaging at least twelve other vessels as well as many army and navy planes on the ground. Immediately the Americans were at war, brought into it united as they could have been in no other way.

In Vancouver there was a colony of thirty thousand Japanese, many of whom were Canadian-born. They owned most of the fishing fleets and many small stores. The Sino-Japanese conflict in which Japan seemed to be fighting an unprovoked war of aggression had led in 1937 to a proposed boycott on Japanese goods sold in Canada. The Woodwards had opposed it, believing that it would injure mostly those who were not responsible for and were taking no part in the War and that such a boycott would be most hurtful to British Columbia which exported to Japan millions of dollars' worth of lumber, pulp, paper, fish and minerals.

As a result of Pearl Harbour, however, the first major action of the new Government was to order the immediate removal of all Japanese, both alien and Canadian-born, from the Coast, and transfer them to the interior of British Columbia to camps east of the Cascade Mountains. This decision, later much criticized with the wisdom of hindsight, was probably inevitable and understandable in the circumstances but led to loss and hardship for many Japanese who were loyal Canadian citizens. The distress of the Japanese fishermen was increased by a record run of salmon in B.C. rivers that year.

Before 1941 ended Billy opened a new Armoury at the University of British Columbia. Two Commanding Officers of the U.B.C. Contingent of the Canadian Officers' Training Corps, Lt. Col. Gordon Shrum and his predecessor Lt. Col. Harry Logan, had raised the $50,000 required to build the Armoury. Taking part in the march past which concluded the ceremony was Cadet Charles ("Chunky") Woodward, not quite seventeen, quiet and reticent.

153

He had already had some exposure to Store life during Christmas holidays working in the Toy Department or eviscerating turkeys, or spending the Easter break in a stockroom. Though he was to lead the Company to expansions even greater then those achieved by his father and uncle, he had at this time by no means decided that merchandising was to be his career. His one aim was to go to war, and being an extremely determined young man, he was sure that before long he would achieve it.

The attack on Pearl Harbour changed the whole picture for British Columbians. The War was no longer a remote conflict being fought thousands of miles away. It was right on Vancouver's doorstep.

A total blackout was immediately ordered. At first streetcars were lightless, car headlights covered except for a thin, horizontal strip on each lens, but after about a month, semi-blackout conditions were substituted. There were rumours that the British Columbia Regiment was in Hong Kong but though items to this effect had appeared in the newspapers it was found that no local regiments had been selected for that disastrous expedition. There was a rationing of beer and liquor, a shortage of sawdust which was widely used in Vancouver homes for fuel. Invasion by the Japanese was considered not only possible but probable.

CHAPTER NINETEEN

His Honour
The Lieutenant-Governor

The first guest entertained at Government House by the Wood-wards was Gracie Fields, British singer who was travelling the world and using her vast talent to procure comforts for servicemen. She asked that there should be no entertaining for her. Her visit was followed within the same week by that of the Archbishop of Toronto and Primate of all Canada, Archbishop Owen. Through the war years the Woodwards were hosts to an immense variety of guests. They ranged from the Quiz Kids, four American youngsters able to answer questions on any topic and raising funds to buy milk for British children by so doing, to Crown Princesses and Governors-General.

Usually it is the Lieutenant-Governor who pays for the parties that he attends but before Billy had been in office a week a party was given for him and Ruth. Their hosts were their ever-faithful admirers, the staff of Woodward Stores. The reception was held at Vancouver's Jericho Country Club. Directors' wives, Mrs. R. J. Hawkins, Mrs. W. Sinclair, Mrs. W. Mann, Mrs. A. C. Cox and Mrs. T. McBride "presided at the urns". Brother Puggy and his wife Marion received the guests.

When he was not busy entertaining or lending his presence to worthy causes, the Lieutenant-Governor travelled about the province talking to people or urging them to support Victory Loan Campaigns. The first of such tours occurred early in 1942 when he went with his secretary A.D.M. Fairbairn to the Kootenay District. The meeting at Nelson held memories for both men. Here in 1903 His Honour had been an eighteen-year-old bank clerk before he had persuaded his employers to send him to Cuba. In 1912 Fairbairn had come from his native South Africa straight to Nelson.

"We've got to do more than we are doing now if we are going to win this war," said Billy, looking sternly at the crowd from beneath his bushy eyebrows. "This war can easily be lost. The time to sugar the pill is gone. We want the Government to tell us, not ask us. I'm not going to ask you to buy bonds, I'm going to tell you. It's your job and mine."

The people loved him for his sincerity and forthrightness.

In April, 1942, the Governor-General of Canada, the Earl of Athlone, and his wife Princess Alice paid the first of several visits to Government House. It was His Excellency's 68th birthday but the celebration was dampened by the news of the astoundingly rapid successes of the Japanese who, on the day of the Athlones' arrival in Victoria, gained control of the Burma Road, completed the conquest of Central Burma and forced the British to evacuate Mandalay. People now realized how long the War must last.

Princess Alice was ill throughout the visit. Her letter of apology to Ruth for such a trouble-making indiscretion could not have been more profuse if her illness had been intentional. At the end of the month in quick succession came another royal visitor, Crown Prince Olav of Norway, chased out of his country by the German invaders — and the U.S. Ambassador to Canada, Jay Pierremont Moffat.

"There never was closer cooperation, military, economic and spiritual, between Canada and the U.S. than at the present time," said Mr. Moffat with truth.

That same month two very different men whom Billy especially admired were in the news. One was General McNaughton who had, for a time, commanded him in the First World War and who now became Commander of the First Canadian Army. Billy revered his unorthodoxy, his brains and his unpretentiousness. Another of his heroes, J. S. Woodsworth, founder of the C.C.F., died that April. Woodsworth was a pacifist, a socialist and an idealist. Billy was none of these things but he recognized and respected greatness: his admiration for Woodsworth was intense.

The number of causes supported by Billy and Ruth was increased by their warm hearts. The Blind, the Protestant Orphans, the

Queen Alexandra Solarium for Crippled Children, the Salvation Army, the Red Cross, St. John Ambulance Association, the newly-formed Vancouver Welfare Association and any other good work which might alleviate the distress of the disabled or the disadvantaged were espoused. Equally urgent were the causes associated with the War; and even the claims of history, such as the Vancouver Pioneers' Association, the United Empire Loyalists, the Pioneer Schools and Victoria's Centenary were given their due. Billy was away on the occasion of the last-named event and Ruth spoke:

"We must all feel justifiable pride in Victoria's history and in the character of its founders," she said.

The character of those founders, industrious, indomitable, sacrificing, was much in evidence then in British Columbia. Thousands of Vancouverites gathered in the Malkin Bowl on October 19, 1942, to renew their pledge:

> I solemnly pledge myself earnestly to fulfil to the limit of my power each wartime duty that faces me and so to stand shoulder to shoulder with those of my fellowmen who are defending with their lives our mutual cause.

It was a time of war, of tragedy and disaster, yet there was a sense of common purpose which dignified the daily round. Sacrifice, service, cooperation abounded, and other ennobling qualities which are far less evident in the somewhat sour times in which we live today.

Billy was applauded warmly as he moved about the province making speeches and often tongue-lashing his audience.

"We will suffer on this continent," he said. "We cannot live here complacently when the island of Britain is the only thing between us and abject slavery under the heel of the Hun."

Condemnation of the Allies' inability to launch a Second Front he rejected totally.

"Now is the time to close ranks, be charitable to one another and end this destructive criticism of the Dominion Government."

That summer a Japanese submarine shelled isolated Estevan Point on the west coast of Vancouver Island: two weeks previously the Japanese had occupied Kiska and Attu, two of the Aleutian Islands between Japan and the northwest coast of America.

"British Columbia will be bombed within six months," declared Billy, and he was not the only one to make this wrong prediction. But for Japanese reverses in the Battle of Midway and in New Guinea, raids on Victoria and Vancouver might well have been attempted.

The Fiftieth anniversary of the opening of Woodward Stores in Vancouver was celebrated on June 7, 1942, three months later than the correct date, in order to coincide with the Golden Jubilee Tea of the Vancouver Pioneers' Association.

Puggy acknowledged the Association's congratulations:

> Most of you pioneers went through the hard school to establish yourselves in Vancouver, the same as my father. Our destiny has been linked up with your own through the past fifty years. You have been good friends to this institution.

The following March Puggy was called away to War work. He was pleased to have this recognition. The Financial Times on the occasion of his being appointed a Director of the B.C. Telephone Company had commented:

> This decisive man of action . . . has often basked in the reflected glory of other members of his family.

That such should be his fate Puggy resented deeply. He therefore promptly accepted an invitation to head the Northwest Purchasing Company even though secretly he suspected that the project was not likely to make any significant contribution to the War Effort.

The Northwest Purchasing Company was a Crown Company designed to centralize the purchasing of property, materials and supplies for Northern development. The Company would do all the buying for the United States and Canada in the North and would provide a clearing-house for supplies ordered for construction projects such as the Alaska Highway.

"A large part of our job is goodwill," said Puggy to reporters, giving them a glare that indicated that without efficiency and purpose there would be little goodwill as far as he was concerned. Then he departed to his new headquarters in Edmonton, on loan from Woodward Stores.

Though Billy found his deepest satisfaction in the Anglican

158

Church, and especially in the services held in St. James' Anglican Church, Vancouver, his religious beliefs were not confined to any one sect. More than once he gave the address at Christ Church Cathedral (Anglican). At Hastings Park Forum he headed the United Church of Canada's Crusade for Christ. He attended Pontifical Mass in Victoria. But his attempts to bring about exchanges between Anglican and Roman Catholic clergy brought some angry rebukes.

"Dear William," wrote one enraged critic, "your stock has gone down 80% in the eyes of the decent people of Victoria, bringing that damned Catholic priest with his Romish vestments to celebrate in our church. We all know you have gone over to Satan in connecting up with St. James and Cooper. It is a disgrace to your office.

"You should set an example, not that you are capable of much with your face.

"I am an old friend of your father and am very disgusted.

"P.S. Tell that damned Fairbairn to get a shave. He looks like a freak."

John Cody, Bishop of Victoria, felt differently.

"You have no idea how much pleasure you gave our people by assisting at Pontifical Mass," he wrote.

Billy continued to admire all Christian faiths. Many years later when in Rome he begged for an interview with the Pope and brought back a rosary which His Holiness had blessed for Herbert Legge, a devout Catholic employee in the tie section of Woodward's Men's Furnishings Department. It was the most valued present Legge ever received.

"The great strength of Great Britain and the U.S." said Billy, "is the fundamental belief in our religion and way of life."

The Athlones came to Government House again in May, 1943. The Governor-General presided at an Investiture at which Ruth was made a Dame of Grace of the Venerable Order of St. John of Jerusalem. This imperial order which has the reigning monarch as its sovereign head particularly appealed to her, for throughout its many hundreds of years of existence, it has been dedicated especially to work in the medical field.

Other guests at that time were Herbert Marshall and a group of Hollywood actors who raised $8,500 one afternoon at Government

House in aid of the Red Cross; and Crown Princess Juliana of Holland who launched R.C.N. Frigate *St. Stephen* from Yarrow's Shipyards.

Comedian Jack Benny's visit made history because the Woodwards invited to a luncheon given in his honour another well-known comedian, Benny's radio negro valet, Rochester. It happened that on the very same day an exclusive Toronto Club had refused admission to world-famous singer Marion Anderson. The press of the world gleefully seized on the coincidence. One important U.S. paper reported:

> A strong blow has been struck for racial equality in Canada by King George's own representative, the Lieutenant-Governor of British Columbia.

Another visitor was British Ambassador to the U.S. Lord Halifax, with whom Billy had travelled in the battleship *King George V* and whose immense height, made even more immense by his top hat, caused him to tower above his host.

Billy considered a top hat a regrettable piece of apparel and wore one as infrequently as possible.

News of Allied successes was coming from all fronts. By the spring of 1944 the Russians had recaptured Odessa, were gaining control of the Crimea and the Ukraine and were advancing into Poland and Romania. The launching of a second Front in Europe was obviously near; in fact RCAF dive bombers had begun the attacks which were to lead to D-Day.

That April two family events occurred of considerable significance to Ruth and Billy. One was the birth of their first grandchild, Rebecca May McDonald, daughter of their eldest daughter Elizabeth, who in November, 1942, had married Glen McDonald. Two of the baby's godparents were her Uncle Chunky, now fighting as a trooper in Northwest Europe and her mother's headmistress, Miss Gildea, founder of Strathcona School on Vancouver Island. McDonald who later became Vancouver's City Coroner was at this time serving overseas as a Lieutenant in the Royal Canadian Navy.

The other family event was the death of Charlie Wynn-Johnson. He had been retired for several years. He had built Alkali Lake into a famous ranch, had run a herd of purebred Herefords numbering three thousand head and had made a notable contribution to the development of the livestock industry in British Columbia. Wynn-Johnson had had a lonely retirement since his wife had died ten years previously. Often he would climb the hill where she was buried, look out over the range and valleys they both had loved, contemplate the inscription on her tombstone, "Beloved by All", until at last he decided that life there was empty without her and he sold the ranch.

His family was widely scattered. Betty Wilson in Coburg, Ontario, Paddy Cripps at Big Lake in the heart of the Cariboo and Ruth much involved in Victoria. One of the pallbearers at his funeral at St. James' was H. V. Riedemann, who had bought Alkali Lake and was continuing its traditions.

As the end of the Second World War seemed to be drawing closer, the number of Investitures at Government House increased. At one of these Billy presented a Victoria Cross, awarded posthumously to Major Charles Ferguson Hoey, M.C., of Duncan, B.C. It was the first time in Canada that a Lieutenant-Governor was privileged to present this, the highest of military decorations, and as Mrs. Hoey, mother of the dead hero, advanced to receive it, dry-eyed and erect, Billy whispered a few words to her and gently patted her shoulder. On the same day, he pinned the Cornwall Badge, the Boy Scouts' V.C., on fifteen-year-old Ross Brown who had earned the award for his gallant battle against incurable disease and pain.

On another occasion he decorated Vancouver's "Three Musketeers" — Lieutenant-Commanders Douglas Maitland, Cornelius Burke and Tom Ladner who won respectively the DSC and bar, DSC and two bars and DSC and bar.

Billy was invited to visit troops of the First Canadian Army in Holland and Germany and to make a three months' tour of the battlefields. He set out in April 1945 with T. C. Douglas, Premier of Saskatchewan as his travelling companion, and crossed the Atlantic in a bomber. His old friend General McNaughton had been retired for over a year, victim of political skirmishing, and General Crerar was in command of the five Canadian Divisions and two Tank Brigades overseas.

It was realized that hostilities in Europe would last no more than a few weeks. The Allies had crossed the Rhine, the Russians were at the outskirts of Berlin, the British had taken Bremen, the Canadians were sweeping through Holland. In the midst of this resounding success, President Roosevelt, architect of much of it, died.

In England W. A. McAdam, British Columbia's Agent-General, greeted Billy and Premier Douglas. Then they went as fast as possible to the Continent and were met at Brussels Airport by Trooper C. N. Woodward whom his father had not seen for two years.

The greater part of those two years Chunky had spent with the 12th Manitoba Dragoons as driver of a Staghound Armoured Car. He had reached the rank of Sergeant in the Canadian Officers' Training Corps, had been sent to an Officers' Selection and Appraisal Centre at Chilliwack, B.C., and then to Dundurn, Saskatchewan, as an officer candidate. The training period was supposed to be for two months' duration but when the two months were up and the authorities showed no signs of sending him to Europe, Officer-Cadet Woodward applied to be released and sent overseas forthwith. His request was refused but he paraded to the Commanding Officer with such monotonous regularity that eventually it was granted.

The 12th Manitoba Dragoons exactly suited him. It was a Reconnaissance Battalion; raids, protection of road convoys, patrols to gain tactical intelligence were some of its functions. Almost all his summer holidays Chunky had spent with cowboys, riding the range. He had an excellent eye for country and keen powers of observation. He enjoyed life in the ranks and had no hesitation in turning down another invitation to undergo training for a commission, this time at Sandhurst. He was a capable soldier, well-liked, courageous and not easily rattled. He had already survived the battles of the Falaise Gap, where some of the bitterest fighting of the War took place.

Father and son spent a brief time together in Brussels, then each departed to his duties. Though there were strong ties of respect and affection, there was at times some shyness between them.

V.E. Day came on May 8, 1945. In a twenty-minute ceremony Colonel-General Gustav Jodl, Chief of Staff of Admiral Doenitz' Government (Hitler had already committed suicide), surrendered at Rheims all German Armed Forces on land, sea and in the air. Characteristically Billy went to the B.C. Canteen in London to congratulate the women who had run it with devotion and courage.

He sent messages back to British Columbia:

"The Black Market reigns in France and Belgium. Prices are fantastic. It will be at least two years before those two countries can resume normal world trade . . ." The Citizen's Rehabilitation Council, which he had opened shortly before he left for Europe, must "ensure proper protection for returning servicemen and women." The Veterans of the First World War had been "thrown to the wolves" and that must not happen again.

CHAPTER TWENTY

An End and a Beginning

During the Lieutenant-Governor's absence in Europe, Ruth carried on with many of his duties and performed them with her usual gentle charm. She received the Athlones who paid their third visit to British Columbia in May 1945. She entertained Major-General Sir William Dobbie, Governor of the much-bombed island of Malta, Hollywood actor Dick Powell, her old friend Father Whitehead of St. James' Church, doctors and their wives from all over B.C. and members of the Vancouver Symphony Society. She took the salute at a march past of Girl Guides and Brownies, accepted the Vancouver Branch presidency of the I.O.D.E. and spoke to the women of Canada on the World Day of Prayer. She was a modest woman who never really enjoyed the limelight. It was considerable effort for her to face such constant exposure to the glare of publicity. She was happy to see Billy back at the end of June, happier still to know their five-year regime was drawing to a close.

Often in her mind was the thought of retiring to the Saanich Farm which they had bought earlier that year. The purchase of Woodwynn was a happy event for the whole family. This farm had been developed in 1856 by Angus McPhail, a retired Hudson Bay factor believed to be the first white settler on the Saanich peninsula. It comprised 550 acres of which 350 were arable, its gardens ran down to the sea. Billy who for all his generosity detested waste and extravagance as much as his father had detested them, declared that this was to be "no luxury establishment that eats up money more than it can produce but a farm that must pay its way."

Ruth was delighted with their new home. She would develop another, smaller Alkali Lake Ranch which would give as much pleasure to her grandchildren as Alkali Lake had to her own family. Hopefully Woodwynn would be profitable; at any rate she would try to make it so. The name, compounded from Wynn-Johnson and Woodward, was her invention.

One function that took place soon after Billy's return to Victoria was the reception of K57000 Private Wallace, the 150-pound St. Bernard, mascot of the Canadian Scottish Regiment who would have no home after that Regiment had been demobilized and was therefore invited to take up permanent residence at Government House. Wallace was brought in by the pipes and drums of the Regiment and strode ahead of them quite content with the look of his new abode. Once inside the gates he was put on a leash and handed to former Commanding Officer Brigadier F. N. Cabeldu. Wallace created a diversion by slipping his leash and going off to make his own private investigation of the premises. While doing so he met Mitzi, Ruth's minute Yorkshire terrier, who was not prepared to share with a stranger the domain of which she was the undisputed mistress and sprang into battle. It was some time before order was restored. Eventually Mitzi accepted Wallace and sometimes rode happily in a saddle on his broad back.

The final ball of the Woodward regime was given in honour of Governor-General Viscount Alexander, especially brilliant because Billy considered this man to be the chief architect of victory and because this was the occasion of the debut of Mary Twigg, his youngest daughter.

There had been no let-up in the Woodward's employees' drive to continue making their one hundred per cent Victory Loan contribution. In November, 1944 film star Gail Patrick had presented them with a pennant for winning the War Finance Victory Award with a substantial over-subscription of their quota. They won the pennant again in 1945.

Puggy's stay with Northwest Purchasing Company had not lasted long. There were three other directors and he had disagreed with all of them. He had found his duties unrealistic and insufficient challenge to his keen intelligence and vast energies. He was appointed administrator of consumer rationing for Canada but held the appointment briefly and without enthusiasm. Woodward Stores was his life and he considered that there he could contribute most usefully to the War effort.

He could not avoid flaring up from time to time. Occasionally he would decide that there had been interference with his management of the Store, would resign as General Manager and remain "on part-time".

However, for all his comings and goings it was Puggy who steered the Store through those difficult War years of restrictions and shortages and who hired and schooled men capable of meeting the challenge of the future.

He and Billy had decided that since both of them were involved, and likely to become more involved, in public affairs, the number of directors should be substantially increased. These new directors should be men who had worked their way up in the Company by their own abilities and would know the Store intimately at every level. Their education, background or outside experience counted for little in selecting them. In fact a University training was a liability, as Billy and Puggy considered that some men who had received this advantage would turn up their noses at menial tasks.

The new directors were: J. W. Butterfield, C. A. Vine, Edward Martin, J. C. Haddock, W. T. Whitehead, J. B. Drain, A. R. Mitchell, T. R. Farrell and G. D. Glanville. The other directors were W. B. Sinclair, W. Mann, D. Blackburn, T. McBride, R. J. Hawkins, G. T. Duncan and A. C. Cox.

Every one of these men gave the Store total devotion and a competence which would be hard to match. Almost all the new directors Puggy had promoted and trained. Though he bullied them unmercifully they respected and admired him. He was always on the lookout for talent, was quick to spot it and tireless in recruiting it for the Store.

One of his recruits was Isaac Lipovsky who started his career hawking candies and ice cream up and down the aisles of Vancouver's old Empress Theatre and who became one of the most successful restaurateurs of his day. The Lipovsky brothers invented the ice cream slice and sold it to patrons in a small cardboard box complete with wooden spoon. After a period of selling peanuts and pop at Athletic Park Lipovsky gradually edged towards the restaurant field and there attracted Puggy's attention.

166

Lipovsky not only knew a vast amount about people's preference in food but was also deeply concerned with nutrition and balanced meals. At first Puggy allowed him only a sandwich concession, then, realizing he had found a man with sincerity, intelligence and energy, permitted him to run a restaurant on the Food floor. Himey Koshevoy, Vancouver journalist, who interviewed Isaac Lipovsky on his retirement, wrote about him:

"Lipovsky has strong theories on food, some of them odd to me but he never forces the deal on his customers. For instance, he feels that milk is strictly for the young but he'd sooner impale himself with a fork than refuse you milk if you ask for it.

"He had devised rolls and buns chockablock with whole wheat and brimming over with vitamins and, strangely, the eaters swallow them by the carload and like them so well that they rarely ask for pale, glutinous slices of bread."

Another Woodward manager equally notable was J. McTaggart-Cowan, father of two eminent British Columbian scientists and himself a product of a well-known Scottish public school. For many years he ran the Garden Shop in an unorthodox way. Customers would wait patiently in line while he administered a lengthy rebuke to someone who had planted his peonies too deep or neglected to fertilize an azalea. McTaggart-Cowan employed almost no staff because he trusted few to give the right advice. As a result his department was incredibly untidy and his customers would often have to burrow among discarded sacks and cardboard cartons to find for themselves what they wanted. But he knew his subject so well that people flocked to be served by him.

Lipovsky and McTaggart-Cowan were vastly different from each other and from the usual type of department store employee, yet both were men of outstanding talent. It was Woodward's ability to attract and retain such men that made the Store itself different and outstanding.

At last in August 1945 came the surrender of the Japanese and the end of the Second World War. Former staff who had been stockroom boys and girls when they enlisted, came back as men and women, matured and seasoned by their experiences. Back they came from every branch of the armed and of the women's services. They seemed to bring with them a sense of responsibility which

167

suggested that their war years had not been barren ones. They remembered the parcels and cigarettes the Company had sent them. They remembered that their families had continued to enjoy discount privileges while they were in the forces.

When they returned, the Company gave them back their former jobs, and in many cases better jobs, with all the increases they would have received if they had never volunteered.

By the time of the 1945 Annual Meeting the number of staff shareholders had swelled to five hundred. They had good reason to be enthusiastic for they received full dividends as soon as they were awarded shares, even though some might not finish paying for those shares for many years. Stockholders paid only 4% on their unpaid balance but received dividends which were never less than 7% and often larger.

The first issue of the Beacon Magazine was published also in 1945 and did much to foster the family feeling which the Woodwards tried in many ways to instil throughout the organization. They sent flowers to their people when they were ill or had babies. They arranged for inter-departmental soccer and softball matches to be played on days off, for banquets, and an annual picnic usually held on Bowen Island. A newspaper article noted that even when Billy was Lieutenant-Governor he found time to attend the Store picnic or the funeral of a janitor.

This attitude might be branded as "paternalism". Nevertheless it let staff members know that the boss cared about their happiness whether on or off the job and it elicited a reciprocal loyalty.

At a post V.E. Day Directors' Meeting, Billy spoke of the progress of the firm and compared its size and financial condition with that of forty-one years ago.

"Our opportunities and plans for expansion are unlimited," he said. "But we don't intend to limit expansion to the stores in Vancouver and Edmonton. We are going to build department stores all over British Columbia, in Alberta and maybe in Eastern Canada as well. We have the know-how and a good name. Our greatest need is for men who can accept responsibility and give leadership."

Chunky took his discharge from the Army as soon as he was permitted to do so and was demobilized in England. A Woodward buyer, Courtney Haddock, had been sent by the Company to start the task of re-establishing pre-war relations with manufacturers. Haddock had been with Woodward's for twenty years. He was the china and glassware buyer and had such a knowledge and love for his merchandise that later, when wartime restrictions had been removed, his department became unique in Vancouver. He was a genial, extroverted man with a zest for life and laughter. His laugh could be heard a block away. The austere atmosphere of some of the staid, old English firms with which he did business in no way restrained his ebullience.

On this visit he was buying not only chinaware but toys, textiles, carpets, leather goods, boots and shoes, hardware, clothing . . . in fact merchandise for the whole store. This warm and sympathetic man was the ideal person to take 21-year-old Chunky under his wing and show him how to make friends and good deals for Woodward's at the same time.

They travelled in England and on the Continent. In Great Britain alone they placed orders to the value of one and a half million dollars. One order placed with J. and E. Hall of Dartford, Kent was for the installation of lifts and escalators for the Vancouver and Edmonton stores. Courtney Haddock was always an Anglophile. At a press conference at British Columbia House he said:

"The population of British Columbia is largely derived from British stock and the sentiment in favour of the Old Country is very strong. The Province is keenly anxious to reciprocate the purchases which Britain makes of its lumber, minerals and foodstuffs.

"We ourselves as a firm have been buying British goods for the past 50 years. In the course of my visit I have been particularly impressed with the fact that in spite of the stress of war, their quality is unimpaired. So long as British craftsmanship remains what it is, there will always be a demand for British goods."

Some of the stately homes of England belonged to the Wedgwoods and other famed manufacturers who were pleased to invite buyers of the calibre of Chunky and Haddock to stay with them. The team from Woodward's had some interesting visits.

Chunky was a somewhat silent partner on the buying expeditions but Haddock noted that he was observant, not easily fooled, made up his mind quickly, and had the family faculty for reaching the nub of a problem with extraordinary speed.

When Billy ended his five-year term as Lieutenant-Governor in August 1946 accolades poured in on every side. During those years he had been promoted Honorary Colonel from Honorary Lieut-Col. of 15th Field Regiment RCA, had been made a life-member of the Vancouver Board of Trade and Knight of Grace of the Order of St. John of Jerusalem. He and Ruth had received ambassadors, Governors-General of Canada, royal personages, cabinet ministers, distinguished officers of Great Britain and the United States, prominent theatrical people, railway presidents, a prince of the Roman Catholic Church. In recognition of "outstanding public service rendered to the Province of British Columbia" City Council conferred on Billy the freedom of the City of Vancouver. The most significant tribute to the Woodward regime was paid by some 300 Victorians who lined up outside Government House for several hours on the day Ruth and Billy left, to shake hands with them.

Billy was urged to accept a second term of office but declined; he could not wait to get to Woodwynn. Already there was a herd of 97 Jersey cows and 80 acres of potatoes had been planted. Billy and his chauffeur Wesley Strickland cleared several more acres, taking it in turns to operate the tractor that was strange to both of them. Billy knew more about beef as it reposed on the counters of Woodward's Meat Department than about beef on the hoof. However, he intended to learn and he was determined the farm would pay its way.

He attended cattle auctions in order to improve the standard of cattle produced in the district by the use of better bulls. At one of these auctions held in Kamloops he bought a 450-lb. shorthorn calf by mistake. He had not realized that auctioneer Matt Hansen's nods and winks were the accepted method of purchase.

Chunky and Courtney Haddock came back from Europe. Haddock had to do some fast talking to explain two of his purchases . . . a gold tea-set valued at $110,000 and a London bus. Fortunately for him he was able to sell the former to King Farouk of Egypt and the latter to the City of Victoria.

The store itself was ready for action. There had been no expansion since 1939. The heavy diet of restrictions on which the people of Canada had been fed all through the war years had prevented that. Now, however, the management was bristling with plans.

Studies were made of growth and population trends in most major cities of British Columbia. In March, 1947, Puggy acquired real estate in Victoria on behalf of the Company for eventual erection of a department store in that city.

In November, 1947, the first section of a new $800,000 addition to the Vancouver Store was opened. This included an addition of 132,000 square feet, a new 11-storey section and the completion of the 7th and 8th floors. The Bakery added ovens which could produce 25,000 loaves of bread a day. The new coffee roaster could handle one thousand pounds of coffee per hour. There were new freight elevators with two-ton capacity and speed of 100 feet a minute and new passenger elevators.

The narrow-fronted, 3-storey corner structure of 1903 was unrecognizable.

CHAPTER TWENTY-ONE

A Branch in Port Alberni

In 1948 Woodward's took the surprising decision to build a branch department store in Port Alberni, a small lumber town on Vancouver Island.

Travellers often miss Port Alberni because they can reach it only by leaving the Island Highway and driving some 40 miles from the Straits of Georgia to the head of the long inlet that almost cuts the Island in half. The journey is worthwhile for the road passes through Cathedral Grove in MacMillan Park, a stand of the most magnificent trees in the world. Hundreds of Douglas firs, some of them 225 feet in height and five feet in diameter, tower over the grove where they have stood for 600 years. Beyond is the Somass River, its banks lined with tall trees; lovely Stamp Falls; Sproat Lake, ringed with lofty mountain ranges, and Mount Arrowsmith, impressive at any season and visible from every part of the Alberni Valley. Even in British Columbia Alberni is outstanding in its natural beauty.

The city region was first settled in 1860 when nine men built British Columbia's first sawmill for cutting export timber. "A disastrous decision," commented the mill manager. With unbelievable inaccuracy he informed the British Colonial Secretary that "there was no wood in the district to supply the wants of a large mill."

A dam was built on the Somass River in 1892 to provide power for a sawmill and for British Columbia's first paper mill which, ironically, was closed down when the supply of cloth rags from England proved too costly as raw materials and local wood was declared unsuitable for a good product! In 1911 the first passenger train arrived and Port Alberni became technically the western terminus of the rail system of Canada. By the next year sufficient people had settled near the harbour to bring about the incorporation of the City of Port Alberni. Then came a succession of lumber mills, plywood mills and shingle mills. In 1947 the construction of MacMillan Bloedel's huge pulp mill was commenced, Port Alberni had 10,000 inhabitants and the Harbour Commission was incorporated by the Federal Government.

Nevertheless, it took considerable foresight at that time to realize that Port Alberni would become British Columbia's third largest volume sea port and that within twenty-five years 231 deep sea vessels would leave it carrying 440,000 tons of lumber, 350,000 tons of paper and 55,000 tons of plywood and shingles; that the pulp mill would be equipped with a $23 million newsmachine producing 526 tons each 24 hours and thus becoming the world's fastest and one of the world's largest producers; and that the lumber and paper mills would have a combined payroll of $42 million.

What could be far more readily realized was the all-pervading stench that hung over beautiful Alberni, the permanent legacy of those same profitable mills.

"You'll get used to it," the incoming Woodwardites were told. Some of them never did get used to it but found it a small price to pay for life in vigorous Port Alberni.

A few of the Woodward directors had favoured building in Victoria or Nanaimo, both larger and older cities, but were outvoted. Lateral expansion was to be the new Woodward policy. Hitherto the two existing stores had been periodically added to or modernized. Now the firm would in addition establish department stores all over British Columbia. Management would be faced with problems of supply, transportation, personnel training, sales promotion, not previously encountered; there would be wrinkles of many types to be ironed out. So it would be wiser to start this new policy in a small town where experiments could be conducted and mistakes corrected more easily. Moreover, the directors argued, Port Alberni seemed to have a potential for prosperity greater than most places and would probably grow faster. They judged the people of the Alberni Valley to be energetic, bold and progressive.

The Woodward directors were right. By 1970 Port Alberni's

average per capita income had climbed to $7,238, ranking it in this scale of measurement seventh out of 99 Canadian cities. The area population was 30,000. Woodward's became the first of the chain stores to establish a branch there. Eaton's, Woolworth's, Simpson-Sears and Zellers arrived at intervals over the ensuing twenty-five years to open stores or order-offices.

Many months were spent in meticulously detailed planning before the Port Alberni store was opened. All through the winter of 1947 and spring of 1948 cars and trucks bearing fixtures, merchandise and all the varied paraphernalia required for the equipping of a modern department store travelled the rough road from Parksville, skidded and slithered over the long steep hill beyond Cameron Lake. It was a severe winter that year and sometimes drivers had to spend the night on the road. Jim Skinner, meat manager, and Bill Latimer, produce manager, moved to Port Alberni six months before the opening for purposes of liaison.

Though only a handful of department managers and key personnel were being transferred from Vancouver to work in the new branch, keen interest and excitement were felt throughout the organization. Every member of the large Woodward staff who was in a position to do so wanted to make his or her contribution to the welfare of the new baby. Many were sent to work for a few days or weeks in order to indoctrinate their Alberni counterparts in Woodward ways.

"On March 1, 1948, after many delays and difficulties," reported *The Beacon,* "the first phase of our expansion plans culminated in the opening in Port Alberni of the most modern store on Vancouver Island."

The *West Coast Advocate* with even greater hyperbole called it "the most modern Department Store in Canada."

Billy presided at the opening ceremonies, exuding confidence that this would be the best thing that had ever happened to Port Alberni or to the Woodward organization, and employing to the maximum his great gift of making everyone he encountered feel the most important person there. Alone on the sideline stood Puggy, his small keen eyes darting suspiciously over the whole scene, looking for flaws, hiding his pride and satisfaction. Well in the background was Jack Butterfield, the Yorkshireman who had

174

managed the Edmonton store so efficiently that now he was General Manager of all the Woodward Companies. His dry, dour manner concealed an excellent sense of humour and a lively intelligence. In spite of little formal education he could quote his favourite author, Emerson, as fluently as a university professor of English. Food Floor Director Tom Farrell, unassuming, immensely popular, who had made his Food Floors unique in size, selection and competence of operation, surveyed the crowd from his 6′4″ of height. Another interested spectator was Garfield Weston, one of Canada's leading businessmen, who was to become the world's foremost foods merchandiser. On this occasion he had been attracted by Woodward's unexpected choice of site and wished to make his own appraisal of the Alberni potential.

Ruth stood by the doors and as they were swung open to admit a crowd of over 1,000, she presented a rose to the first customer, Mrs. C. N. Dane.

As the eager shoppers surged forward one of them mistook a large plate glass window for a door, tried to walk through it and bounced back, thus giving Store Nurse Brown her first patient.

Chunky was not invited. There were to be no special concessions for the boss' son. He was to remain in Vancouver managing the Boyswear Department, serving his apprenticeship, winning his spurs.

The Mayors and Councillors for both Port Alberni and Alberni attended. Mayor Jordan of Port Alberni officially turned the key of the new store.

Ready to receive his customers and treat them according to declared policy as "invited guests" was store manager Ken Whyte. True to the Woodward rule of promoting from within he and his thirteen department managers were all longtime employees. Whyte had been produce manager in Vancouver, had worked for Woodward's for sixteen years and was an Islander who had been born and raised in Nanaimo. His job was no sinecure for he had been instructed to operate his store as a local unit. He had complete autonomy in buying and, within the framework of basic Company policy, could run it as he saw fit. He was to lean as little as possible on the Vancouver store.

Woodward's Port Alberni, though the smallest of the branches,

175

served as a model for the stores of the future and was therefore of special importance. The three-storey building was thus described in one of the local papers:

> Embodying every modern departmental store facility for serving the public, this imposing structure is an outstanding addition to a main city business street which already had reached large proportions in merchandising activity.
> There is a long-range motif in the construction, the plan being so designed to permit additional storeys as the development of the Albernis requires.
> Entering the Store, one is immediately struck with the bright, clean atmosphere which prevails, an achievement brought about by the use of an attractive ivory paint tint on walls and pillars, and fluorescent lighting, flush with ceilings and further diffused by installation of grids in the fixtures.

The article went on to draw attention to the "tremendous range of goods"; to the terraza flooring, a type of tile flooring polished with a fine sand; the self-service carriers in the grocery department in which are incorporated seats for small children; the absence of turnstiles; the meats and provisions displayed in scientific coolers for self-help; the unique refrigerated salad and sandwich unit; the automatic electric soup tureen which kept soup at a constant temperature; the 500 plywood counters; the air-conditioning; the call system for summoning staff; the conveyor belts and cold storage rooms; the 69 tons of equipment in the 1000-sprinkler unit.

The eulogy filled six full columns of the *Twin Cities Times.*

The new staff were almost all local people. When they checked in at the Time Office they were delighted to see a poster on the wall portraying a wild-eyed, rednosed man punching his timecard and obviously nursing a monumental hangover. Underneath was a caption coming from the lips of the Time Office supervisor:

"I said, 'Put a tie on, *not* tie one on'."

The people of Alberni were forthright and vigorous with little use for ceremony and formality. They appreciated being able to joke with management and liked unconventional ways especially coming from a firm as dignified as Woodward's.

Said one of them many years later: "The nice thing about Woodward's is that you feel you are working with the bosses and not for

176

them and since I am starting my 28th year I feel I am an expert."

Equally popular was the decision taken almost immediately to spread Woodward service to some of the remote places on the West Coast of Vancouver Island, many of which could be reached only by boat. So a small cabin cruiser was hired and manned by Hazel Ritchie, personal shopper, the Store Manager and a few "models". The *Ucluelet News* later published a leading item:

"The *Otter Point* skippered by Captain Porritt called at Ucluelet government wharf yesterday loaded with merchandise of all descriptions from Woodward's Store at Port Alberni. The boat was crowded all afternoon and evening with shoppers."

Sarita River, even smaller than Ucluelet, was even more enthusiastic:

"Something new came to Barclay Sound on Monday . . . a floating department store on a small scale but nevertheless effective. Woodward's Store Port Alberni sponsored this innovation and from our point of view was a complete success. The *Otter Point,* literally crammed to the portholes with merchandise for sale and order reference, was the market place and the clerks seemed to enjoy the venture as much as the customers. Where else could one go for a swim between rush hours? Several acquired degrees of sunburn and splintery feet. To Mr. Whyte and Mrs. Ritchie and the rest of the crew we offer thanks for the service and look forward to a repeat performance."

Tofino, Port Albion, Long Beach, Bamfield and other settlements which could not be reached at that time by road were also visited by the Woodward team. During the fifty-eight years of operation in Vancouver the firm had become widely known. It was an integral part of British Columbia with a name that inspired confidence. One young Frenchman handed Hazel Ritchie $2,000 in cash to choose furnishings for his house. "Buy me a suit," said another. He was convinced that if it came from Woodward's it would be sure to fit.

The trust of the people in these remote areas increased the personal shopper's determination to justify it.

After only a year of operation in Port Alberni Woodward's staff had almost doubled its original complement and numbered 14 managers and 160 employees.

177

The directors knew that this was the start of a new era, that the times were changed and would never be the same as before the War.

The First World War had been a stepping stone which brought Canada from colony to nationhood. The Second World War, in which Canada made even more substantial contributions of men and materials, still further enhanced her status.

Now that it was over, separate Canadian citizenship, a distinctive flag and a Canadian Governor-General were demanded. A Canadian Citizenship Act was passed by which a new distinct nationality of Canadian citizen was created.

Both in and out of Parliament the replacement of the Red Ensign which had served Canada since Confederation with a flag which reduced or eliminated the Union Jack was angrily debated though not approved until 1965.

Billy was strongly opposed to the idea of a new flag.

"It stems from a part of Canada which was not known favourably for its manpower response during the War," he commented with unusual acidity.

The ten years following the end of the War were years of great prosperity for Canada. Woodward's prosperity increased correspondingly. Prosperous or not, the firm had always been opposed to frills or extravagance in any form.

Most senior executives still had offices little larger than cupboards. Advertising kept to a minimum of space and maximum of wordage. City deliveries were organized from a half-acre space on Cordova Street and a dilapidated building on Water Street known as the McLean Building. These conditions were more suited to the days when deliveries were made by a few horse-drawn wagons instead of the 105 trucks now required.

Puggy was his father's most faithful disciple in upholding the principle of economy. The story goes that on one occasion when he was making a purchase the salesman tried to upgrade it.

"No!" declared Puggy. "What do you think I am? A millionaire?"

"Well, aren't you?" demanded Alex Ross, the salesman, looking him in the eye. Puggy made no reply. He liked a man who stood up to him and Ross went on to a long and distinguished career in the Company.

The decision in 1949 to modernize delivery methods was overdue. Six acres of ground were purchased north of the Grandview Highway at Kaslo Street. During the Fifties stores were planned for West Vancouver, New Westminster and Central Vancouver. The Grandview Service Building was well located, being more or less equidistant from the main store and each of the proposed sites, but after less than two years proved to be too small.

Steel was still in short supply. As a temporary measure Woodward's decided to add a Quonset, a simple building which could be erected with maximum ease, speed and economy as had been proved by its use by the Services in wartime. The Grandview Service Building included the largest Quonset in Canada. Part of it was a warehouse, part a delivery centre through which all items of delivery were cleared.

A high speed delivery system was designed to make the best possible use of the Woodward truck fleet. It was a unique operation, until then not generally used, and involved a system of droploads at the end of each run. Merchandise for sale was taken from the warehouse to the Store. On the return trip, after the driver had switched trailers, the delivery parcels were taken to the delivery centre where an endless conveyor belt took them to the appropriate loading bin. A growing number of delivery items could be handled and cleared each day more efficiently and at less cost.

Before long the Grandview Service Building covered ten acres, the number of trailers had grown to fourteen and they were traveling a million miles a year.

CHAPTER TWENTY-TWO

In Search of Merchandise

As soon as the Grandview Service Building was opened and the new delivery system rolling, Woodward's set out on another project. This was to extend its search for merchandise by establishing agencies all over the world. A London office from which these agencies could be controlled had been opened in 1946 and Ernest Pool appointed manager or, as he preferred to call himself, "Woodward's resident representative." An elderly man with courtly manners and a vast knowledge of London, he was well-known in Vancouver which he had often visited as Canadian representative for the London firm of I. and R. Morley. In this capacity he had done business with Woodward buyers for years.

"I am the official bloodhound for our Stores," he said. "Produce a bit of rag and give it to the hound to sniff and off he goes in a gallop. That's me. One of my so-called friends in Vancouver gives me the rag and off I go. If it's cotton I dash to Lancashire: if wool then it means Yorkshire."

Soon his peregrinations would include most of the major cities in Europe until the job became too exhausting. In 1952 he was succeeded by Aidan Robinson under whose direction the London office became a major link in the chain.

At first the office was shared with Thomas Meadows on Cheapside: then it was moved to 9 Colemen Street. Both locations were in the heart of the City. The 1950 European tour promoted a move to Lower Regent Street.

"If the European business develops, as I am sure it will," Billy told John Butterfield, "it may be better for the foreign people who come here and do not know London to see us in the West End." Many years later, because of extremely expensive West End rents, the London Office was moved to a barge on the River Thames.

The first world tour in search of merchandise which would be more varied, probably less expensive, undoubtedly different was carried out in 1950 by Billy, Ruth, Alex Mitchell and Courtney Haddock.

The year 1949 ended with the marriage of Mary Twigg to Robert White. Though Billy subsequently became good friends with his son-in-law, he was a devoted father who could not at this moment consider any man good enough for his beloved daughters. So he had grumbled his way through the pre-nuptial festivities and Ruth was glad to get him away from Vancouver.

Though Ruth's position on the team was unofficial and her presence unassuming, all leaned on her taste and discernment.

"Your mother's help I must say is invaluable," wrote Billy to Chunky from Paris. "Mitchell's idea of fashion possibly runs to Sporting Goods and Kitchenware and he could not see himself spending a great deal of money on the things your mother liked to have. But your mother won the day."

Alex Mitchell served Woodward's for 34 years with tremendous zeal and competence. As a youth of 18 he had emigrated from Lossiemouth on Scotland's east coast and found his first employment cutting bacon in Woodward's Provision Department. Thence after cutting a great deal of bacon with a diligence and enthusiasm which caught Puggy's eye he was promoted Section Head of the Cheese Counter. After that he never looked back.

Courtney Haddock had started as an extra on 95-cent days and managed to hang on. He was the China buyer who had acted as young Chunky's merchandising mentor. With Haddock on the team there would never be a dull moment. His purchases of a London bus and a $110,000 gold tea-set had been followed by the acquisition of a hurdy-gurdy and a taxi-cab scarred by the 1941 Great Fire of London. Scarcely had the directors recovered from these shocks when they received information that Haddock had acquired two unwrapped Egyptian mummies of Pharaohs Antiochus I and Philadelphus II. Hastily Billy wired him:

"Forget them. They are not exactly in our line." He sent a letter

Ruth Woodward and younger daughter Mary Twigg who in 1949 married Robert White.

after the cable in which the same thought was expressed considerably more strongly.

It was too late, the Pharaohs were on their way to Woodward's China Department. They were rushed out of sight whenever either Billy or Puggy came anywhere near the department. Eventually the mummies found their way to the Pacific National Exhibition where they drew large crowds and earned substantial sums for local charities.

Billy enjoyed Haddock's enterprise and appreciated his flair for merchandise. Though his extravagances were frequently at variance with the Woodward policy of thrift there were times when they paid dividends. One such occasion found him at the British Industries Fair on the same day as Queen Mary, a noted connoisseur of fine china. Every time the Queen made a purchase — and there were many — Haddock bought the whole set exhibited and placed a sign on it "Sold to Woodward Stores, Vancouver, Canada."

Mitchell and Haddock had in common only their total devotion to Woodward's and were often opposed in their opinions. But their experience and abilities were complementary and outstanding.

Billy and Ruth, Mitchell and Haddock started their tour in March, 1950 by visiting the Woodward's Toronto office which had just been opened at 220 Bay Street as an initial step in the round the world buying programme. Don Junker was its first manager. He had graduated summa cum laude from Woodward's Merchandising Classes and this appointment was his reward.

"We covered over three thousand miles in the first three weeks," Billy wrote to Chunky "and opened accounts with at least 150 new firms.

> . . . It was a weird trip motoring up the Rhine through the ruined cities of Germany. It will certainly take a long time before they are able to rebuild them, but the German youth is beginning to march. We saw several groups out with flags along the roads as I used to see them in 1926. Personally I think we were crazy to keep on dismantling their plants unless we have something to do for the millions of Germans who are just wandering aimlessly about looking for trouble. I have no great sympathy for the people but would hate to see them go wrong a third time. Mr. Churchill was 100% right when he

said we should help our enemy to a certain extent and get them on their feet. They are working in the factories, especially at the places we went to — Nuremberg and Frankfurt. The Italians are also working very hard and they are all desperately keen to do business.

Your mother is very glad to hear of the great progress of Wynn. I think she spends a great deal of her time buying, or trying to buy, something for the grandchildren.

To John Butterfield he wrote:

Mitchell and Haddock seem to be doing very well and they are looking forward to our experiment in Italy and Germany, also Switzerland. As you know — they will make some mistakes but they will not buy a great deal to start with, but I am perfectly certain that the German trade is quickly coming back again and we cannot afford not to inspect it very closely.

Haddock and I went to a textile show by the Indian Government. They had plenty of white cottons, such as sheetings, pillowcases, etc., and some very nice fabrics and draperies.

These Indian people had a tremendous display; a great deal of their merchandise will be of no use to us whatever . . . the colours are not right . . . but the quality of the merchandise struck both Haddock and me as being particularly good.

Agencies were appointed in Belgium, Austria, Switzerland, France, Spain, Holland, Germany, Italy and Scandinavia. Two years later, Ruth, Billy and Alex Mitchell completed another tour, this time 225,000 miles in 17 different countries and Woodward agents were appointed in Siam, Japan, Turkey, India, Malaya, Pakistan and Hong Kong.

Gowns from Sweden, knitware from Italy and Austria, tools from Copenhagan, locks from Germany, shears from Italy, scarves from Pforsheim, jewellery and china from England, carpets from Persia and India, toys and smallware from China and Japan, glassware from Sweden . . . Merchandise indeed from all over the world was making its appearance on the Woodward counters.

But Billy was 67. He found the 1952 tour hard going. When Ruth met him for the last part of the journey and then herself became seriously ill in Toronto, he was alarmed. He had been nominated as a possible successor to Viscount Alexander as Governor-General of Canada but declined to let his name go forward.

Ruth's recovery was speedy and complete but he decided that life must become less strenuous for both of them. He began to spend more of his time at Woodwynn Farm.

Charles Namby Wynn Woodward, 6 feet 2, slim and athletic, known by the inappropriate pseudonym of Chunky, was as different from his father as Billy had been from his. For instance he lacked Billy's exuberance and flair for public relations. Where, old timers would ask themselves, as they observed with some misgivings this serious, reticent heir-apparent, were the smiles and jokes and little compliments so freely disbursed by Billy as he strolled through the Store? Was Mr. C. N. going to be a stern taskmaster like his Uncle Puggy? Would they live in awe of him and fear for their jobs? Some had heard that he had not wanted to work in the Store at all. He had wanted to be a cowboy.

But when any staff members got close to him and had a face to face conversation, their fears began to dissipate. They found him frank, ready to listen, quick to comprehend and unexpectedly humorous. There was no thought of firing someone who had made a mistake, no refusal to listen to a point of view which differed from Store policy. If a successful merchant's chief characteristics are, as is generally conceded, integrity, sound judgment and quick comprehension, he was the right man to run Woodward's. These were qualities he had in no small measure. Moreover, and in this respect he did not differ from his father, he could talk to a man in a man's language and his tone did not change whether that man was Prince Philip or a night watchman.

After his return from Europe in 1946, Chunky took a lengthy post-war vacation at Alkali Lake Ranch. At last his father had telephoned him and asked with characteristic directness and with some asperity: "Are you going to be a cowboy all your life or are you coming to work for the Company?"

This was no joking or idle enquiry. If ever a man had ranching in his blood with good reason, that man was Chunky Woodward. Both his great-grandfathers, John Woodward and Donald Anderson, had been prosperous farmers almost a hundred years before, in Wellington County, Ontario. One grandfather, Charlie Wynn-Johnson, had made Alkali Lake an exceptionally fine ranch. The other grandfather, Charles Woodward, had had as his first venture the two-hundred acre farm on Manitoulin Island. Raising cattle at Woodwynn was his mother's love, second only to her family.

Billy waited for an answer to his vital question with some apprehension. Could the line of succession in store command be broken? He might have had more faith in his son's reaction.

Chunky returned to Vancouver at once as duty dictated and abandoned his ranching dreams. He occupied a desk in the Merchandise Office and from this vantage point, the heart of the Store, he studied the ramifications of the Woodward organization. His final decision was not prompted solely by filial duty. As a buyer he had found that picking winning merchandise could be as exciting as picking a winning horse. That same satisfaction which his grandfather had experienced when at age fourteen he had triumphantly merchandised his father's farm produce, by some quirk of heredity Chunky felt when he made a good buy or better still a good sale.

Chunky learned with approval that the Company's next expansion would probably be in West Vancouver. Woodward's had been approached by the management of British Pacific Properties who planned to build a Shopping Centre at Taylor Way and Marine Drive. Would Woodward's be interested in operating a department store as its main feature?

Would they be interested! This was exactly the type of development the directors had been looking for, one which would take place in a part of Vancouver bound before long to treble or quadruple in size, one which would immeasurably benefit the whole City, one which was part of a new merchandising trend. If the negotiations were successful this department store in West Vancouver would be Chunky's first command.

British Properties was well financed. Its major stockholder was the Guinness family, a family of Irish brewers whose fortune was one of the largest in the British Empire. They had already made substantial investments in Vancouver by building the Marine Building, by developing a large luxury suburb on the North Shore and, in spite of determined opposition from shipping interests and others who protested the felling of trees in Stanley Park, by erecting over the First Narrows the Lions' Gate Bridge, "the longest suspension bridge in the British Empire."

The decision to build a Shopping Centre was farsighted, for in

186

1949 the very term itself was virtually unknown. This retailing trend was a post-World War Two development brought about by the movement of population to suburbs, the increased use of the automobile, traffic congestion in cities and the high cost of parking. Such Shopping Centres or Shopping "Plazas" as existed were in the United States. In fact it had been necessary to employ a planner for the project from Seattle, Hugh Russell, who had laid out the Bellevue Shopping Centre in that city.

One type of Centre was owned by a real estate organization which leased its units to supermarkets, specialty shops and similar enterprises. Another type was owned entirely by one large retailer who operated his own branch store as the focal point and leased the remaining units to tenants of his choice. Woodward's first venture into the Shopping Centre field was of the first type.

British Pacific Properties had spent one and a half million dollars building the Centre, Woodward's leased part of it for a department store and supermarket. In subsequent ventures they often preferred to own the entire complex.

Park Royal, West Vancouver was the first Shopping Centre in Canada. Perry Willoughby, a member of the Guinness family, was its manager. The Woodwards were convinced that this type of retail outlet was the way of the future. As in Port Alberni, this was a pioneer store where there would be much experiment. From it much would be learned.

The trend to decentralize merchandising areas, to relieve traffic congestion and remove trade concentration from the heart of the city had started. It was destined to become the prime merchandising form in Canadian retailing.

The immediate success of the Park Royal Shopping Centre far exceeded expectations. The Centre was a great deal more than just a collection of stores. It became a roadside attraction for the city. Day and night the brilliantly lighted windows attracted hundreds of window shoppers. Even on Sunday or holidays the 700-car parking area was often almost filled. The stores were smartly finished with facades of glass, stonework brick and turned wood. Exclusive specialty shops, a Woolworth store, hardware, drug and dress shops and restaurants offered variety and competition to the Department store.

Motorists cheerfully paid the 25-cent toll to enjoy a beautiful

Rosemary Woodward with elder son John. Her father A. E. (John) Jukes was a school friend of W. C. Woodward. She married C. N. Woodward in 1948 and is shown here with their elder son, John. She is now Mrs. John Devlin.

2½ mile drive from the centre of town over the Lions' Gate Bridge with free and easy parking at the other end, an advantage becoming ever rarer in congested Vancouver.

Especially the motorists came on a Wednesday. By Provincial statute, stores in British Columbia had to close one working half-day each week and Vancouver merchants had chosen Wednesday. By a further ruling instigated by the Retail Merchants Association, Vancouver received the right to enforce closing all day on Wednesday. Thus the Park Royal Centre being outside the city limits was one of the few spots where Wednesday shoppers could go.

Woodward's of course dominated the Centre. On 11.8 acres they built a bright, modern store all on one floor with provision for a second storey as soon as it was needed. No permanent fixtures were higher than four feet for easy visibility throughout. The adjoining supermarket, always a chief feature of a Woodward store, covered 12,000 square feet of postless space with large, readily accessible food bunkers. Its most apparent innovation was the electric-eye exit door, common in the supermarkets of today but then almost unheard of. Another unique feature was the 135-foot long self-service refrigerator, stocked with every conceivable kind of meat, fish and cooked commodity, most of them prepackaged. It became known as the "talking fridge" because if an article was missing the purchaser could speak into a wall phone and out from the warehouse would come the missing commodity.

The location of the Park Royal Shopping Centre had been chosen after months of research. Since the opening of the Lions' Gate Bridge in 1938, West Vancouver had grown from a small section of summer homes in a forest to an area of mansions stretching 15 miles or so west and affording residence to some 12,000 high-salaried persons. They all had to pass Park Royal on their way to Vancouver because Marine Drive was the only route. In addition there were now 26,000 residents of North Vancouver. West and North Vancouver were expanding particularly rapidly.

Woodward's policy of expansion had required the formation of an architectural department with at one time as many as six full-time architects. Jim Page, manager of the department, assisted Charles van Norman, a leading Vancouver architect to design the store. Chunky was himself included in every phase of the planning.

He scanned the Woodward organization, now numbering 3800 employees for the very best men and women to be his department managers. He moved his home to West Vancouver and lived with his family a short distance from the Centre. In 1948 he had married Rosemary Jukes, daughter of another prominent pioneer family and their first child, Elizabeth Wynn, celebrated her first birthday in the same week as the Park Royal Centre opened. The marriage ended in a divorce twenty years later.

Construction was started in the summer of 1950, with opening planned for the early months of 1951. Such was the enthusiasm of the Store, the young manager and the people of Vancouver, that the Centre was opened in September 1950, six months ahead of schedule.

The omens for success were propitious. The next seven years were years of prosperity for Canada during which the Canadian Gross National Product more than doubled.

CHAPTER TWENTY-THREE

The Opulent Fifties

Louis St. Laurent, the aging Prime Minister who succeeded Mackenzie King and whom many Canadians had believed to be too mild and ineffectual to achieve much more than maintain the status quo, was the leader under whom the titanic growth of the Canadian economy occurred during the years 1948 to 1957. He quickly persuaded the United States to join Canada in building the St. Lawrence Seaway, long a pending issue on the project list. He instituted universal old age pensions and hospital insurance, piled up budget surpluses, substantially reduced the debt of the war years and made his nine-year regime the most prosperous era Canada had ever known.

In British Columbia another unlikely leader, W. A. C. Bennett, brought about equally surprising advances. When in the election of 1952 no political party secured a majority and Mr. Bennett was asked to form a Social Credit government, it was not known whether he favoured the theories of monetary reform propounded by Major Douglas. He soon made it clear that his promise, quoted by Dr. Margaret Ormsby in her history of British Columbia "to form a government which was not of the extreme right nor of the extreme left but a middle of the road free enterprise government," and his slogans "Progress not politics" and "Pay as You Go" were more than mere catch-phrases. Several vexatious problems such as the Medicare problem were solved with speed and sound common sense. British Columbia prospered during those years more spectacularly than any other part of Canada.

Nevertheless prices were rising and an inflationary trend, almost

191

negligible when compared with that of the 'Seventies, made its appearance. Billy Woodward was quick to denounce it and give a warning of its consequences.

"The way to bring prices down is for people to stop buying," he said in a widely-quoted talk to the Vancouver Board of Trade. "It may seem strange for a merchant to say that but I feel strongly that it must be said. There is no justification for these high prices."

During the Second World War as a member of the Wartime Prices and Trade Board he had seen a suspension of anticombines activity. He had realized that production, the allocation of resources and the setting of prices in time of war had to be made subject to direct controls. But he knew that price-fixing agreements were still being maintained in certain areas of the economy. Herein lay the danger and one powerful reason for rising prices.

Such agreements were as opposed to Billy's oft-repeated merchant's maxim: "Buy the best that you can, sell it for as little as you can and make a profit" as they were to his father's principles of offering low-priced goods, honest value and fair dealing.

The Canadian Government took action. It appointed the Mc-Quarrie Committee to recommend any amendments desirable to make the Combines Investigation Act "a more effective instrument for the encouraging and safeguarding of our free economy."

Immediately Woodward's sent a supporting brief to Ottawa, expressing a view which the Company had held since its inception and holds today and which is therefore quoted in full:

> James Sinclair Esq., M.P.,
> Chairman:
> Special Committee on Resale Price Maintenance,
> Houses of Parliament,
> Ottawa.
>
> Sir:
>
> For many years the Woodward organization has sought by every means in its power so to conduct its business that it can offer the best merchandise to customers at the lowest possible prices. This we believe to be the major purpose of the merchandising profession.
>
> Price maintenance, however, has made it impossible for the merchant to reduce his prices below an arbitrarily fixed mini-

mum, and has nullified his constant search for new techniques which will enable him to sell for less. We wish therefore wholeheartedly to endorse the recommendation of the McQuarrie Commission against resale price maintenance.

Experience has taught us that business interests are best served by placing first and foremost the interests of the public. Whoever else may benefit from maintained prices it is not the public. It is possible that certain manufacturers may benefit by their ability to command a predetermined price for their product, whatever its quality may be. It is possible that certain retailers may derive advantage from the restriction of effective competition. But it is also sure that the consumer is frequently denied savings he might have enjoyed through the efficiency which only competition can promote. The use of competitive methods in bringing merchandise to the public is a powerful weapon against inflation.

Many forms of retail outlets are to be found in Canada. There are stores where customers serve themselves in order to save, and stores where they may receive exclusive individual attention. There are stores where they may order by telephone, have delivery, purchase at the same price for credit as for cash, and there are stores where none of these advantages are offered. Is it reasonable to compel them all, irrespective of the amount of service they offer and irrespective of their widely different operating costs, to sell their product at the same price —and that price the highest the market will bear?

The whole of our Canadian economy is geared to a free enterprise system. It is the basis of our political creed. The man in the street has faith in it. He believes that sooner or later unfettered competition and the laws of supply and demand will defeat the bogey of inflation. The freezing of competitive selling is the very antithesis of free enterprise. For these reasons we oppose and have opposed it in principle and practice for 60 years.

We strive to sell merchandise in an efficient manner and at minimum margins consistent with good business. This too is the aim of many manufacturers with whom we do business and who have built up for their products an enviable reputation respected by retailers and consumers alike.

Many products that have no resale price set by their manufacturer have sold successfully and profitably over a long period. There is no reason why the merchandise sold at maintained prices today would not enjoy a similar success when freed from resale restrictions.

Much of our merchandise is not price controlled; yet the practice is growing and as it grows, so surely is the stimulus of competition eliminated. So too grows the prevalence of excessive trade-in allowances, of premiums and prizes offered with major purchases to present an illusion of extra value, of exaggerated advertising claims and other devious practices. Sound business ethics demand that savings effected by competent merchandising be passed directly to the public.

The foregoing brief is respectfully submitted for your consideration.

(Woodward Stores Ltd.)

The McQuarrie Commission's recommendations made it an offence for a manufacturer or other supplier "to recommend or prescribe minimum resale prices for his product; and to refuse to sell, to withdraw a franchise or take other form of action as a means of enforcing minimum resale prices."

Charles Woodward who had often been boycotted by powerful drug combines, who had to make some of his purchases at corner stores and sell them at a loss in order to maintain these very principles, must have raised a ghostly cheer at this result.

An amendment to the Combines Investigation Act was passed in 1951 which made it an offence to fix minimum resale prices though suggested resale prices were still allowed.

Another battle waged at this time was the battle to preserve the five-day business week. Vancouver was the only major Canadian city closing its stores by law for one full day each week. There were many non-retail groups who considered that their interests would be better served with a six-day week and who resented the fact that when the shops were closed there was a dead day all over the city. A number of retailers agreed with them.

"All very well for Woodward's," they grumbled, "they can keep their branch stores open when their main store is closed. Most of the rest of us are not in such a happy position."

To remain open six days a week even though employees would be guaranteed a five-day working week shattered several basic Woodward principles. The Company believed that:

194

1. Customer service would deteriorate. Customers who preferred to deal with a certain salesperson would come to the Store only to find that it was his or her day off. Service could not be as good with a staggered staff.

2. The public would pay higher prices for its needs or retailers would have to work for less money. The average consumer spent all she could afford in a five-day week. The cost of extra wages with the additional operating expense of a sixth business day could not be covered.

3. The six-day shopping week would increase the number of part time staff but decrease the number of full time employees.

4. A heavy blow would be dealt to the teamwork which was the heart of Woodward's efficiency.

The battle raged for weeks and months.

"You're impeding progress in your own selfish interests," cried the angry opposition.

"You're forcing a return to the times when retailers never closed their doors so long as there was a customer around," replied Woodward's. "Thirty years ago Vancouver merchants took the lead in securing a half a day holiday. Now in the era of the 5-day 40-hour week, they have set another standard to the advantage of the general public and their own profession."

On June 23, 1954 the issue was taken to the people of Vancouver and a plebiscite held. Woodward's lost. The climate of the times was such that defeat was inevitable. Vancouver stores could remain open for six days a week as in other Canadian cities. It was feared that the day would come when they might have to be open for seven.

Reluctantly Woodward's followed suit and stayed open six days a week "on a trial basis." Then after six month's operation in this way, management decided to return to a five-day week and to close the main store on Wednesdays. An editorial appeared in the staff magazine:

The Store's decision to close on Wednesday was a bold one. Though Woodward's is a large and powerful organization, to stay closed on shopping days when many of our competitors are open required the courage of conviction. Our management is to be congratulated.

195

The move was made in the interests of customer service and for the benefit of our staff.

It is scarcely necessary to point out what a bitter blow to Woodward's efficiency was dealt by the coming of the six-day week, and the consequent necessity for staggered "days off". By top executive and junior stock boy alike it has been regretted. A compact, hardhitting organization like ours thrives when we are all working together and all relaxing together, for team work binds together our structure.

Many of us have been ashamed of our service over these last few months. That bitter remark, "I am sorry, it is his day off", which has been used as an alibi so frequently, has produced a wave of apathy in our Store which never existed before. The energy and aggressiveness which have flowed all through the organization have started to bog down in a morass of excuses and frustration.

These worries are over. As you read these words, customers should once again be enjoying the keen personal service which over the years has played so large a part in our success. Staff members should once again be able to meet their friends and share with them the pleasures of the same day off. Store sports leagues which had disappeared will soon doubtless be revived.

This is good news but we must repeat the warning at the head of this message, "It's up to you."

It's up to you to make this decision of the management a success, by adding new lustre to the name for good service for which Woodward's is well known. It's up to you to do your job so conscientiously and cheerfully that our customers will realize the difference between this and other stores. Many of them sympathize with our desire to have the same day off at the same time.

It's up to you not to give your store a black eye by buying on the day we are closed at one of our competitors. It's up to you to banish the apathy and irritability which have been increasingly in evidence. It's up to you to give your Store all the loyalty you have, because in the final analysis Woodward's does the same for you.

We know beyond a shadow of doubt that the return to a five-day week will be welcomed throughout the Store, and envied by the staffs of our competitors. So, do your part in making this experiment a success.

But eighteen years later mounting competition would bring back the six-day week.

The early 'Fifties were momentous years for the Store and for the City of Vancouver. The old Granville Street bridge was replaced by a modern structure eight lanes wide. Commercial television made its appearance in Vancouver with the Canadian Broadcasting Company opening its T.V. station, CBUT. Queen Elizabeth II was crowned and many of her Vancouver subjects attended her brilliant Coronation. An exceptionally beautiful Aquarium was opened in Stanley Park.

Sport flourished too during this eventful decade. Vancouver was the site chosen in 1954 for the British Empire Games. On a scorching August afternoon Bannister and Landy ran what came to be known as the Miracle Mile, breaking all records by completing the distance in less than four minutes. That same day an appalled crowd watched as in their clear view Jim Peters totally exhausted but unvanquished reeled, staggered and crawled his way to what he believed to be the finishing post of the 26-mile Marathon, giving an example of courage unequalled in the annals of sport. Billy Woodward who was a spectator was so impressed that he financed the Jim Peters Fund which gives financial help to boys and girls who have been in trouble with the law and provides Christmas hampers and Easter gifts for needy families, meals for junior softball teams and outings for athletic teams from Oakalla Prison.

The British Columbia professional Lions' Football team made its debut as members of the Canadian Football League, and Woodward's sponsored the Boys' and Girls' Quarterback Club which enabled its 8000 young members to view the games at a special low price.

Eric Nicol in his comprehensive history of Vancouver quotes this significant statistic; "In 1956 the value of property within city limits topped one million dollars for the first time. During the year $68 million was spent in construction, much of it large buildings."

The coming of the giant T. Eaton Company to downtown Vancouver did not offer Woodward's the predicted shattering competition. Business at Park Royal and at the Main Store continued to increase. Two more branch stores were opened, one in the capital, and one in the former capital of British Columbia.

Victoria had long been marked as an obvious site for a major Woodward store. But statisticians reported that population growth in this city was relatively small though its per capita income made it the richest city in the province. There was debate among the directors as to whether this was the right time for a department store there.

Woodward's Victoria, opened on June 29, 1951, was different from the other branch stores. It employed no more than thirty people and specialized in British Imports of interest to American tourists. It was built on one floor with a frontage of little more than one hundred yards. The people of Victoria were disappointed. They had been eagerly awaiting a Groceteria and anticipated the usual impact a Woodward Store had on the cost of living in any city it served. Nevertheless this small store of specialized departments, a precursor to the Mayfair Centre built in Victoria twelve years later, enabled the Company to keep an eye on growth and shopping trends in the capital city.

Courtney Haddock was appointed manager of the new branch which stood, appropriately but purely coincidentally, on Courtney Street where it meets Douglas. Since its operation was too small to occupy fully his considerable energies and talents, he devoted much time to public works, becoming president of Royal Jubilee Hospital, an alderman, and after retirement, mayor. In October 1951, when Princess Elizabeth accompanied by the Duke of Edinburgh, visited British Columbia, she shopped at Woodward's, Victoria; and four Freemen of the City of Vancouver, Hon. W. C. Woodward, Hon. E. W. Hamber, W. H. Malkin and John Bennett were presented to her.

The same month the Main Store held its first post-war, one-price sale day, now known as $1.49 day.

"The results," said Denny Glanville, the then Merchandise Manager, "were excellent and compared favourably with our old 95-cent days."

Soon afterwards, as if to emphasize Vancouver's opulence, the last of the old streetcars left its streets forevermore.

CHAPTER TWENTY-FOUR

Some Notable Woodwardites

The Park Royal Centre was soon running so successfully that in less than one year from its opening a second storey was added and Chunky was able to turn his attention to his next assignment, the management of the branch department store projected for New Westminster. Steel restrictions delayed construction for a year, but early in 1952 Billy and Mayor Jackson performed the customary ceremony of turning the sod and plans went forward to build as soon as release of steel permitted.

New Westminster was of special interest to the Company. In 1891, when Charles had paid his first exploratory visit to British Columbia, he had considered building his store in the Royal City, once the capital of the Province, rather, than in Vancouver. He had written in his memoirs:

"The place which seemed to appeal to me before I came to Vancouver was New Westminster on account of having so much good agricultural land tributary to it and Vancouver had not; New Westminster also had access to the mighty Fraser River and where large ships came in and loaded and discharged their cargoes. The Canadian Pacific Railway ran into New Westminster as it did into Vancouver and it seemed a much more preferable city than Vancouver which I thought at the time was only a C.P.R. boom town."

Later Charles had changed his mind. Nevertheless there were historical associations of importance to a firm as intimately tied up with British Columbia's history as Woodward's. The site chosen at the junction of Sixth Avenue and Sixth Street was several blocks from the then heart of the town but was its geographical centre.

At the turn of the century Bussey's Grocery, a familiar landmark, had stood at this corner.

The store was opened on March 11th, 1954. When the great day arrived, crowds began to line up at 8:30 for the 10 o'clock opening. Not only did they come from New Westminster and Burnaby. Residents of the Fraser Valley poured in from as far up river as Chilliwack, crowding the roads and hindering the official cars which carried Woodward's directors and New Westminster dignitaries so that the commencement ceremonies were delayed by twenty minutes.

" It was like the opening of the first city market more than 60 years ago," reported the *Vancouver Province*. "Thousands came today to inspect the colourful, sprawling building which is Canada's most modern 'corner store'." The heart of the two-storey building, the newspaper predicted, would be the Grocery department covering an area 30,000 feet square, New Westminster's largest food market. The reporter went on to rhapsodize over the magic-eye doors, the 125-foot vegetable counter, the 100-foot self-service meat counter, and the 50-foot frozen food display case.

The most popular of the several innovations was the rooftop parking, the first of its kind in a Canadian Department Store. 300 vehicles could be accommodated on the roof of the 400 by 225 foot building. This space by no means satisfied Chunky who held strong views on the necessity of providing ample space for customers' cars. Three auxiliary adjacent lots would have space for 450 more.

Mayor Jackson who was ill on opening day was represented by his wife who cut the yellow silk ribbon and by Alderman Courtney who was especially lavish in his praise of the parking provisions. New Westminster was growing fast and its streets becoming more and more traffic-congested.

Architect Jim Page had done a good job. Wide aisles, high ceilings, and light, bright interior decoration provided a general air of expanse. A new technique in flat plate slab construction permitted the use of extra-slender support columns and reduced their number, thus giving an unobstructed, wide view on both floors.

Other novel attractions included a "Kiddy Park", the building's fifth parking area, where a mother could deposit her child to watch television while she shopped, an underground conveyor belt which carried customers' parcels to a central depot for loading into cars, a public address system and electric check-outs.

Three hundred people were employed at the new branch, bringing the total Woodward staff to almost 6000 in the Company's six stores. 3500 of them worked in Vancouver, 1000 in Edmonton.

Chunky arranged for a special faked edition of the *Columbian* to be delivered to the directors in Vancouver which read as follows:

According to an authentic report Woodward's Stores (Westminster) will now be referred to as the Main Store, having branches in Park Royal, Port Alberni, Victoria, Edmonton and a subsidiary store in Vancouver.

Mr. C. N. Woodward, Store Manager, points out that this radical change will necessitate the promotion of more staff to Executive positions.

The outrageous article then explained how most of his managers (the majority of whom had come with him from Park Royal) would replace present senior officials. It concluded:

Mr. Handford will be Director of Directors' cars. Messrs. Ashby, Charles and Elliott have been named to the Ulcer Control Committee because of their deep inner understanding of these problems.

A cartoon showed Woodward executives rushing to get aboard the Royal City Band Wagon.

Chunky had found that a touch of humour improved most situations.

With Billy spending more and more of his time at the farm, Puggy more and more of his with the P. A. Woodward Foundation and Chunky fully occupied opening and running branch stores, the directors had greater responsibility than ever before for making Company decisions. The same directors who had been appointed to the Board when it had been reconstituted in June 1942 were still serving in 1954 and would continue to serve for many years to come. Only George Duncan, Company Secretary, had retired in 1946. He had been replaced by William Swannell who had already had a close association with the Store, through his duties as chartered accountant in the firm of Paisley and Company, Woodward's auditors. Additional directors were W. G. Skinner and Chunky Woodward.

It was in some ways a unique board. None of the directors had a university degree. All but one had been promoted after serving long years in the ranks. All were rich men who owed their prosperity totally to the Company and whose devotion to it was no less total. One of the few who had had a previous job of consequence was Gordon Skinner, a chartered accountant of the first rank who came from a position with the Alberta Government to succeed A. C. Cox as Controller. It was doubtful if elsewhere in the Province could have been found a group of men who combined fewer years of formal schooling with sounder judgment or wider vision.

At the 32nd Congregation for the Conferring of Degrees at the University of British Columbia in March 1947, Mary Twigg Woodward was awarded a Bachelor of Arts degree, thus becoming the only Woodward to receive this distinction. Chunky had left U.B.C. after one year to go to war and did not return to its halls.

By 1954 almost all of Charles' original associates had died or retired. John Little, who had worked for him at the Main Street store and had backed him all the way when faced with bankruptcy or when quarrelling fiercely with his partners, was dead. So was Silas Folkins, Charles' office manager. One of the current directors, however, had served the Store since 1913. Bill Mann, an emigrant from Ireland, had paused in June of that year in his weary round of job-seeking to take a look at Woodward's. He found it so different from the country stores of Armagh and Dublin that he felt intrigued and sought an interview with W. C. Woodward who was then manager of the General Office and in charge of the staff.

These were days when jobs were hard to come by, when applicants were many and openings few, but Bill Mann lacked nothing in confidence. At school he had been a good student, especially able in mathematics. He had had a thorough professional training too, having served a five-year apprenticeship in Keady. There he had lived over the store and in return for room, board and no pay, had learned with painful thoroughness the drygoods business. Though he was young he had acquired some knowledge of customers' ways when he managed a ladies' store in Dublin called Hannagen and Shackleton. As he stood before the man who was to be his employer for nearly half a century there was a flash of mutual esteem. The next day found Bill Mann in the Men's and Boys'

202

Clothing and Furnishing Department, determined to earn his $14.00 a week salary, dusting, tidying, sorting with his usual eager energy.

Charles Woodward liked him, made it clear that he could have a future with the Store and encouraged him to send back to Ireland for his bride. On arrival she surveyed the mass of merchandise which filled Woodward windows . . . clocks, shoes, carpets, lace . . . and privately decided that compared with Dublin merchandise, it was "junk".

Charles took a fatherly interest in the young couple, even reprimanding Mrs. Mann for buying too many hats.

"How can your husband continue to make his payments on the Woodward shares he is buying if you are always getting new hats?" he demanded. The hat that was about to be purchased was returned to stock.

Bill Mann was a considerate manager.

"My first recollection of Mr. Mann," said one former member of his staff, "is a window had to be trimmed and the deadline was one o'clock. I don't know what went wrong but on this occasion I found myself in that window surrounded by tickets and heaps of merchandise with fifteen minutes to go. Then who should look in but my Manager, Mr. Mann."

"Have you finished?" he asked.

"Finished!" I replied, "I haven't even begun" and I burst into a flood of tears.

"He didn't say a word but in less than a moment we were hard at work together trimming that window. I had a lesson in window display and in human kindness all at the same time which I have never forgotten."

During the 'Thirties Mann travelled for the company more than any Woodward buyer and established contact with fashion houses in Winnipeg, Montreal, Chicago, New York and other major cities on the North American continent. On Charles' instructions he practised strict economy on his trips. If the stated price of his hotel room was $6.00 he looked amazed and horrified until it had been brought down to $4.00. He sent his heavy luggage ahead of him so as to avoid the need of a porter. His evening and weekend entertainment was walking. Some of the junior buyers who accompanied him to Montreal retain vivid memories of riding to the far end of the subway and then walking back to town, of tramping over Mount Royal in the snow, of starting the Sunday morning walk at 8:30 a.m., and stopping only at 11:00 a.m. when they would attend service at whatever church happened to be nearby.

Occasionally Mann would follow another of Charles' habits and go to an inexpensive variety theatre. Sometimes the results were embarrassing. On one of these occasions he sat next to an impressive Ukrainian lady who was surveying the show through a magnifying glass on a string. She insisted that he take a look through it and as the transfer was taking place the glass dropped under the seat. While the shy but ever courteous Bill Mann was searching for it with the aid of a match he set fire to a candy wrapper on the floor. When order was restored he signalled his companions to leave and complete the evening with a long walk.

Mann was a shrewd, perceptive buyer. In 1954 he was appointed Merchandise Manager. He was also senior director, having served on the Board for thirty-five consecutive years. He stayed on long after retirement age: Woodward's was his life. He took a newly created position of Store Manager of the Main Store and spent much of his time greeting and being greeted by hundreds of customers whom he knew or whose parents he knew.

"So good to see you in the Store," he would say and beam at them in a way that could not but enhance the pleasure of their shopping.

Working with Bill Mann in the Merchandising Office was another director, one who later would be an outstanding President of the Company, George Dennison Glanville.

He had come to Woodward's in January 1929 from Portland, Oregon. His father, owner of a small department store in New Westminster, had suddenly decided to sell his store and go to the United States to study for the ministry. This meant a dramatic change for the family in income level.

All through school Glanville worked every Saturday and in the summer months at Brink's Pharmacy in one of the rougher sections of Portland, making sundaes, washing windows, sweeping. There was no hope of his attending University. When he left school he worked in a Portland department store where he sold ties, shirts, socks, and ladies' shoes.

Then he found the pay was better at Jantzen's Knitting Mills so he got himself a job in their knitting department running a machine that sewed and cut ladies' bathing suits. He was fast with his hands and a good knitter. After a while Jantzen's arranged to send him to Australia for further training.

But he had observed that most of the best promotions went to relatives of the management. He was 19, married, and ambitious. In spite of his years in the United States he was Canadian. So he asked permission to go to Vancouver for a day where he was interviewed by Billy. The fact that he was willing to leave a good job to come to Woodward's, that he was experienced in Fashion and keen on retailing impressed Billy.

"Something may turn up," he told Glanville at the end of their interview and when the opportunity arose five months later he did not forget.

After a few months in the stock room Glanville was made Assistant Manager of the Fashion Department. This meant getting to work at 7:30 each morning in order to have the floor ready for an 8:30 store opening. It meant pulling the heavy racks of coats and suits into position by means of a long-handled hickory stick with an iron hook, trimming the window, supervising the staff and staying on the job each night until 6:30. It was excellent training.

An incident occurred during his first week which almost cost him his job. At the back of the department was a wooden elevator shaft where, because Woodward's used every corner for storage, straw hats, bathing suits and other seasonal items had been stacked. A plumber with an acetylyene torch had set the shaft on fire. Always prompt to act, Denny Glanville pulled the fire hose from its hook and directed it with unerring aim at his Manager who suddenly appeared on the scene to be immediately knocked down by the powerful jet of water.

A fire Sale followed and was so successful that Denny was forgiven. Such a tremendous crowd of women invaded the store to take advantage of the special prices that the windows had to be barricaded. There were few booths where they could change their clothes but the bargain-hungry women refused to be embarrassed by such a trifling omission and many of them changed right on the floor or behind the portable mirrors.

205

In 1932 while on holiday and on the golf course he received a message:

"You're wanted at the Store immediately."

He rushed back to find himself promoted to Manager of the Notions Department. There was some debate about salary increase.

"After all," it was pointed out to him, "you will know nothing about your new duties. You will be going to school at our expense."

He pressed for the raise and got it.

His new department was seriously in the red so immediate action was necessary. One item that struck him was the $15,000 charge for advertising which the department had paid the previous year. It was very near the amount of loss sustained that year. Why advertise at all, he thought to himself? Much of the merchandise consists of small items such as buttons, pins, spools of cotton and so forth. So he cut out advertising for a year and turned in a profit.

Denny Glanville retired in 1972, after more than 40 years of most distinguished service and leadership.

Second in seniority only to Bill Mann was director Davey Blackburn who was appointed to the Board in 1930 and had joined the Store ten years prior to that. He was a Yorkshireman who had spent his life in the 'rag trade', had an unusual knowledge of materials and was a most dedicated man.

The writer of this history who was at one time Personnel Manager of Woodward's remembers an occasion which illustrates Davey Blackburn's total immersion in his work. A new staff member had been sent to his department and soon after her arrival there, either because of the heat of the day or because she was nervous, or for whatever reason, she fainted in the middle of the floor. Without hesitation Blackburn reached for the telephone and called the Personnel office.

"Mr. Harker," he said, standing over her prostrate body. "Do you remember Miss So-and-So, the young woman you sent me this morning?"

Yes, Mr. Harker did remember Miss So-and-So.

"Well," continued Blackburn, a look of shocked surprise on his usually bland countenance, "she has fainted. How do you expect me to conduct my business in the best interests of Woodward Stores if you send me girls who faint?"

206

CHAPTER TWENTY-FIVE

Builders of the Food Floor

Though many of Woodward's most successful merchandising policies came about, as has been shown in these pages, through the unique genius of his younger brother, Puggy, "people" policies were more often Billy's brain-children.

One of his happiest ideas for the promotion of good staff relations was the formation of the Staff Advisory Council. At a dinner in 1972 celebrating its thirtieth anniversary Rose Bancroft, president of the Council, described its history and explained its function in these words:

> In 1942 the Hon. W. C. Woodward visualized the future expansion of the Company and the problems that could occur as a result of expansion. Communications was one of the major areas of his concern. Therefore, there would be need for a medium by which staff could be informed of Company policies and the Company be advised of staff problems and requests. He chose to follow a programme of having the Company appoint seven employees:
>
> Miss M. McMaster, Mrs. K. Samworth, Miss L. Daly, Mrs. F. Smith, Mr. J. James, Mr. E. Hayes, and Mr. E. Lister. They were chosen for their interest in people, length of service, sound judgment and ability to cooperate.
>
> It was soon decided that members should be elected to the Committee, not appointed. Thus in 1943 the first elected Staff Contact and Advisory Committee was formed, consisting of 25 members, one representative from each department.

It is impossible to list the many benefits and advantages introduced and promoted by the Staff Advisory Council. They ranged from conveniences such as the opening of a sundeck or the provision of wired music to financial decisions involving millions of dollars. No major change was introduced without prior discussions with the people who would either suffer or benefit from it, no request from the Committee that could be implemented safely was denied.

The first part of every meeting was held without any member of management being present. Thus the Council never became a rubber stamp. At least once a year Advisory Council Presidents from the various Woodward Stores in British Columbia and Alberta came together for discussions.

Another of Billy's people policies, no less farsighted, was the Profit-Sharing and Savings Fund Plan. As soon as it became obvious that the growth of the Company would necessitate putting its shares on the open market and changing the policy of restricting Woodward shares to staff members, he started to search for some other method of sharing the Company's success with them. Profit-Sharing appeared to be the answer and the plan evolved in early 1953 after a great deal of study and research has become a model and a major staff benefit.

The basic principle was to make employees partners in the fortunes of the Company they worked for. If the store prospered so would they; if earnings for whatever reason diminished then less money would be distributed. The Profit-Sharing Plan was to be entirely separate from normal salary increases, Cost of Living Bonus, Group Insurance, Shopping Discounts, Pension Plans, Sick Pay Plans or other benefits. Times were so good in Canada in the mid-fifties that there was a tendency for people to consider financial success inevitable. Billy wanted his people to understand that profits were subject to the law of supply and demand, that no Company could survive without them, that they must be worked for, and that they depended on diligence, foresight and team-work. The Plan worked like this: for every $100 of salary earned by each full time staff member, one "unit" was allotted. For example an employee earning $100 a week and thus having an annual salary of $5200 would be allotted 52 units. If he had been with the Company three years or more he would receive additional units for service.

Twice each year, on days which came to be known as D-Days, each of Woodward Companies would distribute a percentage of its earnings among staff members. The value of the unit was determined by dividing the total number of units of all participating Woodward employees into the amount of the company contribution. If, for instance, the value of the unit were $5.00 the employee with the 52 units would receive $260.

This money was put into Savings accounts set up for each individual employee. If he was buying a house, had heavy medical expenses or was paying off a mortgage, he could draw out his money and use it. But normally the money must remain in his Savings Account where it would accumulate and earn interest. He could if he wished add his own savings, the limit of such contribution being two weeks' pay each year, four weeks' after he had reached age 50. Thus when he retired or left the Company's employ he would have a substantial sum in addition to the non-contributory pension he received from the Company.

Some Woodwardites at first received the Plan with reservations. Old-time staff members who had become accustomed to receiving large dividends on Woodward's shares which they had bought for five dollars a share regretted that now they would have to buy their stock on the open market at a much higher price. Managers and part time staff were unhappy that they were excluded from the Plan. The fact that their money was banked and not distributed in cash was regarded by a few as "paternalism". But the response to the Voluntary Savings idea, a unique feature, was astonishing. Usually 95% of the participants chose to add their savings to the Company contribution.

Woodward's Profit-Sharing and Savings Fund, fed by regularly distributed portions of Company profits, by employee savings, by investments and by the earnings of the Fund itself, grew rapidly. As successive D-Days rolled around and each employee watched his nest egg grow until in some cases it reached well into five figures, he realized that such paternalism was to his decided advantage. Staff turnover was substantially reduced.

The development of the Food Floor into a major part of the organization continued. Many department stores on the North American continent have no food department, others sell food in a limited way because the markup is minimal compared with the markup in fashion or drygoods. But Charles and his sons had from earliest days been keenly interested in offering a variety of top-quality, low-priced food stuffs for a simple reason: though the profits might be small, a thriving food department brought customers into the Store.

The Woodwards were fortunate in finding some remarkable men who were not only top-flight merchants but were able to invest their merchandising activities with a certain flair for the dramatic. For instance in the 'Thirties, beef and mutton from Australia were cut up by a huge bandsaw right in the public gaze. A conveyor belt was pioneered by which customers' parcels were brought to a central place and claimed by ticket. At one time a corral was built on the sales floor for the prize-winning steer that Woodward's had bought at the Williams Lake Stampede. With this vigorous black animal enrolled as a member of the staff there was never a dull moment for shoppers or workers, though the steer provoked a bitter debate between the Maintenance and the Meat Department as to who should clean up after it.

The first architect of these unusual but customer-attracting ideas was John Leaman, a tall, bulky Englishman who ran the Meat Department so successfully that in 1930 he was made a director of the Company. He and his two colleagues, a Scotsman, John Tosh, who ran the Provisions and Bill Ells, the Grocery Manager, quarrelled incessantly but the three men were imaginative and indomitable.

Not all of Leaman's hirings were successful. One man who started as a helper on the midnight shift on a December night in 1930 made Woodward history. "You're to burn all those cardboard cartons," said Leaman, showing him around and indicating a vast pile of old, worn-out cartons awaiting disposal in the Furnace Room. Then Leaman went home and the new man went to work.

There was another pile of cartons in the Furnace Room. They were neither old nor worn. All five hundred of them were neatly packaged and contained Christmas turkeys. They had come frozen from Alberta and had been placed there to thaw, ready for next day's sale. The new man did not hesitate; they were cartons and they all had to burn.

210

Leaman returned just in time to see him thrusting the last of them into the furnace.

"Well, I done it, guv'nor," he said triumphantly, mopping beads of sweat from his brow.

All that day the staff of the Food Floor went about their work tantalized by the fragrant aroma of roast turkey.

Leaman ran classes for his helpers. At a time when other stores gave little thought to training their staff he used to give instruction in the evening after store closing to any of his young assistants who seemed to have leadership potential. Standing at a blackboard he would teach them how to figure out profit and loss, how to price merchandise, how to calculate selling cost. It was these classes that brought into prominence Thomas Farrell who later made Woodward's Food Floors internationally known and among the foremost on the North American continent.

As a tall, shy schoolboy of 14, Farrell had come to Woodward's at 7 a.m. on a Saturday in 1928 looking for a part time job. He had loitered at the employees' entrance until he caught Leaman's eye. Leaman was not in the best of humour that particular morning. He came roaring over, asked him what the heck he wanted, bawled him out for getting in the way and whisked him behind a counter all in the space of a moment. The bustle and excitement of those busy Saturdays combined with his admiration for Leaman led Farrell when he left school to look to Woodward's Food Floor for his career. Two or three years later he became a full time member of John Leaman's staff.

He was the green boy who was sent to look for a left-handed cleaver, a leg of liver, a bucket of steam, to the huge enjoyment of his fellow workers. He was the freshman made to wear, whenever he was working in the cooler, a collar of bones as all other new boys in the Meat Department had to do when the boss was not around. He learned to sweep a floor, handle a knife, serve customers so that they would come back. On his relief period he brewed tea on an old burner and served the other men as they reclined on sacks of sawdust in the stockrooms behind the selling floor.

Much of the day he spent at the parcel chute where he became a familiar figure, benevolently towering over customers as he handed them their purchases.

He was thorough and conscientious. He further enhanced his reputation in Mr. Leaman's eyes by winning a meat-cutting contest held annually on the Food Floor when he had been with the firm for only a few months. Billy Woodward too had made enquiries about Thomas Farrell when he had spotted an invoice for a $10 book on Meat Retailing passing through the General Office. Who was this young man who bought books that cost more than half his monthly salary, he wanted to know?

Farrell was invited into Leaman's classes. In 1935 he was promoted Assistant Manager of the Provisions Department. At once he began to develop a number of ideas which created public interest. He had the butter packed under ultra-violet germ-killing lamps before a high window so that customers could see the butter moving along a conveyor belt, being sliced, weighed and packaged by girls in immaculate white smocks. He was the first to buy orchids from Hawaii, fly them to Vancouver and sell them at prices which could be afforded by people who did not usually buy orchids. He was the first to put baby seats on the buggies, indeed to use buggies at all, the first to fly French pastries from Paris and grapefruit from Italy. He collected from Woodward's agents around the world native dresses so that customers could see the girls in Italian, Dutch, Swiss, Norwegian and other national costumes when shopping for the products of those countries.

The mechanization of the Food Floors and Grocery Warehouse, with their conveyor belts, rollers and tunnels, the employment of full time home economists to advise customers about diets — he was always abreast of the times or ahead of them.

Though he had a mild and kindly manner he was determined. Once when he was a young manager one of his favourite ideas was stolen by a competitor. It was the "Bacon-and-Egg Day", a very special event, which had been shamelessly imitated. Farrell seized his hat, set his jaw and sallied forth to call on the President of this large firm.

"What do you mean by stealing my idea?" he demanded of the venerable but startled executive who received him.

To the surprise of all concerned, the competing Bacon-and-Egg Day was halted immediately.

Farrell who had great powers of leadership became the undis-

212

puted Czar of all the Woodward Food Floors and could with justification use the term "Canada's Foremost Food Floor". A survey taken in 1955 revealed some interesting highlights:

In the Vancouver operation, over 50,000 square feet are devoted to the selling of foods. Over 300 regular people staff this floor, plus many extras. Four hundred shopping carts are required to keep the flow of over 4,333 grocery items moving to the 22 grocery check-outs. In total, there are 36 check-outs on the Food Floor, plus 19 cashiers and registers. Between 2,500 and 4,000 empty cartons are required daily in the Grocery for the packing of groceries and every hour an average of over 200 parcels move 250 feet underground on conveyor belts to the Parcel depot in the Garage."

(On one occasion an absent-minded parcel boy threw a large parcel of groceries down the chute and forgot to let go of them. He too travelled the 250 feet underground on a conveyor belt and arrived, alarmed but uninjured, in the Parcel Depot.)

It takes more than the entire output of the two largest ranches in B.C. to keep the meat department supplied with beef and keep showcases full. Woodward's own sausage, made fresh every hour, has a total length of over 7 miles per week. A bacon slicing machine, capable of turning out 800 pounds per hour, operates at capacity to cope with peak selling days. One hundred and sixty varieties of cheese from 13 different countries; all makings for ready-cooked meals such as roast chickens, barbecued spareribs, pork, chicken and steak pies; every popular salad known, including Waldorf and mixed jellied fruits; 30 varieties of bread, ranging from low calorie Holgrain to egg milk twist; cakes, plain or fancy; a complete assembly of national brand groceries as well as snails from France, rattlesnake meat from Florida, cockles and mussels from Devon and poppadums from India — these are but a small part of the variety presented.

The Grocery Mail Order stands ready to fill the entire food needs of the hundreds of people up coast and inland from the Arctic Circle to Australia. (Woodward's ships to both.)

Some of the Food Floor extras include our Bea Wright Kitchen, which not only gives cooking assistance to the hundreds who call or phone, but also advises them on the usage of all

213

new foods, makes up food requirements from prospectors'
grub lists to fashionable garden parties, plans menus for fishing
trips or for wedding receptions. Over 10,000 recipe sheets
are distributed weekly.

Woodward's own Supreme Brand products range from coffee
and teas to Norwegian sardines, from English-made orange
marmalade to Canadian strawberry jam, from super-colossal
olives and extra-large prunes to salad dressing and spices.

Tom Farrell's talents brought him to the position of President
of the Woodward Companies from 1972 until his retirement in
1975.

CHAPTER TWENTY-SIX

Puggy's Superb Philanthropy

At the 1954 Annual Shareholders' Meeting P. A. Woodward announced his resignation from the Company. He had retired and returned many times in the course of his various family quarrels but this time his resignation was final.

On the day after the announcement he took a walk around the Store as he had done so often, hat on the back of his head, keen eyes behind rimless spectacles darting searching glances into every corner as he went. He thought back to the days when as a boy, fifty years ago, he had helped the workmen dig the foundations and after school had delivered parcels on his bicycle. Now he was 64, his temper, never very good, had not improved with age. One day his nephew would hold the reins and he realized that Chunky had a mind of his own. They had already clashed over the next item in the Store's expansion programme, the decision to build a ten-million dollar Shopping Centre in Central Vancouver. Puggy had hotly opposed the plans for Oakridge and lost.

The Store had been his life and he had given it tremendous service. It had brought him some sorrow and much satisfaction and had made him a rich man. Now he would spend his money for the benefit of the people of Vancouver: and spend it he did, with a wisdom and lavishness almost unequalled in the annals of British Columbia.

One of his first acts was to form a small private company by means of which he was able to distribute a large parcel of Woodward shares at bargain rates among staff members who had in his opinion served the Company faithfully and well. This act of generosity which, in return for a few dollars, ultimately put thousands into the pockets of many Woodwardites at all levels, was performed so unobtrusively that it was a long time before the beneficiaries realized what a substantial benefit they were receiving.

But if this same benefactor lost a bet at the Vancouver Club, it was double or quits until he was even and it is doubtful if any of his friends would have had the nerve to try to borrow a small sum from him, as the turndown would have been so rough. Now he turned his full attention to the Mr. and Mrs. P. A. Woodward Foundation which in the next few years would disburse more than five million dollars. Warm-hearted Marion Woodward, who never failed to send flowers and a bedjacket to any lady staff-member in hospital, was his enthusiastic partner in this tremendous enterprise.

One of Puggy's heroes was the late King George VI, a shy man who before coming to the throne had lived in the shadow of his immensely popular elder brother, Edward, Prince of Wales. Perhaps Puggy, fourth and youngest son, saw in him a certain likeness to his own sibling relationships. He too had an immensely popular elder brother.

He decided to donate a statue of King George VI to the University of British Columbia. At an impressive ceremony on the University campus the statue was accepted by Dr. A. E. Grauer, Chancellor of the University and unveiled by Hon. Frank MacKenzie Ross, Lieutenant-Governor of British Columbia. So great was Puggy's reverence for the late monarch that it seemed to him presumptuous publicity to present his gift himself. So he arranged for the statue to be presented by the Vancouver branch of the War Amputations of Canada, an association which he had long supported. He had these words written on the programme:

> Few men have worked more selflessly for their fellow-human beings than His Late Majesty, King George VI. He ascended the throne following the unhappy circumstance of Edward VIII's abdication. Three short years later he found himself at the head of a Commonwealth and Empire plunged into its second struggle for existence within a quarter of a century. Throughout the War . . . sharing the full dangers and sufferings of his subjects in bomb-shattered London, he inspired free men everywhere to fight on for ultimate victory. The post-

216

*Marion and "Puggy" Woodward. He arranged for a statue of King George
VI, a man whom he greatly admired, to be presented to the University of
British Columbia by the War Amputations of Canada, one of the many
associations which he supported.*

217

war era brought political change and social revolution, undreamed of a mere decade earlier. Yet the Commonwealth itself emerged stronger and more virile than ever before.

Today the debt which our Commonwealth family of independent nations, freely associated through the person of the Sovereign, owes to the outstanding personal dedication of George VI is one that can only grow with each passing year.

Puggy had a hand in the composition of these appropriate words. In all his philanthropic projects he gave most careful thought to exactly how his money would be spent. When he was satisfied that the need was there and the means of filling it effective, there seemed to be no limit to the amounts of money he was prepared to spend. But because he hated waste of any kind — money, time or effort — he was never easily satisfied.

The local hospitals were the first to benefit. At St. Paul's Hospital, Vancouver, he financed an automated laboratory testing system so that patients could be tested on admission in a unique testing programme. To the Royal Columbian Hospital, New Westminster, he gave an acute trauma unit. The Health Centre for Children at the Vancouver General Hospital received an Intensive Care automatic nursing unit. There followed reading machines for the blind, a school for retarded children, and an interest free loan to permit the construction of a Civic Marina in Vancouver.

The Woodward Library was given to the University of British Columbia, in memory of his father. Property that he owned at Kelly Lake, on North Pender Island and on the Capilano River provided summer camps for veterans, especially amputees, and for Boy Scouts. His charities ranged far and wide aiding the needy and disadvantaged.

His ultimate and superlative gift was to the University of British Columbia, a donation of 3½ million dollars, the largest single contribution it has ever received, to construct the Health Sciences Centre. Now at last U.B.C. could begin to build a large well-equipped modern Centre where teaching and research would be provided for the Faculty of Medicine. Puggy did not see the 410-bed hospital and research centre opened on the University Boulevard in 1969, one year after his death, but he did sit for many months working with the planners and watching every detail. The

Foundation continued to spend at the rate of $250,000 per year to support the Health Sciences Centre.

Puggy was also an active executive Vice-President of the Downtown Business Association. In 1937 he had persuaded the three Vancouver Department Stores, Woodward's, Spencer's and the Hudson's Bay, and Birk's Jewellery Store to form an Association and thus have a united way of approaching City Hall. During the Second World War the group had languished but in 1947 it was revived and enlarged, though still financed mainly by the three large stores. Rehabilitation for the downtown area, transportation and real taxes were three of the main projects. Tempest de Wolf, who had been a lifetime friend of Puggy, was the main drive.

"At his insistence," said de Wolf, "I did a survey of the incidence of sales taxes through the Provincial house. We could not get anywhere with John Hart but when "Boss" Johnson took over, our lobby was successful. Puggy can well be known as the father of the sales tax in British Columbia."

He also backed de Wolf's idea for a Downtown Parking Corporation, helped to put through a bylaw by which the City was allowed to borrow a million dollars to buy land for parking purposes and lent the Corporation $30,000 to get it started.

Though he moved from the Woodward scene in 1955, this distinguished merchant remained an outstanding contributor to the development of Vancouver until his death thirteen years later.

In December 1956, two months before his death, Billy received yet another honour. The officers of the 15th Field Regiment (R.C.A.) held a dinner attended by representatives from all the Greater Vancouver militia units, to mark his retirement as the Regiment's Honorary Colonel, and the appointment of his successor, Brigadier Aeneas Bell-Irving. Defence Minister Ralph Campney who had come from Ottawa for the occasion made this announcement:

"We have decided to create a special military rank for Colonel Woodward. I have approved his appointment as Colonel-At-Large of the Canadian Militia. This means he will be a Colonel not as a courtesy, but as a rank. It is probably a unique rank in Canada."

Billy was presented with the Canadian Forces Decoration and with two mounted miniature brass cannons.

Two months later he went to Hawaii on holiday and while there suddenly died. There was a family funeral on the Island of Maui.

When the news of his passing reached Vancouver, flags were set at half mast not only at the Woodward Stores but all over downtown Vancouver. The British Columbia Legislature stood in silent tribute to him. So did Vancouver City Council. So did the Salvation Army at its evening service in the temple. The Directors of the Royal Bank halted their meeting in Montreal to record their sympathy and their appreciation. Members of organizations and institutions all over B.C. and Alberta whose lives had been touched by this simple, generous man paid similar respects.

A small private service took place at St. James Church in the east end of Vancouver; a memorial service held at Christ Church Cathedral, Vancouver was filled to capacity. Friends were requested to send contributions to the Patients' Comfort Fund at Shaughnessy Veterans' Hospital instead of flowers.

The Beacon Magazine, Woodward's staff journal, published this tribute:

WE SHALL REMEMBER HIM

When Hon. W. C. Woodward, the Chairman of our Board, died on Saturday night, many hundreds of us felt that we had lost a friend. At every level of our organization there was a sense of personal loss, such as cannot often accompany the passing of a leading citizen, for he had a rare gift of shedding warmth, and kindness, and friendship, wherever he went.

There were many moist eyes among us, but they were not for him. He lived a good life and went as he would have wished, in the best possible way, at the height of his powers, without lingering illness or wearing pain. He was a good man, and we do not doubt he has passed on to better things.

So our grief is not for him but for his family, who have lost a devoted husband and father, and for ourselves, who have lost a friend whom we loved.

The *Vancouver Sun* said: "Vancouver is honoured to have known him."

CHAPTER TWENTY-SEVEN

The New, Young President

Shortly before his father's death two events occurred which placed the operation of the Woodward Stores squarely and suddenly in Chunky's lap. Billy, mindful of his own father's reluctance to retire, had appointed General Manager John Butterfield President of the Company and assumed the position of Chairman of the Board. But in October, 1956, Butterfield, who had been ill for some time, decided he could no longer carry on and resigned. Thus at the age of 32 Chunky found himself President and Chief Executive of the fourth largest department store chain in Canada. His senior director Bill Mann, who was 69, wished to continue serving the Company, but in the field of goodwill rather than decision-making. However, Chunky had Glanville and Farrell and Clarridge and many other young men as aggressive and dynamic as any in the Company's history. He needed them, for changing and uncertain times lay ahead. Denny Glanville became General Manager, Tom Farrell Assistant General Manager of the chain.

Billy and Puggy had marked their father's death by presenting the staff of the downtown store memorially with an Auditorium for entertainment, recreation and meals. Chunky's memorial to Billy also took the form of a staff benefit. He offered two scholarships to the University of British Columbia, one to the University of Alberta, open only to the sons, daughters and legal dependents of Woodward staff members. The scholarships were worth $500 per year for five years. They were later increased to four in British Columbia and three in Alberta and the amount raised to $600.

A recession began in Canada in the autumn of 1957. The Liberal

Government had been in power for more than twenty years. It had already forfeited the respect of the Canadian people by its behavior during the famous Pipeline debate over a bill designed to bring huge quantities of natural gas from wells in Alberta to Central Canada. Whatever the merits of the bill, it was forced upon the Canadian people with an arrogance which spelled the doom of the Government.

Though it was not then fully appreciated, Canada was living beyond its means. The march of inflation, which would become a gallop in the 'Seventies, had commenced and was accompanied by growing unemployment, recession and a mounting foreign debt.

The new President of the Woodward Stores faced an era fraught with world economic problems greater even than those which had marked the years of the World Wars or the Depression. Though he was young, and looked younger than he was, he did not lack confidence. He had received a thorough training and was the most widely experienced executive in the Company. The previous year he had appeared before the Gordon Economic Commission which had been established by the Federal Government "to determine the course of Canada's economic development during the growth and change in domestic and external markets."

Alone he had confronted the five elderly and distinguished members of the Committee and found himself by no means overawed.

"Canadian customers are being lost because British goods are not up to specification and do not arrive on time," he told them. His remarks were placed at the top of the *Financial Post's* weekly comment and received wide publicity. The *Vancouver Sun* in a leading editorial in December 1955 called them "the best gift that went across the Atlantic to Britain this season."

His first act as President was the placing of a million-dollar contract with John Laing and Son (Canada) for the construction on the site of the present garage on Cordova Street of the largest parking garage in the British Commonwealth. Work began immediately and the six-and-a-half storey building was completed by August 1957. Customers entered the Store by a skywalk at the third floor. The old garage which at the time of its erection 26 years ago had been the first of its kind in Canada was torn down.

Though the new garage accommodated 800 cars and had a parcel pickup 100 feet long servicing 12 cars at a time, within fourteen years it had to be enlarged by yet another garage connected to it and to the department store by 9,000 square feet of overhead walkways and selling areas, once again almost doubling Woodward's downtown parking facilities.

Before the curtain was rung down on the 'Fifties other events important for the store and for the City occurred. In 1958 British Columbia celebrated its one hundredth birthday. That summer Princess Margaret, the Queen's younger sister, paid a two-week visit to British Columbia to take part in some of the festivities. She reviewed the Fleet from the deck of H.M.C.S. *Ontario* and was guest of honour at a ball given for her by Lieutenant-Governor Frank Ross at H.M.C.S. *Discovery*. Bill Whitehead, Woodward's Display and Publicity Director, was given the job of decorating the Naval headquarters for the occasion. A number of young men-about-town were instructed to practise dancing with girls five feet tall and weighing one hundred pounds. Her two favourite partners appeared to be John Turner, Montreal lawyer, and later Minister of Finance in the Trudeau Government, and Chunky.

The Princess spent a pleasant unscheduled Sunday afternoon relaxing with Ruth at Woodwynn Farm.

In 1959 the Grandview Service Building was extended to cover ten acres.

In the spring of the same year Woodward's Marine Division was opened at the Columbia Yacht Basin in Coal Harbour, at the foot of Cardero Street, to cater to the ever-growing number of Vancouver boating enthusiasts. Andrew Jukes, manager of the Capilano Shipping Company and Chunky's brother-in-law, became manager of Boatland, as the new complex was called. The Marine Division had the distinction of being the only Woodward store which could be approached by boat.

Vancouver marked the end of the 'Fifties with the opening of the 23-million dollar George Massey Tunnel linking the downtown area with a freeway to the U.S. border and of a magnificent Civic Auditorium named for and opened by Queen Elizabeth II.

Hon. Frank Ross was soon due to end his term as Lieutenant-Governor, and the newspapers began to make suggestions:

"As for the high office of Lieutenant-Governor," remarked

Princess Margaret, who visited British Columbia in 1958 to take a part in the Province's Centennial celebrations, dances with C. N. Woodward at a ball held in her honour at H.M.C.S. Discovery.

columnist J. Nesbitt in the *Colonist,* "we've never had a son succeed his father at Government House, so how about Charles N. W. Woodward? Perhaps he'd like the job if he isn't too busy running his vast department store chain . . . Young Woodward is frequently mentioned as a natural."

Chunky knew he would not like the job at all. Moreover, he had become the owner of Douglas Lake Cattle Company, one of the largest ranches in the Commonwealth. Thus he could at any rate spend some of his time riding the range.

The major event of the 'Fifties for Woodward's was the opening of the $10 million Oakridge Shopping Centre, the biggest project in its history. Two years earlier Chunky had lifted the first spadeful of earth using the same $1.49 day shovel his father had used at the sod turning for the New Westminster store.

In April 1955, the Canadian Pacific Railway announced that a 32-acre site on Cambie Street running from 41st to 45th Avenues was to be put up for sale. The C.P.R. had received this land from the City in 1886 in return for an agreement to bring the railway to Vancouver, instead of terminating at Port Moody as had first been planned. The land was part of 6400 acres sold to the Railway for $1.00 an acre and extending from the Burrard waterfront to Langara golf links. Gradually the C.P.R. had disposed of the downtown area, moving farther and farther south until this site, the geographical heart of the City, came up for consideration.

Conditions were attached to the sale. In an era of strictly controlled planning there was to be no haphazard development. The site must be used for a Shopping Centre, the entire project must be completed by the end of 1959 and the plans must be acceptable to the City Planning Committee. Oakridge was to be part of the Comprehensive Development District, the first of its kind in Vancouver.

This was a commercial venture of major importance. Tenders were submitted by most of the leading retailers of Canada.

To obtain these 32 acres was vital for Woodward's. Already the Company served the downtown area, the North Shore and the Eastern approaches. Expansion to the south was all that was needed to complete its development programme in Vancouver. Bids were to be made in secret so that no bidder would know what any other had offered. Denny Glanville who had the unenviable task of calculating an appropriate figure decided on a tender of $2,108,750. Sketches, drawings and plans were submitted and Woodward's learned that the Canadian Pacific Railway had accepted its offer.

Oakridge would not be the type of Shopping Centre owned by a real estate organization which leased its units to tenants as was Park Royal. Woodward's would own and operate the entire complex. This was the point which brought dissension from Puggy.

"We are merchants, not real estate developers," he declared. "This venture will lead us into trouble."

His brother and his nephew disagreed. Chunky had learned much from his years at the Shopping Centre in West Vancouver. Park Royal, named by Guinness chairman the Earl of Iveagh after the district of London where the Guinness breweries were situated, was a most unlikely phrase to describe the site before construction began. The whole venture had been an experiment, uncertain and risky, especially for the small specialty shops. Would people take to this type of shopping? Were there enough potential customers in the area? Would anyone come from elsewhere than the North Shore to shop? McDonald's Menswear had waited three days after the opening for its first cash customer.

But in less than two years not only had Woodward's added a second storey but another 10,000 feet of space had been needed for the other stores. Park Royal had become a Canadian pioneer prototype for all the shopping centres that had sprung up across Canada. Bernadette Sanderson, who had joined Woodward's Park Royal in 1950, twenty-five years later had seen the original 22 stores grow to 114.

Chunky had no doubt that Shopping Centres were the new trend in merchandising.

"Centres are for family shopping, informal shopping," he told the Directors when called upon to give them his impressions of the Park Royal experiment and his opinions on the Oakridge purchase.

"When people go down town to shop they get dressed up and it is a planned activity. But in Shopping Centres they may go in slacks or without a coat.

"Centres are for convenience shopping. Everyone is on wheels these days and once a person is in a car, an extra mile or so doesn't bother them. It's being sure they get parking that matters. Although geared to serve people of the locality, a Shopping Centre draws many from outside. We find at Park Royal that many customers are from New Westminster or Kerrisdale. Some are families who wanted to take a short drive in nice weather but don't want to fight downtown traffic."

Uncle Puggy's objections to Oakridge seemed especially valid when, before even one bulldozer had moved onto the site, Vancouver City Council rezoned the land from residential status to commercial use and increased the assessment from $47,850 to $478,500, a jump of 1000%. Lawyer F. K. Collins appealed the assessment as premature. The City he said had put in no sewer or drainage installations yet. The property had at that time no commercial value whatsoever.

But Government is often anxious to get its pound of flesh from a rich operator and Woodward's lost the appeal.

Water presented another problem. There seemed to be no ground water. Not until the workmen excavated the boiler-room did water appear. And how it appeared! It poured into the excavated room at the rate of 10,000 gallons a day. Special equipment had to be borrowed from the George Massey Tunnel operation to get the flow under control. Then water geologists, the electronic age's answer to the forked willow stick, were hurried to the site from Tacoma. They found seven artesian wells on the property capable of producing one million gallons of water per day and providing an electronic-filtered air-conditioning system. Dust- and lint-free air-fresh stores were the result. Things have always had a way of turning out well for the Woodwards.

Four acres of Oakridge were set aside for beautification. A wide frame surrounding the shopping area was landscaped and planted with a profusion of azaleas, fuchsias and rhododendrons, evergreens and annuals, beech, birch and dogwood, yew and prostrate juniper. Japanese cherry trees presented by the Japanese government, masses of floribunda roses, cacti, succulents and yucca interspersed with great rocks and sand combined to make Oakridge on a summer day one of the sights of Vancouver. At the south end of the main mall was a pool with spray-type fountain and changing lights.

227

For the centre of the main mall architect Jim Page, who had designed the department store and all the specialty shops, turned his versatile abilities to designing a mural almost as long as the mall. It was made of glass tile and depicted the mountains, the industries, the sunsets and the lashing seas of British Columbia. The mural was handmade in Venice and to his distress arrived late for the opening ceremonies.

Forty different kinds of independent shops and a wide variety of services clustered around the Department Store. They included an Auditorium seating 300 and available for entertainment and meetings, an Adminstration Building, a branch of the Vancouver Public Library, of the Trans-Canada Airlines, of the Royal Bank and the White Spot Restaurant.

So that customers could shop free from the fumes of trucks and the noise of delivery vans, a collection and delivery area was constructed 20 feet underground. It was the first tunnel built in Canada for a shopping centre to remove truck traffic, was one-third of a mile long and high enough to accept the highest trucking van. An ingenious communication system enabled drivers to speak directly with any one of the mall's small shops. Food floor customers could also use this "Ask It" system by making their enquiries into one of the microphones on the Food Floor and receiving an immediate answer. But as children liked to use them for playing pranks and adult customers did not seem interested, the microphones were discontinued.

The Shopping Centre had a pedestrian mall as its core with three shorter malls branching from it and a 19-acre parking area surrounding it and accommodating 2500 vehicles. A service garage could take care of 20 cars at a time. The Food Floor, housed in a separate building, included a giant-sized dairy case, an open refrigerated area for dairy products, 106 feet long and unique. Almost all Food Floor checkouts fed to a conveyor belt which moved parcels directly to the parcel pickup depot in the parking lot.

The contractors, who had moved 300,000 yards of earth weighing 405,000 tons, used 3000 pounds of reinforcing steel and laid 25,300 yards of cement to erect the buildings, sat back and surveyed their handiwork with pride. It was surely the last word in shoppers' comfort. They could wander in a beautiful garden with wired music playing to them in the background and choose from an array of immensely varied merchandise. Not even the sound of a truck would be allowed to disturb their peace. There were no steps to climb. A water-type smoke eliminator permitted not one smudge of smoke to issue from the 6-foot stack. Six hundred insulation vibrators reduced all noise and vibration, 125 complete and separate air conditioning and ventilation systems kept the Oakridge air pure.

Old Charles would have approved. As early as 1893, realizing that people wanted to enjoy shopping, he had offered door-prizes and even hired a band to play in the Store on an occasional Saturday evening. But the means of providing for customers' shopping pleasure in a modern Shopping Centre might have surprised him.

Reginald Clarridge was appointed manager of this newest jewel in the Woodward chain. Like Denny Glanville, who had been his boss for several years, he had made his way up through the Fashion Division, starting as stockboy in the Cosmetics Department. He had been born in Calgary, lived as a boy in New Westminster, joined Woodward's as an extra during the Christmas rush of 1934, made the full time staff and married pretty Beverley Lee from the hosiery counter. During the Second World War he interrupted his career at Woodward's to serve four years in Canada, the U.K. and Europe with the Royal Canadian Air Force.

Chunky had spotted Clarridge when he was manager of the Notions, liked his unassuming way, quick wit and quiet intelligence and asked him in 1954 to work at the New Westminster store as Merchandise Manager and Second-in-Command. Later he became President and Chief Operating Officer of the Company.

Ten thousand people came to see Oakridge opened on May 6, 1959 by Vancouver Mayor Tom Alsbury. Traffic jams were caused even more severe than those that occurred when John Woodward's promotional stunt had closed Westminster Avenue for three hours 65 years before.

CHAPTER TWENTY-EIGHT

Woodwynn Farm

Woodwynn is part of one of the oldest farms in British Columbia. The farm was pioneered by William Thomson, a stalwart, black-bearded ship's carpenter who, in the middle of the Nineteenth century, was shipwrecked on the wild West Coast of Vancouver Island and enslaved by the Nitinat Indians. The year 1855 found him settled in Fort Victoria working for the Hudson's Bay Company whose men had rescued him from the Indians.

One day that same year he walked twelve miles along the Indian trail which is now the West Saanich Road and from a hill by the side of a burn looked over a land where he knew he wanted to live. The land was named Saanich which in the Indian language means "plenty". It was well named. There was an abundance of salmon and deer, of acorns and wild blackberries, of game and fertile soil.

He built a cabin in the woods, went back to Victoria for his wife, young son David, and their one horse which they rode in turns to their new home. Whoever rode the horse carried the baby.

At first William Thomson was only a squatter, the sole white settler in Saanich, but as soon as the land was surveyed, he bought 200 acres for 25 cents an acre. The Thomsons made friends with their Indian neighbors and Margaret learned to speak their language.

Before Thomson died he owned 2000 acres of Saanich peninsula and had cultivated most of them. He had raised a family of ten sons and five daughters and built the finest house in the district which he called Bannockburn, in honour of another Scottish victory also bought by courage and determination. In 1862 he gave part of his land for the erection of St. Stephen's Church, one of the loveliest churches on Vancouver Island. As saplings he had planted the two towering fir trees which shelter it, his team of oxen hauled the timber and his numerous progeny received their first lessons there for he had stipulated that the church must be used for a school as well as a place of worship.

Remembering that the Church was built of California redwood, he had accepted on its behalf a redwood cross bearing the inscription, "In memory of General James Garfield, president of the U.S.A., presented to St. Stephen's Church by teachers and scholars of Calvary Memorial Church, Philadelphia, U.S.A. . . . Easter Day 1882."

In 1870 he started the Saanich Fair, still held annually, the high spot of the local calendar and now the oldest Fair west of the Great Lakes.

The Woodward house, black-beamed, partly white brick, long, low, somewhat Elizabethan in appearance, stands just across the road from St. Stephen's. When the Woodwards bought 550 acres of Bannockburn and named their farm Woodwynn, a combination of their two names, they knew they were acquiring part of the history of the West, and they respected the Thomson traditions. They too worshipped at St. Stephen's and were pleased to do so, preferring small churches to large ones. Woodwynn remained a place for young people. Though Ruth and Billy could not match the 15 Thomson children they had 14 grandchildren who would find as much joy and perhaps be as strongly influenced by Woodwynn as Ruth and her sisters had been by Alkali Lake Ranch. Ruth was especially devoted to Indian causes and Indians continued to find friendship, help and respect at Woodwynn.

Above all, it remained a productive, well-run farm.

So Billy, banker, merchant, former King's representative, who had lived in cities all his adult life, became a farmer. On his 255 arable acres he grew wheat, oats, barley. He learned to drive a tractor and a baler, and assisted by his chauffeur Wes Strickland, as urban a type as he, and by local help, he put up 200 tons of hay the first summer. Strickland operated the cutter from the back seat. The crops Billy sold to Ruth for her cattle.

Mr. and Mrs. W. C. Woodward at their farm Woodwynn, Saanichton, B.C.

"That is why," Ruth would say, looking at him with feigned distress, "I can't make any money."

"It must be poor management," he would retort, "I sell you the stuff at cost."

This was a long-standing and oft-repeated joke between them, but Billy truly was determined that Woodwynn should be operated at a profit. Otherwise it would make no contribution to the general good and he and Ruth would be "playboy" farmers, a role he heartily detested. Moreover, he had his own share of the family dislike of waste and extravagance.

Ruth was completely and immediately at home on her farm. Though no woman in British Columbia had had a fuller or more demanding social life, she did not really enjoy such activities. Next to her family she loved cattle and at Woodwynn she was in her element. She decided to start with Jerseys, the most popular breed in the district and to have a dairy farm. She and Billy built good buildings, well-planned in every way and soundly constructed. The Jerseys were practically all purchased from Island breeders and care was taken to select a foundation with capabilities for high production. The milk was of top quality and could readily be sold in nearby Victoria.

Before long Woodwynn had a calf herd and a herd of heifers which according to the Canadian Jersey Breeder of January, 1950 "would charm the heart of a good Jerseyman anywhere." Ruth entered her cattle at the local shows on the Island and did well. In 1949, three years after their retirement from Government House, Frasea Standard Model, the senior herd sire, was grand champion at the Saanich Fair and at the Duncan Exhibition. Woodwynn was recognized as one of the better breeding establishments in Canada.

Ruth loved it all. There would be no more receptions, no more fancy teas, or an absolute minimum of them. Every day she would spend in old clothes, performing numerous chores among her beloved cows.

She found one aspect of farm life greatly and distressingly changed since her days at Alkali Lake. A plethora of records, unending, minutely detailed, had to be kept. At the end of every month lengthy forms had to be completed and sent to Ottawa with duplicates kept on file. There were RCP (Canadian Records of Performance) on yellow forms, one of which was sent to Ottawa as soon as a cow calved. It described her whole lactation. There was another record breaker on white paper requiring the name, breed and tattoo (ear tag) of every cow on the farm. For each cow there had to be a separate form stating when she calved, was bred, was last milked, the weight of her daily yield, if she had been or would be entered for RCP daily herd test, if she aborted, died or had been sold.

Then in blacker ink came the statement: "If this cow is NOT to be entered on RCP daily weighing or RCP daily herd test, state reason."

Finally, in even blacker ink: "I hereby certify that this report is true and correct as completed in every aspect."

"I sign it trembling," Ruth told a press reporter who visited her, curious about the new life of the former chatelaine of Government House. "The report is supposed to be a protection but it's also a pain in the neck."

Characteristically, she added, "What it must be like for the farmers who have to do all their own work I don't dare to think."

The big barn which Willy Thomson and his friends had built in Queen Victoria's Jubilee year still stands. Ruth had it painted white with red doors to match the other Woodwynn barns and buildings and added a row of calving pens down one side of it.

The Woodwards spent seven years, from 1945 to 1952, raising Jerseys. Though the farm was primarily Ruth's concern, she was much helped by her husband's shrewd judgment and unexpected enthusiasm.

Lack of water, one of the chief reasons why Saanichton farmers did not specialize in dairy farming was at first a drawback. The rain distribution was such that often their farms were overgrassed in June with minimal pasture growth in July and August. It was not uncommon to have 90% of the total yield produced by June 1st. So Billy acquired a private irrigation system, the only one on the peninsula and a highly successful way of overcoming the problem.

In 1953 many cattle records were set by animals from Woodwynn. Prize cow Rosemont La France, whose ancestors had been famous local producers for many years, completed a record by producing 11,255 pounds of milk and 515 pounds of fat. Rosemony

Ruth Woodward and her grandchildren in 1960. LEFT TO RIGHT: John Woodward, Melanie White, Andrew White, Philippa Morgan, Deborah McDonald, Nicola Morgan (standing), "Becky" McDonald, Rhegan White Mrs. W. C. Woodward, "Kip" Woodward, Robyn Woodward, "Rusty" McDonald, Susan White, Wynn Woodward, (only grandchild missing is Joel White who was not born at the time of this picture).

Golden Polly bettered it with her record in 365 days of 12,978 pounds of milk and 714 pounds of fat, and won a gold medal certificate. Bream Lad, Journal's Jill, Model's Fairy, Model's Justice did almost as well. Quilchena Forward, a two-year-old bull, was grand champion of the Jersey class. Fury's Jay was junior champion cow at the Saanich Fall Fair.

But though 1952 was the year of her greatest successes, it was also the year when Billy decided that the Jerseys must be sold. Ruth had 115 animals . . . at times there had been as many as 160 producing 140 gallons of milk a day . . . and her job kept her busy from morning till night. It was difficult in those lush days of full employment and general prosperity to find people who wanted to work on a farm. As for keeping trained workers to help Tom O'Reilly, the Farm Manager, that was impossible. The economics of dairy farming she had discovered were so strained that the industry was in the hands of a few men who had battled a lifetime to make a bare living from it. There was nothing to be gained from running a large herd unless a farmer was totally dedicated to his work in a way she could not be.

Woodwynn was Ruth's home. She had children, grandchildren, a host of friends and a multitude of commitments, most of them charitable. She agreed that the herd must be sold and made a decision eventually to replace them with Aberdeen Angus. The black compact Angus was a beef breed of the highest rank. She would concentrate on beef breeding rather than dairy breeding.

One principal trouble had been finding people to do the milking. This problem would not occur with a herd of Aberdeen Angus. She did not immediately confide her plans to Billy. She knew he had had enough of cows for a while.

It was decided to hold an auction in the fall, though the thought of parting with her beloved cows filled her eyes with tears. Tom O'Reilly was sad, too. All his farming experience had been with Jerseys.

It was not a good time for a sale. The previous February there had been an outbreak of foot-and-mouth disease in Saskatchewan and the U.S.A. had placed an embargo on Canadian cattle. As a result there were no American buyers present and most local breeders were adequately stocked and therefore hesitant in buying.

The prize of the herd was still Frasea Standard Model. By now he was sire of the first prize-winning get of sire, five times grand champion of the Saanich Fair, his daughters had won silver medals and countless prizes, and he himself had sired the first prize senior get of sire at Saanichton.

Auctioneer Jack Gibson received but one bid for Frasea Standard Model, a bid of $200 from a buyer who was interested only in the beef.

"Completely unacceptable," snorted Gibson, echoing a much stronger comment from Billy. So Frasea returned to the barn to await another occasion.

Prices were far below the value of the stock and many cows which had repeatedly won honours at exhibitions went for bargain prices. Model's Blossom along with her newly-born calf fetched the highest price, $350 for the two of them.

Billy went to bed that night in a bad humour. He knew that Ruth would miss her Jerseys. Moreover, he disliked selling cattle or anything else for a great deal less than they were worth.

He was even angrier when he awoke next morning to find his tractor gone. A young sailor who had been on an all-night binge decided that it was a suitable vehicle for a joyride and was apprehended at 5 a.m. just as he was about to launch himself and Billy's tractor into Government Street.

When at last Ruth broached the subject of Aberdeen Angus, Billy was not hard to persuade. She assured him that they were noted for their superior quality of meat, smooth fleshing, fine bone and high dressing percentage and that Angus cows were reputed to have a remarkable longevity. She had read that Grannie, the first Aberdeen Angus cow ever registered, born in 1832 had died at the age of 36 in a thunderstorm, having produced 29 calves every one a prize-winner.

"People are eating a lot more beef these days," Billy declared, becoming more and more enthusiastic. "George Hull tells me that the per capita consumption has risen from 51 to 74 pounds and that British Columbia, with nine per cent of the national population, produces only three percent of the nation's beef. Over 100,000 head have to be imported every year from Alberta."

Hull, manager of Woodward's Meat Division, was very knowledgeable about his subject. Ruth was the cattle expert but often found it was useful to have a merchant for her husband.

He bought the first Aberdeen Angus from E. P. Taylor who had been his wartime companion when together they had been torpedoed in *Western Prince*. Billy made a good buy which pleased him. Doug Locke who had had much experience in dry farming came from Saskatchewan to take charge of the fields and to be farm manager. Tom O'Reilly remained in charge of the cattle and together they made a good team. The herd began to grow and the omens for success were good.

On November 6, 1954, two years after the auction, Blackbird Strype was born. This noble Angus bull, son of a supreme champion Perth bull, became the Woodwynn senior sire.

In 1957, that eventful year which saw the passing of Billy, the turning of the sod at the site of the Oakridge Shopping Centre, the opening of the 900-car parking garage and Chunky's purchase of Douglas Lake Ranch, Ruth was invited to become honorary president of the B.C. Angus breeders. The first B.C. Aberdeen Angus field day took place and was held at Woodwynn. She was by now the well-informed owner of an outstanding herd of fine cattle. Nearly 200 enthusiastic fanciers of the breed gathered at Woodwynn and were surprised to see that some of the finest examples of this famous beef breed were being raised there and that sons and daughters of grand champions were the rule rather than the exception.

The head of the federal livestock branch, R. K. Bennett, came from Ottawa to attend the exhibition and complimented Ruth, Tom O'Reilly and the other Angus breeders on the way they had improved the quality of the beef being marketed.

"It takes faith, ability, love of cattle and integrity to succeed with purebred beeves," he said: "I have long been impressed with the integrity of the men in the registered livestock business." Even in cattle-breeding, integrity, the preeminent Woodward quality, was the main requirement for success.

Each pen contained a bull, his cows and their calves. Ruth wished that Billy could have seen the smooth, black, shining, polled cattle eating contentedly while visitors milled about listening to the commentary. She had been a widow now for several months.

J. P. Sackville, from Calgary, president of the Canadian Aberdeen Angus Association, also added his respects. In the last five years he said, British Columbia had made greater strides in the extension and improvement of the breed than any other province except Quebec. Much of this success could be attributed to the example of Woodwynn.

Ruth's friend and neighbor, Grace Moses, whose grandfather Daniel Moses had settled in Saanich at almost the same time as Willy Thomson, whose maternal grandmother was a full-blooded Indian, and whose farm was as much a part of British Columbia's history as Ruth's, admired the Aberdeen Angus but decided to make no change in her own farm. She had an exceptionally fine herd of Jerseys which she raised when she was not teaching school or handling a milk route.

The fine herd at Woodwynn eventually numbered 250 animals. To Ruth's pleasure and profit it inspired others to increase their Aberdeen Angus holdings. Soon after the field day she sold a grand champion female, Mayflower B S Woodwynn, to Quilchena Farms for $2000.

Ruth's concern over the plight of the Canadian cattlemen led her to visit Australia and New Zealand to observe their methods of sheep and cattle-raising. Ranchers in British Columbia and Alberta worked harder than any section of the community yet barely made ends meet. In the mid-1960's many Canadian growers were receiving 3½ cents less for cattle on the hoof than the actual cost of production. Why?

At many cattlemen's meetings she heard over and over again the various reasons advanced for this unhappy situation.

"It's the fault of the supermarkets. The whole beef industry is in the grip of these big supermarket chains. They have a monopoly and can set prices to suit themselves. They have pushed the price of Canadian beef up to $1.25 per pound when 85 or 90 cents would be ample."

"Four per cent of Canada's total beef supply comes from New Zealand and Australia. New Zealand beef is being sold for 45 to 65 cents. How can we compete with that?"

"The Canadian housewife will accept nothing but red meat with white firm fat. That kind of meat can be obtained only from beasts fed on grain and from a feeding programme which requires 35,000 to 40,000 bushels of barley a year. Every animal has to have a ton of hay annually! And the cost of grain goes up all the time."

"We should impose restrictions and set a quota of beef allowed in from abroad."

"Annual land taxes are levied up to one dollar an acre. Last year I paid the Government $6000."

"Our rainfall averages 18 inches a year."

"Our high wages are the trouble."

"Canadian beef is the best in the world but we are not getting a fair return for it."

And so it went, the long, unending, justified lamentation. Ruth believed that for men who performed such essential service to be so miserably rewarded was intolerable. British Columbia cattlemen had overcome the difficulties of the past . . . the wolves, the rustlers, the hard winters, the drought. This problem too could be defeated. New Zealanders were said to be able to produce cattle for 11 cents per pound live weight, less than half the Canadian cost. Why not visit them and find out how they did it?

When she joined a tour of Western Canadian farmers and ranchers to Australia and New Zealand in 1964, she was 67 and living an exceptionally active life. This was to be no luxury tour but a business trip with a serious purpose. The group, mostly from Alberta, numbered 32. She persuaded her friend Mrs. W. C. Pitfield, who ran a herd of 150 polled shorthorns at her farm near Montreal to go with her, thereby swelling the number of women on the tour to eight.

It was strenuous. The cattlemen visited freezing-works, all weather meat-loaders and breeders all over the country, saw some of the finest Aberdeen Angus in the world, were amazed at the lush New Zealand pastures and enjoyed vast hospitality. It is hard to assess how great an impact the three-week tour had on solving the problems of the Canadian farmer but it cannot have failed to provide some solutions.

Ruth's decision to go with the ranchers was characteristic. If the reader has decided that the Woodwards deserve to be called great Canadians because they have made impressive contributions to their country, she should certainly be included, though she would have been amazed to hear herself so designated. She was a modest woman. But it is indisputable that she did much to improve conditions in the cattle industry in Western Canada.

Her performance as wife of the Lieutenant-Governor of British Columbia was outstanding. She omitted no duty, knew instinctively what must be done and supported an incredible number of ventures and people. The more unheralded the enterprise the more firmly she backed it.

She managed to find the time to be Lady Provincial Superintendent of St. John Ambulance Brigade, treasurer of the Women's Auxiliary to the Vancouver General Hospital, driver for the Community Chest, organizer of the Junior League Thrift Shop, sponsor of Girl Guides and 4H Clubs, and while living in Ottawa, organizer of the Red Cross Thrift Shop. She held the title Dame Grace of the Venerable Order of St. John of Jerusalem.

To a newspaper reporter she once declared:

"I'm a feminist. I think we've had a pretty poor show by the men. Young women are getting educated . . . they'll soon be taking over everything. Look at the fuss they've made over abortion laws. But I think they'll win out in time and I think they should.

"But with free abortion and education to give woman independence from her husband, modern woman will just stop having babies. And I think she's going to be sorry when she's an old woman."

Princess Margaret, the Princess Royal, herself a cattlewoman with a herd of Red Poles, and Princess Alexandra visited Ruth at Woodwynn. So did Prime Minister Lester Pearson. So did her Indian friends, Mrs. Modiste and Mrs. Francis Bob.

Ruth had been brought up with Indians at her father's ranch. Said one Cariboo paper, "It is doubtful whether any other ranch in British Columbia has had a more friendly understanding among their Indian employees." This happy state of affairs was attributed to both the Wynn-Johnson family and to Tommy Johnson, a ranch employee who worked there for 43 years. Ruth was one of 500 people from Kamloops, Anaheim, Canim Lake and all the surrounding country who attended the funeral of this most respected Indian. He was the first man to help her as a child to gain an understanding of Indian ways and a sympathy with Indian problems which were lifelong.

Many of the Indians who lived on the East Saanich Reserve

only a few miles from Woodwynn were her friends. She urged that one of them, Chief Ed Underwood, should be appointed to the Board of Directors of the North and South Agricultural Society, sponsors of the Saanichton Fair. She started an Indian Brownie pack, sat on a committee of Indians and whites to help Indians organize a cooperative for the sale of their crafts and arranged for Mrs. Modiste and Mrs. Francis Bob to go to Nanaimo personally to present sweaters they had knitted for the Royal Family. When the Six Nations Council of the Grand River officially opened Chiefwood, home of Pauline Johnson, the Mohawk Indian Poetess, Ruth was an honoured guest. She and her friend Irene Rogers helped to revive the Indian Days' celebration at Hamiltchasen Park and both were made honorary Indian Princesses. The welfare and acceptance of Indians was one of her life-long concerns.

Ruth had a favourite saying, not often pronounced for she never pontificated, but it was strongly held:

It is the greatest of all mistakes to do nothing. Because you can do only little, do what you can.

"I have tried to live my life by that quotation," she once told the writer.

In February 1972 Ruth went to Scotland to attend a Cattle Show and planned to be away for seven weeks. It was unusual for her to be away so long. While she was there she was not well and suffered pains in her legs. "Robbie" Robinson, manager of Woodward's London office, was worried about her. However, she insisted on being allowed to accompany some Woodward buyers who were going to the Continent. She had not been on a buying trip since she had helped Billy and Alex Mitchell eighteen years earlier set up the Round-the-World agencies. She wanted to experience once again the excitement of the market and the search for merchandise.

Perhaps she knew it would be for the last time.

As soon as she was home, she went to Douglas Lake Ranch. On the way she stopped at Kamloops and watched Tom O'Reilly receive the Country Life Trophy, Voice of the Federation of Agriculture in B.C., for the highest training group of five bulls of all breeds at the Tranquille Testing Station. It was a tall, magnificent cup, the most prestigious trophy she had ever won. She beamed with pride and pleasure.

Ruth stayed at Douglas Lake only for the weekend, then came home, telephoned her sister Paddy Cripps, took one last look at the Country Life Trophy, went into her room and died in the night.

St. Stephen's is the oldest church in British Columbia on its original site and holding unbroken services. In a simple grave beside the church, overlooking Woodwynn Farm, are buried two of its most faithful parishioners, Ruth Wynn and William Culham Woodward. A lamp placed in the sanctuary by their faithful friend Nanny Lloyd burns perpetually in their honour.

CHAPTER TWENTY-NINE

Venture in the East

Though the Provincial Government in the 1960's was strong and capable, some feared that it was placing itself above the law. British Columbia was the only Canadian province where no verbatim account of parliamentary debates was permitted, where citizens were not allowed to sue the government, where Cabinet decisions must inevitably prevail. The B.C. Electric Company, despite previous protestations that such expropriation would not happen, was arbitrarily taken over.

When the government decided to tax Puggy's estate for money which he had left to his Foundation, Premier Bennett ruled that it was not a charitable foundation and was therefore subject to taxation. Chunky fought this ruling vigorously but the government simply passed a Bill stating that no ruling of the Finance Minister could be challenged in court and made the Bill retroactive to cover the Woodward case.

The year 1959 saw the end of an era and the dawn of social and economic revolution which at this writing is in full swing and likely to continue. That year the success of Woodward's was such that the Company was able to give one million dollars to the Profit-Sharing Fund.

In announcing what was probably the largest contribution ever made by a Canadian Company to staff members the President might have been excused if he had shown a touch of complacency. But there was no hint of it in his speech. At the 1959 Advisory dinner, attended by past and present members of Advisory Councils, he outlined some of the troubles which in his opinion lay ahead for

Canada and British Columbia and how he thought they should be faced. Sound judgment, forthrightness and foresight were evident in his remarks, qualities which he had inherited in full measure from his father and grandfathers. Though he was a young man, speaking to a small group of men and women at no executive level, at a meeting of little significance outside the Store, his words might well have been heard and heeded by a larger audience. This is what he said:

This year your Company will be 67 years old. From a very small beginning, on the corner of Harris and Westminster, now Georgia and Main, it has grown to be a major industry in British Columbia and one of the largest retail industries in Canada.

You might ask, how has all this come about? Well, I think there are probably two main factors involved. One, the principles of merchandising laid down by the founder have been carried on and extended by the present management, and secondly, the loyalty of the staff has not wavered. We can look back with pride on our accomplishments. We have laid a solid foundation of mutual respect and trust, both with our customers and with our staff, and are able to look to the future with confidence. Although we know that our Company is ready for the future, and the staff can be sure that whatever success we have, they will be a part of it and share in it, it must not be forgotten that our future is bound with the future of this province and to the rest of Canada.

I do not want you to construe my remarks tonight as sounding off, or being anti-this or anti-that, but it is time we sat down and did some serious thinking about our future, not only in this province, but as Canadians. The last two years seems to have been embroiled in continual bickering by both management and labour. It is hard for us to understand this, as we have had no disputes for close to 70 years. The future of every one of us, regardless of what side of the fence we are on, is tied to one another. Let us stop thinking of personal glorification, and start thinking what is best for Canada and best for us all.

One must realize that B.C. has become the highest cost province in Canada. I am not saying that it is too high. Maybe the rest of Canada is too low; but in respect to further expansion, one must watch that costs do not get so far out of line as to discourage industry or investment.

B.C. is a primary producing province, depending on world markets and world distribution. Some years have been good — some bad. So far we have done fairly well, but what we need are many more secondary industries, and they will not come unless we can be competitive with the rest of Canada. One of these days there must be a solution, but so far none has been found nor do we seem closer to reaching one. Everyone seems to have a pet theory on how to improve labour practices, but in the thought I am a Canadian, and proud of it, and want to make Canada a better place to live, I want to have more control over the destinies of my country. I think that everybody should be a little more nationalistic — should think a little more about our country and less about our neighbor to the south; what she is doing or what she has.

We have a situation in Canada where most of our unions and many of our companies are U.S. controlled. What happens to us here depends on the political expediency of what has happened in the U.S. I have no wish to stop foreign investment, but if they are investing money here, the money should not be invested in some subsidiary of a large American or foreign corporation. It should be invested in a Canadian company, with a Canadian makeup. This company is 100% behind the future of Canada. Too many of our American subsidiaries are little more than frosting to the parent company's cake, and no thought is given as to what happens to Canada or the people of Canada if they decide to close down or curtail business. Too many subsidiaries are here to see what they can put in; but the most successful American and foreign investments in Canada are those which have complete Canadian makeup and have tied their future with the future of Canada.

Labour, I feel, is in the same category, and what I have said about foreign investments in Canadian corporations holds true with regard to our unions. They should be completely Canadian controlled, and their leaders should be looking out for the good of the Canadian workers only, and not taking orders from their U.S. superiors. If the present trend continues, we will end up no longer as a Canadian nation, but will be virtually enslaved economically and politically.

246

We believe both parties could do a lot more as Canadians and could give more intelligent thought to what is best for our country — how best we can increase our industrial capacity and the number of available jobs. This will never come about at the rate we are going. It will never come about if we fail to think about the other person or if our orders always come from the U.S. It will only come about if we work together with mutual respect and a genuine interest in working together for the future.

I believe Canada is our heritage and our heritage for generations to come. Profits and benefits should be shared by all classes in our democratic way of life. They should be shared by the people who put up this capital; by the industries, and by the people who work in them. Canada is a rich country and there should be no need for want or hunger or sickness. As long as a man will work there should be a job for him.

I suggest that both management and labour take a leaf out of our book, regardless of how distasteful it may seem to either party. We don't think we are perfect, but we have gone a long way in the right direction. Just stop and take a look at what both management and staff have got out of working together for close to 70 years. The management has a highly successful and prosperous company; unbounded faith in the future; a staff whose loyalty and devotion is second to none. The people who have put up the money have received dividends never anticipated in the growth of the company. Our staff is one of the best paid in this trade in Canada. They have profit-sharing and are able to share individually in the success of the company. They have sick pay — medical benefits for themselves and their families, which does away to a large extent with worry about illness. They have group life insurance. They have pensions provided by the company which alleviates the worry of what to do when they pass the working age. If the next ten years are as profitable to both of us as the last ten, we shall be the best looked after staff in Canada. All of these benefits were attained because of the management's genuine interest in the people who work for it and the staff's genuine interest in the prosperity of their company. This has been tried and true success for us all. Do not let anyone or anything change this, as if we do, in later years we may live to regret it.

And later in the year at a shareholders' meeting, he declared:

"Shareholders must realize that under today's economic conditions, staff should and do share to a greater extent in the earnings of our business."

That remark was widely quoted in newspapers and business journals across the country.

When the people decided to throw out the Federal Liberal Government and "follow John" Diefenbaker, as they did in the election of 1957, the new Prime Minister inherited troubles which were not of his own making and which he could not cure. Recession in Canada continued. During the early 1960's the Canadian dollar was devalued. In three years general elections were held and during those three years a minority government ruled with all the compromises and weaknesses inherent in minority government rule.

Two grave Canadian problems came to a head. One was the sudden thrust of a strong nationalist movement in Quebec which terminated in kidnapping, murder and the passing of the Emergency War Measures Act. Some called the decision to bring in the Armed Forces "overkill"; others claimed that without such a measure there would have been revolution in Canada.

Another equally serious concern was the extent to which Canadian industry was controlled by Americans. There came a sudden widespread realization that much of the economy, including the vast oil industry in Alberta and the Canadian automobile industry, was almost completely American-owned. The struggle for Canadian identity, for a Canadian citizenship, flag and governor-general was of little moment if Canadians did not control their own economy.

The growing recession hit British Columbia less seriously than other parts of Canada. The boom gave every appearance of continuing. Fine new roads, additional ferries, giant dams appeared all over the Province. The railroad to the North at last was constructed. Expensive season tickets to Canadian National Hockey and Football games were sold out. Eight jets flew from Vancouver every week to Hawaii, taking an ever-increasing number of prosperous winter vacationers.

But there was some caution in evidence, too. In 1962 the voters turned down a proposal to buy from the Canadian Pacific Railway the old Shaughnessy golf course for a public park because the land was considered too valuable. There was reluctance to meet the needs of overcrowded students at the University of British Columbia. Unemployment rose. There were fewer housing starts.

The high cost of doing business in British Columbia did not prevent Woodward's from achieving an expansion over the next fifteen years which can fairly be described as phenomenal. From 1959 to 1975 net sales increased in volume almost four and one half times, from $117,000,000 to $504,000,000. In the same period total assets climbed from $62,000,000 to $205,000,000. This growth, certainly the greatest experienced at any time in the Company's history, had been achieved by a man who was devoted to his vast ranch and yet managed to combine the roles of business leader and cowboy.

For the first three years of the 1960's, after the opening of the Chinook Centre in Calgary, no new Woodward stores were built in British Columbia or Alberta. There were several reasons for this pause. One reason was Oakridge. This addition was a tremendous venture and though it was succeeding beyond all expectations, it needed to be absorbed and fully integrated within the family of Woodward stores before the Company moved on to further levels of expansion. The new President needed to catch his breath and get his bearings. He had no illusions about the magnitude of his job nor the difficult economic climate in which he would be operating. A third reason was the opening of a branch store in Eastern Canada.

The idea of Woodward's invading the densely populated areas of Montreal and Toronto was not new. As long ago as 1950 Billy had discussed the feasibility with Sam Steinberg, President of the largest food chain in the Province of Quebec. Steinberg's, founded in 1917, had 123 food markets in operation by the end of the 'Fifties. But Woodward's had too many plans for expansion in the West for the venture to be given a high priority.

Finally, after many lengthy discussions, in 1961 Woodward's decided to form a joint-venture company with Steinberg's and operate a number of self-service department stores to be known as "Woodward-Steinberg Ltd." Woodward's would manage the department stores, Steinberg's would own outright the food supermarkets adjacent to them. Since both companies were widely experienced and leaders in their field, the stores would be assured of all the newest improvements and techniques for shopping convenience. But self-service was the operative word.

Several Woodward directors had misgivings. Though Woodward-Steinberg Ltd. was to be entirely separate from Woodward's British Columbia or Alberta operation and would not be allowed to defer or delay the expansion programme planned for the West, there were some formidable objections. One was the three thousand miles distance from Vancouver to Montreal. Another was the fact that food merchandising, an area in which Woodward's had every right to consider itself pre-eminent, would be handled by another company. A third was the subtle difference in merchandising creed and policy never specifically stated but known by both partners to exist.

The plan went ahead. The first Woodward-Steinberg Store opened in July 1961 in Pont Viau, suburb of Montreal and was followed shortly afterwards by a second branch at Greenfield Park. Five more stores were expected to be in operation in Quebec and Ontario by the end of 1963. Reg Clarridge was appointed President, Mel Dobrin, a Steinberg executive, General Manager, and Harry Martin moved from Woodward's Vancouver to become General Merchandise Manager.

The general policy was to apply supermarket methods to the selling of hard and soft goods. Customers wheeled their purchases to checkout counters in carts such as are found in the supermarkets. Though there were salesclerks circulating the sales floor, they were instructed to act as "shoppers' aides" offering advice or assistance only as requested.

All twenty-five departments were on ground level with no partitions and few pillars, so that an uncluttered view of the entire shopping area was provided. Signs and showcards were in French and English.

No telephone orders were accepted, no delivery service was offered, charge accounts were not available and operation costs were kept to the strictest possible minimum.

Uniformed male guards patrolled the store for security purposes.

Chunky backed the W. and S. idea for several reasons. He liked adventure and challenge and the new company would provide plenty of both. The overall plan followed the line of some of his own

250

C. N. Woodward — Chairman of the Board of Woodward Stores Ltd.

strongly held convictions, such as the trend for stores to move away from downtown to the suburbs where land was less expensive and parking space more available, and the trend in department store building to "the horizontal."

"I think we've seen the last of the large department stores," he said when interviewed by the *Financial Post* after one year of working with Steinberg's. "It's easier to move people horizontally than vertically and it saves the cost of escalators and freight elevators. The trend is toward, say, five stores of 200,000 square feet each rather than one store of one million square feet."

He was sure that department stores would have to sell more and more merchandise by self-service to remain competitive. Whether they liked it or not, the customers of the future would sometimes have to accept the idea of waiting on themselves. The W. and S. stores provided an opportunity for experiment in the important and difficult field of well-directed self-selection.

But Chunky too had serious doubts about the Eastern venture. Some of his remarks made in his interview with the Financial Post could not have been pleasant reading for his Steinberg colleagues.

"Department Stores have to maintain the romance of merchandising," he said." Price is not the most important thing to customers. Convenience is No. 1 and personal service makes for convenience. There's a lot of merchandise that cannot be sold by self-service. People want to understand and appreciate what they are buying. Nothing can help them do this as well as a salesclerk."

Moreover, Steinberg's wished to expand more rapidly than he considered advisable.

At the 1962 shareholders' meeting he announced: "In May of last year we withdrew from the enterprise on which we had embarked with Steinberg's of Montreal under an agreement whereby we were reimbursed for the amount of our commitment."

CHAPTER THIRTY

Woodward's Goes to Alberta

When Charles had bought a second store in Thessalon in 1885 and tried to operate that, in addition to his store in Gore Bay, by means of a manager, the experiment had not been successful. Nevertheless, he was still attracted to a plan of lateral expansion, the policy by which his sons and grandson would in 1975 see eighteen Woodward stores spread across British Columbia and Alberta. So in 1922 he made a private, unheralded trip to Edmonton. He mooched around by himself for several days and reached the conclusion that here he could profitably build another Woodward Store. He decided not to mention his plan to Billy or Puggy. They would say he was too old for a new enterprise and would want to interfere. Too old! Why he was barely seventy.

C. Woodward (Edmonton) Ltd. was duly registered by Charles and his wife Alice Farrow Woodward. On the morning of Friday, the 2nd of June, 1922, in the office of Messrs. Pelton, Archibald and Stanton, Barristers and Solicitors, 720 Tegler Building, at a meeting attended only by themselves and lawyer Gerald Pelton, the two elderly people elected each other the sole directors of the new company. A few days later Charles had Silas Folkins despatched to Edmonton from Vancouver. He sent for him reluctantly because the visit would take Folkins away from his duties in the Vancouver Store where he ran the General Office and was Secretary-Treasurer of the company. But Folkins was needed in Edmonton to have a quorum. So Folkins was made a Director and allotted one share in C. Woodward (Edmonton) Ltd. Charles elected himself Chairman of the Board. Alice became Secretary, later Vice-President.

253

Thus did this unobtrusive lady, the second Mrs. Charles Woodward, make her brief appearance in the Woodward Story. She was to die before the Edmonton Store opened.

Messrs. Pelton, Archibald and Stanton became solicitors for the Company. Before the end of 1922 Gerald Pelton and George Archibald joined the Board of Directors, and James Glanville, a local merchant (not related to G. D. Glanville, later President of Woodward's). In return for 321,000 shares Charles turned over to the new company the site at the corner of 101st and Elizabeth Streets, Edmonton, which he had purchased and several parcels of land which he owned in California. Mrs. Woodward, James Glanville and the two lawyers were allotted one share each.

But the decision to build was deferred for four years.

1926 was a boom year. In Vancouver and in many other parts of the world, the British Empire was solid, there was peace everywhere and the stock exchanges were buzzing with buyers. Lindbergh had flown the Atlantic.

But in Edmonton that year there was little growth and little indication of future prosperity. Alberta's population of 607,000 had been almost static for five years. Edmonton's population which in 1914 had been 72,000 had dropped to 65,200. There were no large industries, few new buildings. The streets were much as they had been before the War. Building permits had declined from $3,236,000 in 1920 to $1,854,000 in 1926, bank clearings by a similar percentage. When the Edmonton Grads, the girl graduates of McDougall Commercial High School, won the first official world title ever awarded a basketball team and became world-famous both for their victories and for their sportsmanship, this achievement seemed to be Edmonton's only claim to fame.

Charles Woodward, however, had made some other observations. He had read in the 1926 issue of Henderson's Directory that "Edmonton lies on the edge of the greatest natural gas fields in America, holds the key position geographically to about one quarter of the area of Canada and will always have a reasonable cost of living because of the great production of foodstuffs . . . wheat, flour, meats, fish, etc. . . ."

He had noted that Edmonton had begun to use its natural gas, had opened a municipal airport, had started to operate CJCA, its first radio station. The 1926 number of automobile licences had exceeded the 1925 quota by 10,000. The 1925 crop had been excellent and the farmers were prosperous. Alberta coal was being shipped to Ontario and subsidized to enable Alberta miners to compete with the United States. Edmonton was the gateway to the rich, the fabulous North.

On May 4, 1926 Charles the gambler, Charles the businessman with the intuitive hunches, made his announcement. Woodward's would start construction of a store costing $100,000 on 101st Street. He had of course picked a site which subsequently became almost precisely the centre of the City.

The *Edmonton Journal* greeted his decision enthusiastically and a week before the opening of his store editorialized:

> A City in which established department stores are enlarged and new department stores are established is a city whose present and prospective position as a business centre is beyond all question. Edmonton is the scene of the most active mercantile development anywhere in the West.

Abraham Cristall, proprietor of the Royal George Hotel, was equally delighted. Cristall, a Russian emigrant from Odessa, had met Charles on a train travelling to Los Angeles.

"My father was a spell-binding salesman," writes Cristall's son in a book about him, "and he convinced Charles Woodward that Edmonton was a grand place to build a department store, even though there were more department stores per capita than in any other city in Canada."

The Royal George was a near neighbour of the store. The two men became close friends. Charles usually stayed there and insisted on booking a room on the alley from which he could keep a watch on his latest enterprise. Their friendship did not prevent Cristall from purchasing property on the other side of Woodward's in order to try to sell it profitably to Charles at a later date.

Both men might have been surprised had they known that Edmonton would become "Canada's fastest-growing major city", or at least a strong contender among the many claimants to that title, with a population in the mid-1970's exceeding 500,000. 1926 seemed to be a turning-point. Three years later building permits stood at $5,670,000, three times the 1926 figure.

Charles' announcement was made in May, construction commenced in June and the store opened on October 15. Not only the speed of completion but the price was of another era. The store was a three-floor building with basement, occupying a half-block on 101st Street and almost a complete block on 102nd Avenue. It had an entrance on each street, seven display windows and eight bays on each floor.

The opening day's advertisement was characteristic:

"Small profits and quick returns," it proclaimed, and then tersely listed a variety of inexpensive, everyday commodities. The most costly of them was Men's Dress Oxfords at $3.95 but most items cost considerably less; a can of Libby's pork and beans was offered for ten cents, linoleum for eighty-nine cents a square yard and Ladies' Rayon Vests and Bloomers for $1.25. The half-page of small print contrasted strangely with the several pages of alluringly described merchandise placed by the other leading stores.

Charles' first two employees were hired a week before opening. One of them was a boy looking for his first job, named George Plowman. He joined the queue of job-seekers at Woodward's and heard an elderly man say:

"Sorry, there are no more jobs, ladies and gentlemen," and for some inexplicable reason remained after the others had departed. Nervously he approached the elderly man who was Charles Woodward. Charles sent him away, then called him back.

"Just a minute, son," he said. "Come with me."

He took Plowman to a room crammed full of rolls of wrapping paper, paints, boxes, big flat desks, and torsos, arms and legs of female mannequins. The boy was to sort them out. And so began the career of one of Woodward's most successful advertising managers.

The second man to be hired was Jack Barbour, just out from Scotland. He was thirty-six years old, had spent one winter in the North cutting logs and wanted a less arduous job. He walked into the building being erected and wondered what kind of business it would house. Was it an extension of the funeral parlour in the basement where the undertakers were still at work?

"Got a job?" he asked the manager of the construction company.

"No," came the reply, "and we've no water either."

256

Barbour offered to go to the Civic Centre and see what could be done to get water laid on. He came back with the information that ten dollars was required for the connection. The construction manager handed him ten dollars and before long the Store had water.

Charles, who had observed the transaction and realized that Barbour could easily have made off with the money, hired him on the spot. It was Charles' way.

Barbour not only had a job, but before long a room in the Potter Building, where he lived rent-free for ten years. As soon as business was rolling Charles had purchased this nearby, narrow five-storey edifice built of brick, cement and heavy timbers, together with another larger one beside it to be his No. 1 warehouse. From his abode on the second floor Barbour, who subsequently became building superintendent, supervised its many functions. It contained stockrooms for groceries, hardware and housewares, a grain elevator large enough to hold a truck, and a display workshop. It was a centre for furniture and appliance trade-ins and for the despatch of deliveries. As the years went by, it became a most useful catch-all. In 1972 Atlas Demolition's wrecking ball wrecked it to make way for a new municipal Courthouse.

Another "old-timer", Georgia Kay, joined Woodward's in May 1927 as a cashier. On her first day she was given a rule-book and told that she would forfeit fifty cents if she could not return it when she left the Company's employ. She probably did not realize at the time that the day of her departure would not be for another forty-nine years! She read in the rule-book that:

> Whistling, singing or humming must be avoided.
> Always to use the word "Madam" instead of "Lady" in addressing women whose names she did not know.
> Not to go around the Store arm-in-arm.

There were no cash registers and a bill had to be made out for every sale.

Miss Kay enjoyed her work from the start. The Store was like a family. Everyone knew everyone else. Woodward's annual picnic at Alberta Beach or Cooking Lake was a gala occasion, not only for the staff and all their relatives but for a multitude of farmers,

Charles Woodward with his chief carpenter Charles Perrie at the opening of the Edmonton Store in 1926.

neighbours and customers who lived nearby; and for her boss, John Ferguson, known to all as Old John, she had respect and affection.

There had been three Store managers in the first three years. One of them "had taken a two weeks' holiday at a very busy time in the Store. There were ten department stocks being taken and some of them required his attention and supervision." (Minutes of the Board of Directors).

A balance sheet dated December 4, 1927 and showing an overdraft to the Royal Bank of Canada of $27,767.77 with $100,000 in unpaid accounts ended the regime of another.

"Mr. Woodward," recorded the Minute Book, "made the position quite clear that this could not go on damaging the credit of the firm. He would put no more capital into the business on account of handling the financial end in such an unbusinesslike manner."

The position of General Manager was no sinecure. He and all department managers who were engaged in Vancouver had to pay their own transportation each way. This included household goods and railway fare.

"There was no liability on the part of C. Woodward Ltd. for transportation of any kind." (Minutes of the Board of Directors.)

Old John Ferguson took the reins in 1930. He remained Secretary-Treasurer of the Company, a position he had held almost since the Store's inception. After three failing managers, Charles decided that he would retain the title of General Manager, C. Woodward's Ltd. for himself. In those early years seventy-nine-year-old Charles kept a watchful eye on his new baby, startling the nightwatchman by a sudden appearance at 3:00 a.m. or chiding a salesgirl who let him have an orange without making out a bill for it. But for the next decade Ferguson ran the Store for him and ran it well.

In spite of the overdraft and the managers who failed to make the grade, the new store made remarkable progress. In October 1929 an extension was added on the northeast corner. It consisted of three storeys and a basement made of steel and concrete and cost $227,710 ("Exceeding the estimate by $21,000," commented Charles sternly).

At its May 1930 meeting the Board congratulated Charles on his foresight in building when he did and placed on record its appreciation of "the phenomenal growth of the business. First year it doubled our expectations and did a million dollars' business. The second was nearly a million and a quarter and last year was a million and a half."

One month after the passing of this motion Charles granted "an increase of five dollars a week to John Ferguson and his two senior directors, Thomas Kinnear and Hugh Martin." (Minutes of Board of Directors.)

Stock in the Edmonton Company was allotted to Charles' children and grandchildren but he retained $110,000 worth for members of the staff.

In July, 1939, when the strain of administration became too great for his advancing years, John Ferguson resigned and returned to work in the Shoe Department of the Vancouver Store. He had organized further improvements and enlargement in 1932 and on retirement received a letter from Puggy commending him for his "long, loyal and successful connection with the firm."

Ferguson was succeeded by John Butterfield, Vancouver manager of Hosiery and Whitewear. He was no stranger to Edmonton. His first job in Canada after leaving his native Yorkshire had been in that city with Ramsey's Department Store. After thirteen years there he had left to work for Woodward's store in Vancouver.

Within six weeks of his appointment War broke out. Nevertheless, in 1940 the announcement was made that the Store would build a fourth and fifth floor within the next two years. It must have taken considerable courage in the uncertain conditions of a World War to plan a substantial addition. It was badly needed, as was the sixth floor added in 1945.

Butterfield's talents were such that he was recalled to Vancouver in 1943 to become General Manager of the Company.

The War years were difficult for Alberta, with economy so straitened that a general moratorium on debt was established. During that period there was virtually no building in the Province. Woodward's was one of the few companies to venture on an expansion programme.

Then, in 1947, the Leduc oilfield was discovered. Immediately Alberta's economy was dramatically changed. Crude oil soon led all Canadian minerals in value and by the 1960's Alberta accounted for about 85% of Canada's crude oil production. In the next ten years

7,390 oil wells at Leduc produced 144 million barrels per year with reserves of 2,966 million barrels. In the next twenty years Alberta collected two billion dollars from the sale of crown oil reserves, rentals and royalties. Alberta already was known to contain Canada's largest coal reserves.

Suddenly Edmonton became the seventh largest metropolitan area in the country.

Charles Woodward frequently expressed his confidence in the little agricultural community where he had bought his site in 1922. Now his judgment was endorsed in a way few had anticipated. Woodward's expansion in Alberta during the ensuing twenty-five years matched the Province's growth.

CHAPTER THIRTY-ONE

The Alberta Story Continued

The distinguished director of Woodward's enormous development in Alberta was T. K. Campbell, who became General Manager in 1949, later Director of Alberta operations and finally Executive Vice-President of the Company. A lover of the outdoors he had worked in lumbermills and originally intended to seek his future in the lumber industry as a grader. But like several other Woodward executives he went to work in 1930 in the Vancouver Store as an extra on 95¢ Day and was instructed at the end of the day "to keep on coming in until he was told not to."

Campbell's start was inauspicious. On his first day another boy hired at the same time made off with the C.O.D. money and was never seen again. Campbell was questioned about the loss in a way which he considered offensive and he said so. On his second day his manager told him to take a pile of linens down to the main floor. On the way he met Puggy who thought the load unsightly and ordered him to take it back. This instruction he unwisely challenged. John Butterfield, who was present at the time, was shocked.

"The Campbells are coming . . . maybe they'll soon be going," he said ominously.

But Ken Campbell stayed for the next forty-five years.

He served his apprenticeship in the Staples Department, then was promoted Assistant Manager in the Ladies' Ready-to-Wear, the department which at Woodward's was so often a route to success.

Here he experienced the difficulties of managing older women, some of whom were apt to resent a young Assistant unless he were a paragon of discretion and sympathetic understanding. Campbell handled his duties well, learned much from his Manager, Bill **Mann**, and in 1940 was promoted manager of the Ladies' Ready-to-Wear in Edmonton. After only one year he was brought back to fill the same position in Vancouver. When he returned to Edmonton as General Manager it was a help to him to know the store.

In 1949 C. Woodward's (Edmonton) Ltd. was not performing well. The other two large department stores, the T. Eaton Company and Hudson's Bay, set the merchandising pace. Woodward's was a poor third and seemed to be declining. Its gross profit was invariably substantially less than the Vancouver store's.

But in the City itself there was an atmosphere of excitement. The oil boom had attracted people from all walks of life and from all over the world, many of them skilled tradesmen from European countries. The great contrasts in its climate, the new prosperity and unlimited potential, the sudden influx of newcomers brought in by a liberal immigration policy made Edmonton an exciting place. Strangers spoke to each other and made friends in cafés and stores or as they waited at bus-stops, shivering at thirty degrees below zero or sweltering in the ninety-degree summer heat of a central Alberta summer.

"It's a new life and a new country and a new prosperity," they seemed to be saying. "We're all in it together."

With Campbell came John Hopkins. A young engineer promoted from Vancouver to be Building Superintendent, he was speedily infected by the bustle of the expanding city. Not much could be done in the way of massive expansions at Woodward's yet but Hopkins at once started replacing fixtures, renovating entrances and pumping new life into a store which had been static too long. Later he became Supervisor of Buildings and intimately involved in the expansion of the next 25 years.

Ken Campbell lost no time in persuading the Directors that something must be done to give Woodward's its due place in the merchandising world in Edmonton and to keep pace with that rapidly developing city.

The vast potentialities promised by the Leduc discoveries had attracted the attention of a group of New York businessmen who drew up the Dettweiler Scheme, an ambitious plan for expanding and modernizing the central core of the city. They probably planted the seed of a development which subsequently came about but neither the city nor Woodward's was as yet ready for it. Woodward's, with the Royal George Hotel on one side and a parking lot owned by the Cristall family on the other, was restricted from adding to its downtown premises.

Gradually the idea of a Shopping Centre emerged. Park Royal, the first such Centre, had opened in West Vancouver in 1950 and had proved an immediate success. Why not build a Shopping Centre in one of the outlying districts of Edmonton? No such complex had yet been constructed in Alberta and with the city's inevitable opulence just around the corner, shopping centres would probably have a good chance of success there.

So when David Gray, a member of the New York Corporation, approached Campbell and asked him if Woodward's would be interested in leasing premises for a Department Store on thirty acres to be developed in Northwest Edmonton by the First Amsterdam Corporation of New York, he found a willing colleague. The project would be called Westmount and the rental would cost only $1.21 per square foot.

The Edmonton city planners helped by deciding to open the northwest part of the city to residential development. In 1953 services were extended, sewers, water, electrical power and sidewalks put in to what had hitherto been a farming area.

During construction the site of the new shopping centre was a sea of mud. With great difficulty delivery trucks and construction crews ploughed their way through it. Some roads were inaccessible. Several managers appointed to Westmount decided to live near their work. The severe climate and the surrounding gumbo made living conditions there during this period so fraught with difficulties that some of their wives approached the point of nervous breakdowns.

The site of Westmount Shopping Centre was an old lake bed, set in bushland. There were no adjacent houses, no suggestion of urban development.

"Bankruptcy within a year," was the verdict of some of the members of the business community. At times the confidence of the First Amsterdam Corporation of New York and of the Woodward team was shaken.

The opening ceremonies on a blazing August day in 1955 were

264

deliberately "low-key". It had been decided that there should be a minimum of fanfare for a project which might not attain success for a long time. Instead of the surging crowds usually attendant on the opening of a Woodward Store, only the staffs of the participating stores and a few of their relatives were present.

A platform under a canopy had been erected from which the presiding dignitaries would make their addresses. Mayor Hawrelak, mayor of Edmonton, Mr. Paylitz, head of the New York group, and the Hon. W. C. Woodward were conducted to the platform. As construction was still incomplete they had to climb up to it by means of a ladder. Ken Campbell, concealing misgivings behind a cheerful exterior, thought that "they appeared very lonesome up there." The two thousand-car parking lot with its tiny sprinkling of vehicles seemed even more bleak.

Nevertheless, Westmount Shopping Centre never looked back. Soon after its opening a number of massive apartment blocks were built right across the road. Houses and office buildings followed.

The Centre achieved the unusual feat of operating profitably in its first year.

In the downtown store too business was surging forward. This success was in no small measure due to a team of able, aggressive managers nicknamed "The Young Lions" and including Frank Robertson, Alex Weir, Nesbitt McGregor, 'Pidge' McBride and others who were later to attain top positions in the Company.

That same eventful year, 1955, saw a large addition to the South Edmonton Service Building. The old No. 1 Warehouse on 98th Street which had given the department store yeoman service in so many different ways, was becoming less and less relevant as the years went by. Campbell had soon seen the necessity of supplementing it and had pressed for a service building and delivery centre to be built in South Edmonton in 1952. It was enlarged one year later. The 1955 addition increased the size of the South Edmonton Service Building to 161,000 square feet, more than five times the original dimension. A Canadian Pacific Railway spur line ran right into the building, making it possible to unload four freight cars under cover at the same time.

Next the Directors turned their attention to other cities of prosperous Alberta.

Calgary was considered the business centre of Alberta. It was listed in Henderson's Directory as "the largest and most important city between Winnipeg and Vancouver", a claim which Edmonton might dispute. Certainly in 1926, the year when Charles Woodward opened his Edmonton store, Calgary was more populous by some 12,000 residents. But in 1960 the position was reversed and metropolitan Calgary's population was shown as 271,764 compared with Edmonton's 337,568. In 1975, though both cities were more than half again as large, the same disparity existed.

Statistics are not always reliable. But whatever the population ratio, Calgary's claim to be a rich and booming city could not be denied. In 1875, the year of its founding, it had been a little North-west Mounted Police outpost comprising a few tents and shacks. Even when the C.P.R. came there eight years later, on its way to the Kicking Horse Pass, all there was to downtown Calgary were two stores and the Police Barracks. But homesteaders flocked in after the coming of the railway and Calgary was soon the nucleus of a substantial farming and ranching area.

When gas was discovered in 1914 in nearby Turner Valley, and light oil in the same area in 1925, Calgary's function as essentially an agricultural community began to change. After the Leduc bombshell it became the administrative, operations and financial centre of the petroleum industry and was widely known as the "Oil and Gas Capital of Canada".

There were many inducements for manufacturing industries to establish themselves there. Calgary, which lies in the valley of the Bow and Elbow Rivers where the plains meet the foothills, has cheap electrical power and abundant pure water. In fact the city takes its name from a Gaelic word meaning "Clear Running Water". It is the headquarters of one of the largest irrigation projects on the continent. Untold wealth lies beneath its soil.

Calgary seemed as promising a field as Edmonton for Woodward's third Alberta operation. It was decided to build another shopping centre. Such centres, a pioneering development in 1950, in the past ten years had sprung up all over North America. They were now recognized as the most popular merchandising trend.

The Chinook Centre built by Standard Holdings, a leading construction company owned by two dynamic Albertans, Reg Jennings and "Red" Dutton, was opened in 1960. The name was chosen for the dry westerly wind for which Calgary is renowned and which is apt to arrive unexpectedly on the heels of a blizzard, melting the snows in an instant and bringing sudden warmth and comfort. "Chinook" is a happy word in the Calgarians' vocabulary.

At first Woodward's bought land on Elbow Drive near Hays Farm. The subsequent change of location to the McLeod Trail was a wise move. As at Westmount and Park Royal, a site was chosen at some distance from the centre of the city in an area where young families were beginning to reside and where development was bound to take place. The site had been an outdoor movie theatre.

Reg Clarridge was appointed manager of the Chinook Centre but was almost immediately called away to direct Woodward operations in the East. Jack Moxon succeeded him.

During the Second World War, as soon as he was old enough to enlist, Moxon was commissioned with the Seaforth Highlanders of Canada and saw action in Italy. His family home in Vancouver had been almost next door to the W. C. Woodward's. Billy had watched him grow up, liked his enthusiasm and drive, and had offered him a job in the General Office even before he had left the Army. He had been with the Company since 1945, had been Store Manager in Port Alberni, Park Royal and Oakridge, and was well trained for his new challenge.

Moxon remained to play a major role in the Company's expansion in Alberta and in 1976 followed Campbell as Vice-President in charge of Alberta operations.

As at Westmount the opening of Chinook took place on a hot August day, but there the similarity ceased. There was nothing "low-key" about this ceremony. As the Mayor of Calgary, Harry Hays, turned the usual "golden" key, he hailed the day as a "new era in shopping for Calgary citizens." Chunky fired a flare pistol, a natural gas pylon on top of the Centre's sign was turned on and thousands of eager shoppers thronged into the Mall, jamming its forty-five stores and the Woodward Department Store at the end of it. The Chinook Centre was a successful operation from its first day.

Soon after opening, the Centre had an encounter with crime, Western-style. A store detective, believing she had seen a man take a carton of cigarettes without paying for it, challenged him as he was about to leave the Store and asked him if she might look in his shopping bag. The man put his hand into the bag and produced not a carton of cigarettes but a gun. He ran outside, turned and fired. The bullet went through a plate-glass window, hit a column, ricocheted and just missed a salesgirl.

The man fled, hotly pursued by Store Superintendent Fred Wall and Jim Hall, Assistant Manager of the Furniture Department, who had also narrowly escaped the gunman's bullet. Hall was a good runner and the gunman, seeing he was being overtaken, dived into a warehouse. Hall followed him.

Moxon meanwhile had telephoned the police who arrived on the scene promptly and in considerable numbers. The warehouse containing the two men was surrounded by police and onlookers. There was a momentary lull in the action as police decided on their next step.

Suddenly a shot rang out from within the warehouse. Police and pursuers flung themselves to the ground. Fred Wall groaned. That was surely the end of Hall, he thought. But a moment later Hall appeared leading by the arm the gunman who seemed chastened and subdued. Hall held the gun.

This remarkable feat had been achieved by persuasion. Hall had talked him into handing it over. But as the transfer was taking place the gunman, who was new to his job and nervous, dropped the gun on to the concrete floor. It exploded and caused the shot which had sent the pursuers to ground.

Later Moxon congratulated Hall on his courage.

"But," he demanded, "why would you take such a chance for a carton of cigarettes?"

"It made me so damn mad that that guy should take a shot at me, I didn't think about it," replied Hall.

When he heard about the incident, Ken Campbell understood such feelings. Some years previously when Manager of the Ladies' Ready-to-Wear, he had surprised a thief making off with a fur-lined coat and was so angry that he had followed him, even after he had dropped the coat, through the alleys and lanes at the back of the Vancouver store, until he had him cornered. When the thief drew a knife Campbell seized a shovel which happened to be at hand.

The confrontation ended with the capture of the thief and no injuries sustained.

Life in a Department Store is not without its moments of danger and excitement. Not all incidents end as happily as these.

Before long an eight-storey tower, mainly for doctors' offices, and a theatre, were added to the Chinook Centre. The canopies were taken down, the Mall was covered, and an air conditioning system installed. Calgarians could now, even in the most frigid weather, make their purchases in comfort. Here they could buy practically any commodity including a car, have music lessons, get their automobile licence plates, visit the medical clinic. The Centre became even more potent when five years later it joined forces with an adjacent Shopping Centre containing branches of Loblaw's and Simpson Sears'.

Calgary's prosperity went booming along into the Seventies with no sign of let-up. Each month brought 1,000 newcomers. In 1971 building permits jumped from an amazing $173 million to a still more amazing $193 million; thirty-three new manufacturing plants were set up; and Woodward's opened, again in August, Market Mall, a shopping centre in northwest Calgary, so huge that it was described as a "city within a city". It had some novel features in keeping with the new decade and the international flavour — an epicurean and gourmet cookware shop, a Stockholm fish window, a Bombay curry parlour, a computerized paint mixer, a colour television studio, a Paris market, a sound-proof organ room.

It was indeed as Mayor Hays had predicted, a "new era of shopping for Calgary citizens."

Edmonton meanwhile, according to Paul Friggens' article "Alberta: Where the Action is," published in the January 1976 *Readers' Digest,* was doing $1.6 billion retail trade and opening a new plant for every 4.3 working days. Woodward's was forging ahead to keep pace and to provide for an even more spectacular future.

In 1965 and 1970, respectively, Northgate and Southgate Shopping Centres were opened. Both centres were built on the outskirts of Edmonton in areas where at the time of their conception there was no housing except for a few scattered farms set in a vast expanse of flat open country and bushland.

Prosperity had arrived so suddenly and on such a substantial scale that Edmonton had become something of a battleground. Land developers and promoters were watching each other's every move, often striving to distort the City's outline plan, always, to forestall and outguess their rivals. Harassed City planners were endeavouring to keep some shape and uniformity to the continual expansion. If a farmer or a landowner discovered that a large company was interested in his property, the purchase price would skyrocket.

Buying the sites for the two new centres involved lengthy, complex negotiations. Obtaining a development permit was no less difficult. At one stage of the building of Southgate the centre found itself in spite of an agreement with the city without access roads. Campbell made an appeal to Premier Manning who promptly and personally legislated in Woodward's favour.

The first Store Manager both at Northgate and Southgate was Alexander Weir, another Woodwardite who had started in 1934 as a parcel sorter in the Meat Department, spent five years on active service overseas and then worked his way to executive levels. Under his vigorous direction the centres flourished.

Once again the South Edmonton Service Building was proving too small. The whole building was sold to the Canadian Pacific Railway, and in May 1969 the much larger Strathcona Distribution Centre constructed two miles south of it. It occupied nine acres, with another four acres available for expansion, and housed a Delivery Centre, a headquarters for country shopping, food buying offices and a mammoth warehouse for furniture, appliances, carpets and groceries.

Electronic equipment was installed by means of which, under the direction of Woodward's Data Processing Department in Vancouver, a detailed analysis of stocks and sale could be maintained. The modern warehouseman had to be a computer programmer!

Other cities in Alberta wanted to attract a Woodward Store. One was Lethbridge, fifty miles north of the U.S. border. It was not a large city. Even in 1972, when Woodward's commenced negotiations with its Council, there were fewer than forty-two thousand residents. In 1975, when the Centre opened, the population was forty-five thousand. But in the surrounding million acres of irrigated land there were another hundred thousand potential customers.

Lethbridge was a thriving place, the commercial and agricultural centre and supply point of Southern Alberta. Retail sales during the 'Sixties had doubled in volume, in 1971 exceeding $99 million. During the 'Seventies the large plants that had established there included Swift's and Canada Packers.

For many years Lethbridge had been the centre of coal mining operations. Its original name had been Coalbanks and when that name was changed, the new name honoured the first president of the Northwest Coal Company. But now coal was secondary to beef cattle, market gardening, sugar beets and, of course, oil and gas.

Lethbridge called itself with pride and some justification the "Action City". The decision of a go-ahead "action" merchandiser to open a shopping centre there was hailed with enthusiasm. Woodward's did not have to debate with planners or argue for building permits. The City itself assembled the land, 10½ acres of it, three full city blocks, with another ten acres across the street for a parking area, and broke all records by completing $14 million of construction ($3½ million for store fixtures) in twenty months.

In the central business area district, where little more than one hundred years before Cree and Assiniboine Indians had pursued and crushed Blackfoot in the last of the great Indian battles, the Lethbridge Centre, Woodward-owned, was opened on August 27, 1975. It contained in addition to the Department Store an eleven-storey office tower, an enclosed Mall with forty tenants and a twin cinema theatre.

The writer has not found it possible to describe Woodward's activities in Alberta without employing superlatives. The most lavish of them must be reserved for the Edmonton Centre, the largest single project ever undertaken in that city. The site embraces four acres in the heart of the city.

The Dettweiler Scheme designed to rejuvenate the downtown area had lain dormant since 1951. In 1969 its concept was revived. The Oxford Development Group, a major Edmonton real estate company involved in the development and management of commercial real estate in Canada and the United States, with assets of some $400 million, formed a partnership with Woodward's and the Toronto Dominion Bank. Their objective was to provide Edmonton with an integrated retail and office development that would, in the

C. Woodward's, Edmonton. In 1926 Charles Woodward pioneered in Western Canada for the second time and opened a branch store in Alberta.

Model of the Edmonton Centre. Fifty years later a new complex stood on Charles Woodward's original site. It comprised a five-storey Woodward Dept. Store, office towers and shopping malls.

272

words of a press release, "emphasize the creation of a city centre in the heart of the city."

The Centre was planned on an enormous scale, would be ten years in the making (1969-1979) and would cost about $100 million. Planners estimated that a like sum would be spent there annually. Woodward's was the major tenant and would own its premises at the end of sixty-five years.

Edmonton Centre First Phase opened May 1, 1974. It comprised a five-storey Woodward Department Store, three levels of shopping mall containing fifty retail stores, boutiques and restaurants, and the first of three office towers, The Royal Trust Tower.

The new complex meant the removal of a famous old building, the Courthouse. But it was in poor condition and no longer adequate to its purpose. Care was taken to preserve whatever might be of historical interest and so there was a minimum of public distress when the new Woodward's was erected on its site.

The new complex also necessitated the demolition of the old Woodward Store, an equally emotional event. It had stood there for fifty years and held many proud and happy memories. When the hour came for staff members to take their last walk through the empty store, there were some sad faces and a few tears.

There was little time for regrets. The move from the old Woodward's to the new was conducted with only two days' closing, on one of which the staff took a holiday. Moreover, there was a Sale on the final day in the old store and a Sale on the opening day in the new store.

October, 1975, saw the forty-ninth anniversary of Woodward's advent to Alberta, the first-time trading of Woodward shares on the Alberta Stock Exchange and the opening of Phase Two of the Edmonton Centre, with forty additional stores open for business. The unusual beauty of the complex was still further enhanced. Floating glass escalators rose through a sixty-five-foot high, climatically controlled, indoor Garden Court, wherein bloomed tropical plants, set amid thirty-foot fig trees, all illuminated by twelve banks of five-foot square skylights. The open design gave shoppers at any given point a spectacular view of the three surrounding levels of shops and boutiques. A parking area for one thousand cars, two overhead skywalks and an underground tunnel were added.

For the opening ceremonies of Phase Two the Edmonton Symphony Orchestra gave a concert in the Garden Court.

The second of the twenty-eight-storey grey glass towers, the Toronto-Dominion Bank Tower, would not be ready for another eight months. As this was its headquarters and main office the Bank was determined to make it the most beautiful major branch in Canada and the most modern west of Toronto.

Edmonton Centre continues to expand. A second retail mall, a third office tower, a 322-room hotel and another carpark will be added; and somewhere within its vast complex there will be a "people's park" where weary shoppers may relax among the same exotic plants and flowers and in the same warm atmosphere even in the depth of a sub-zero Edmonton winter.

In January 1976 Ken Campbell retired and Woodwardites at all levels and from all stores gathered to pay their tribute to him at a dinner Chunky gave in Edmonton. One statistic will serve to show the extent of growth that took place during his twenty-five years as director of operations in Alberta. In 1950 Woodward's occupied 270,000 square feet of store and warehouse in that province. By the end of 1975 the amount of space had become 3,500,000 square feet, an increase of twelve hundred per cent.

CHAPTER THIRTY-TWO

Douglas Lake Cattle Company

In 1957 an opportunity arose which enabled Chunky Woodward to become a part-time cowboy on a splendid scale. Douglas Lake Cattle Ranch, one of the largest ranches in North America, came on the market.

The Hon. Frank Ross, Lieutenant-Governor of British Columbia, and Colonel Victor Spencer, one of B.C.'s great cattle barons, had owned the historic Douglas Lake Ranch since 1950 and now wished to pass it on to younger hands. Ross and Spencer decided they must be British Columbian hands and turned down an American offer which would have brought them an additional half-million dollars and they must be the hands of a man who would appreciate the responsibility of such a trust. For Douglas Lake Ranch was not only the largest ranch in British Columbia. It was also one of the oldest and one of the most beautiful, with great potential and a famous history.

Chunky, who met all the requirements for ownership, bought it.

John Douglas, for whom the ranch was named (he was not related to Governor Sir James Douglas) first came to the Nicola Valley in 1872, aged 43, hoping that the climate would improve his lung condition. He acquired much land, helped John James of Savona make the first survey of the Valley and survived the exceptionally severe winter of 1879-80. When almost fifty he married Mrs. Julia Cross. She took one look at the little ranch house which was to be her home and declared that under no circumstances would she live in it. Moreover, there was another shack nearby in which the notorious McLean gang of cattle rustlers, who had terrorized the

Douglas Lake Ranch in the Nicola Valley, one of the largest and most beautiful ranches in North America. C. N. Woodward bought it in 1957 from Hon. Frank Ross and Col. Victor Spencer.

neighbourhood for years, holed up and shot it out with the police and settlers till all were captured — and hanged.

"Not for me," said Julia, an urban type who had operated her own boarding-house in San Francisco. She departed to run a similar establishment in Victoria, leaving John to himself and to the tuberculosis which eventually killed him.

In 1882 Kamloops rancher J. B. Greaves, nicknamed "Old Danger", who had come to British Columbia from California, persuaded a number of Victoria businessmen that there was money in cattle. Beef, he maintained, could be profitably sold to the C.P.R. construction crews. A syndicate was formed and the foundations of the Douglas Lake Cattle Company laid. The ranch gained fame by importing the first Clyde horse into British Columbia.

During the next few years Greaves and his associates bought a dozen pre-emptions from original settlers including John Douglas' holdings. Greaves retired in 1910 aged eighty and was succeeded as ranch manager by Frank Ward, son of Curtis Ward, a banker. Douglas Lake became a family corporation with shares owned by Mr. and Mrs. Curtis Ward and their eight children.

When Frank Ward retired in 1940 Brian Chance became manager of Douglas Lake and greatly added to its stature and reputation during his many years there.

The ranch hands soon sensed that Chunky was not some absentee millionaire owner indulging a whim. He was respected immediately as a professional.

A cowboy is a special breed. He is not driven by a love of money or desire for an easy job. He does not demand a shorter work week or go on strike. He is the last of the free enterprisers and free thinkers, independent, self-reliant, totally and incessantly involved in a multitude of tough, demanding duties. Often he rides from dawn to late at night changing saddle two or three times in a day. He keeps the boundary fences in repair, looks for strays missed in the roundup, puts salt when and where it is needed, rides the waterholes and creeks to inspect the supply, pulls cows out of sink-holes, locates lost cows and horses, mows hay in summer, forks it out to the cattle in winter, gathers cattle, earmarks and brands calves.

There was not one of these pursuits that Chunky had not engaged in. As a boy he had sat silent at the night camps, the only touch of group living enjoyed by cowboys at round-up time, and listened to their talk, laconic as his own, their stories, their friendly silence. He had admired their honesty, their humour and sense of fair play. He hoped now that he would be accepted not just as a boss but as one of them.

And so it was. He won their respect and affection not because of the plane that arrived each Christmas-time bringing himself and a vast number of carefully chosen presents but because he understood the challenge of a big ranch and how to meet that challenge.

Douglas Lake Ranch, also known as the Three Bar Ranch, covers 500,000 acres of rolling, hilly land. It is so cut with draws and coulees that although one can look for miles across what seem to be the plains, a rider can disappear from sight in three minutes. This vast spread is bounded by the timberland country of the Douglas Lake plateau to the north with the Princeton highway running east and west. The ranch normally has some 14,000 head of cattle, 250 cowboy horses, 30 lakes and a crew of nearly one hundred.

In addition to the cowboy horses, there are 120 "cutting" horses, trained to separate one particular animal from the herd. Steer-cutting requires a high degree of control and expert horsemanship. Chunky's cutting horses became famous and he himself an expert in the art. Starting with the award of a rose-bowl as the champion steer cutter at the Horse of the Year Show at Vancouver's Exhibition Park, he went on to win championships and ribbons throughout Canada and the U.S.A. including the Canadian championship. One of his horses, Peppy San, in 1967 won more money than any cutting horse in history. His other champion, a mare, might have done as well but was killed in a freak accident, when she fell on a spike, the only snag on the field.

Prince Philip, an enthusiast in steer cutting, has visited Douglas Lake more than once. In 1964 he invited a six-man team from the Canadian Cutting Horse Association, of which Chunky was a member, to give an exhibition in the Royal Windsor Horse Show before Queen Elizabeth and himself.

Douglas Lake Ranch is run as a separate business: its beef is not necessarily marketed through the Store. It is a place where the owner, his family and his friends can fish, hunt, ride and relax. But

278

C. N. Woodward, who has been an enthusiastic cowboy since childhood.

C. N. Woodward steer-cutting. A cutting horse is trained to separate one particular animal from the herd.

279

the ranch is much more than a hobby. Like Woodwynn Farm it is a well-run, productive enterprise, which continues to make an important contribution to the prosperity of British Columbia and is an integral part of the Woodward Story.

Each year of the new decade saw substantial additional features in Vancouver. In 1963 the huge, circular Agrodome, architecturally unique, had been built for Cattle and Horse Shows. One year later the Fraser River was magnificently spanned by yet another great bridge, the Port Mann Bridge on Highway 401, the freeway to the East. In 1965 a university named for the explorer Simon Fraser was built at the top of Burnaby Mountain. In 1966 an aquarium in Stanley Park presented a wonderfully varied display of marine life. In October 1968 the new Vancouver International Airport, designed to handle 994 people an hour, and rated one of the finest in Canada, was opened and that same month saw the opening of the H. R. MacMillan Planetarium and Centennial Museum. The Pacific Coliseum, an all-purpose exhibition and sports building, was a feature in 1969.

In 1963 new Woodward stores started to follow each other in quick succession. First came the Mayfair Centre in Victoria, which replaced the small specialty centre in the area. Victoria, capital of British Columbia since 1871, had a population in 1962 of 154,000 and was reputed to have the highest per capita income in Canada. Woodward's buildings, consisting of a Department Store, a Food Store and a Service Station, shared the Centre with twenty-four other stores.

Kamloops, historic fur-trading post, meeting-place for the gold miners of 1958, and now one of British Columbia's main transportation hubs, was the site for the 1964 store. Ruth Woodward opened it and as she turned the key in the giant symbolic lock, she must have had some happy memories. As a girl she had come here on horseback from Alkali Lake. Kamloops, older than B.C. itself, had a population which had more than doubled in the past decade and would soon have doubled again.

The total area of the site covered two and two-thirds acres and had the customary Department Store and Food Market. Atop the department store a three-floor tower housed a shopping mall, a medical clinic and professional offices. The complex was completely owned by Woodward's. A new City Hall and Public Safety Building were built on a site immediately adjacent which enhanced the whole project.

In 1966 two new centres were added to the British Columbia chain. Guildford was opened in leased premises in Surrey; Parkwood, totally owned by the Company, in Prince George.

Surrey, B.C. had been foreseen by the Mainland Regional Planning Board as a municipality in which a great part of the future growth of Greater Vancouver would occur. For several years Woodward's directors had wanted to have a store there to serve the residents not only of North and South Surrey, but of a large part of the Lower Mainland, from East Delta to White Rock and Langley. The residents were no less enthusiastic. But there were delays in the construction of the Port Mann Bridge and opposition from some members of the municipal council who feared that the granting of a permit to build a large shopping centre might affect the rural nature of their municipality. These obstacles were overcome and the Centre built, with a two-level mall connected by outdoor escalators. One unique feature of the central open plaza was a roller-skating rink which could also be used for car and boat shows and similar promotions. Suspended above the rink and protecting it from the weather was a movie-theatre.

Prince George is as rich in British Columbian history as Kamloops. Alexander Mackenzie stopped there on his passage down the Fraser to the Pacific. In 1807, fourteen years later, Simon Fraser of the North West Company built a fort there and named it after King George III, the reigning sovereign. In 1862 Prince George was described as "a dreary Hudson's Bay Company trading post infested with dogs and Carrier Indians," but one hundred years later the city was experiencing a rapid rate of growth. As Prince George is almost as far north as Edmonton and has a cold winter, Parkwood's covered air-conditioned mall was an essential part of the complex.

"Parkwood will be one of Woodward's most profitable ventures," B.C. Minister of Lands R. G. Williston predicted with some accuracy when he opened it.

No further Woodward stores were opened in British Columbia for the next three years. There were additions and "modernization" made to the thirteen then existing and in 1970, a development took place in the part of the city where Vancouver had first been established, Gastown.

Though it is doubtful if the name Gastown ever appeared on official maps or charts, it was colloquial and persisted even after the little townsite had received in 1870 the more dignified name of Granville. Captain John Deighton, known as "Gassy Jack" because he was a non-stop talker, was the popular pioneer responsible for the town's nickname. His saloon, the Deighton House Hotel, more magnificent in name than in appearance, stood at the intersection of Carrall and Water streets. Just outside was a wide spreading maple tree convenient for the posting of notices and an unofficial meeting-place for the town elders.

Old Gastown included an area between Carrall, Hastings and Cambie Streets and extended north to the waterfront. With the lofty mountains of the North Shore facing it across the harbour and the magnificent stands of timber surrounding it, Gastown was scenically as well-favoured as any community in all North America.

But as Vancouver developed, the commercial centre moved south and west and the buildings in Gastown fell into neglect or were taken over by storage companies requiring premises in low rental districts. It became the slum area of the city; and the slum area of a large port can be a very depressed place indeed. Rubby-dubs and derelicts, shabby rooming houses and tenth-grade hotels, boarded windows and litter-infested alleys pervaded it.

As Vancouver entered the 'Seventies, the restoration of Gastown began.

It is difficult to know where to place the credit for this remarkable development. A group called the Improvement of Downtown East End Society and a number of young architects, artists, university students and businessmen, one of whom, Larry Killam, provided outstanding leadership, succeeded in enlisting City Council's enthusiastic support and eliciting an investment of over one million dollars in capital improvements.

A trend to financing of historic preservation projects through commercial rehabilitation had already been evidenced in San Francisco's Ghirardelli Square, Seattle's Pioneer Square and Victoria's Bastion Square. The developers of Gastown realized that its ancient neglected masonry had been built with sturdiness and artistic perception. Suddenly it was fashionable to have a boutique or a restaurant on Water Street. Maple Tree Square and Blood Alley became popular addresses. At the request of Vancouver City Council, the Provincial Government designated Gastown as a historic area. More tourists visited it than Stanley Park.

Messages came from Prime Minister Trudeau: "You have brought new life and a sense of history to your area of Vancouver," and from Ron Basford, Minister of Urban Affairs: "Gastown stands as Vancouver's lesson to other cities of Canada that downtown can remain a people's place."

Woodward's, the pioneer store which had conducted its business in this part of Vancouver since 1891 and had had its main store right in the heart of old Gastown for seventy years, was delighted at this development and joined it immediately. Chunky saw as a first essential increased parking space. A garage with its front on Water Street, Gastown's main thoroughfare, was constructed. This second garage was connected to the one on Cordova Street by overhead walkways and selling areas. The total of Woodward's downtown parking facilities there now ran to 1450 vehicles.

The new garage contained seven boutique shops. Five of them were leased to firms specializing in unusual lines. Railway World dealt exclusively in model railways, International Coat of Arms in the researching of family trees, Racine-Canapouf in pouffes and similar types of sit-on-the-floor furniture.

The other two boutique shops Woodward's itself operated. One was Maple Leaf House. It had started as B.C. House selling only products made in British Columbia, but because B.C. House is the headquarters for British Columbians in London, England, the name was changed and the merchandise extended to cover products made in Canada.

The other Woodward-operated shop is unique. It is called The Coggery. Its walls painted with bold supergraphics have been profusely decorated with patterns of cogs and gears taken from one of Vancouver's oldest foundries. This foundry closed in 1971. The patterns had been made by hand from pine or fir, teak, birch, maple or exotic rose-wood, formed by laminating meticulously shaped pieces of wood together to make each specific design and

283

painted one of several bright colours to differentiate as to which metal would be used for casting, yellow for copper, red for brass, black for steel.

The beauty and simplicity of the huge cogs caught the eye and fired the imagination of Harry Aiken, Woodward's Display Manager. They could move mountains, turn turbines and steer ships; now they had been almost obliterated by the Electronic Age. As the cogs were lying idle in a warehouse, he was able to buy three trailer-loads of them for a comparatively small sum. He set them up within the walls of The Coggery subtly suggesting a bygone age and boldly introducing a new concept in store design.

The store is devoted to fashion for youth. Shining garbage cans riveted side by side contain such items as jeans, corduroys, levis, skinny ribs and other needs of the 'now' generation.

In 1966 Woodward's became a partner with Marathon Realty Company, Simpson-Sears and other corporations in another project designed to develop the downtown waterfront of Vancouver, Project 200. The development of the twenty-three acre area is a major undertaking which will extend over a period of years and will still further rejuvenate that part of the city where seventy-five years earlier Charles Woodward had established himself and lived over his store with all his children. Office towers, hotels, apartment units, shopping areas, restaurant and theatre have been planned, some of them above the C.P.R. trackage on the waterfront at the very place where passengers alighted from the first C.P.R. train to arrive in Vancouver from Montreal.

The C.P.R. approved the plan and was at first a partner in it. The National Harbours Board liked the idea of improved harbour facilities. Granville Square, a complex consisting of a plaza, high-rise office building, mall and parking area, has already been constructed. So has the Canadian Pacific Telecommunication Building. Gaslight Square was opened in August 1975. At this writing a second office tower is under construction. But the redirecting of major roads which would link the waterfront area with the rest of the City has not yet been approved by City Council.

Old Charles would not have been surprised at this vast expansion for he knew at a time when Vancouver boasted fewer than ten thousand residents that it must come about.

CHAPTER THIRTY-THREE

Mammoth Convoy

Unique promotions have characterized Woodward's Food Department ever since the days when John Leaman placed a prize-winning steer in a corral in the middle of the sales floor and nearby cut up sides of beef with a big bandsaw right in the public gaze. Novel and customer-attracting projects have continued to be devised with ever-increasing ingenuity over the years.

No Food Floor manager has been more zealous or imaginative in this field of endeavour than Allan Eadie, manager of the Produce Division.

To promote papayas, mangoes, whole green coconuts and other Mexican produce, he brought a five-piece Mariachi band from Guadalajara and allowed the musicians to wander around the Food Floor delighting his customers with their songs and guitars. He brought airborne strawberries to Edmonton and had tomatoes flown in from Spain and the Canary Islands. When the price for bamboo baskets and willow baskets normally bought in Poland and Jugoslavia became too steep he found a way of visiting Red China and bought them much less expensively in the Province of Hupeh, along with canned and fresh Mandarin oranges.

In 1972 Eadie devised Farm to Family Express, a momentous event. The idea came to him after he had found himself bringing in a whole trainload of watermelons from Mexico in order to have as many of them as he deemed suitable for a major promotion.

"That's all very well," thought Eadie, "but what about some idea that will sell more B.C. fruits? What about a cargo of B.C. apples brought from the Okanagan Valley by truck in mid-November?

Apples and pears are at their best then and farmers are anxious to sell, because the surge of apple-selling has died down and Christmas buying has not begun."

So he decided to see if it would be possible to bring a million pounds of apples straight from the farms of British Columbia to Woodward's by means of a convoy of trucks. Fifty forty-foot trailers was the number Eadie had in mind and they must all reach Vancouver at the same time; otherwise the impact would be lost.

Moving so many vehicles in convoy from the Okanagan to the Store was a complex and difficult undertaking. He started to plan in May. He had served during the Second World War with the Royal Canadian Engineers as a despatch rider and transport sergeant and was thoroughly familiar with convoys.

C.P. Transport Company turned him down without hesitation. Don Crowe-Swords, manager of Zenith Transport, a firm which had often moved produce for him from California and Mexico, at first thought he was joking but on finding he was much in earnest agreed to make an attempt.

"But," said Crowe-Swords, "I just don't think it's on. I doubt if fifty Canadian trucks can be found for a one-shot deal like that." Eventually, after surmounting many difficulties, he succeeded.

Eadie lined up eight detachments of the R.C.M.P. to help him on the 300-mile route, contacted the mayors of the cities through which the convoy would pass and arranged for parking facilities and overnight accommodation at Hope.

The idea gathered momentum. Trucking companies which had at first declined to be associated with it now begged to be included. Eadie had been working exclusively with B.C. Fruits, the association of farmers through which B.C. fruit is marketed. They had undertaken to fill, in one day, the fifty forty-foot trailers with apples and pears from every packing house in the Okanagan.

Before long Eadie had agreed to include canned fruit and fruit juice from Summerland, cheese from Vernon, potatoes and turnips from the Kootenays, onions from Abbotsford, eggs from Cloverdale, pie fillings, syrups and sauces. By bringing as much produce as possible directly from the orchards, packing houses and processors to the Store and eliminating expensive warehousing on the way, substantial savings could be passed on to the customers.

So the first Farm to Family Express began its journey. The caravan was loaded at various points in British Columbia's Interior and assembled in the city of Kelowna. The Mayor of Penticton was indignant at the plan to bypass his city and insisted that the convoy pass through it. The Mayor of Hope personally supervised the overnight lodging for the truckers. Vancouver police provided a motorcycle escort. B.C. Hydro adjusted its bus service. The Great Northern Railway altered its train schedule lest the convoy be blocked at a railway crossing. A radio control car at each end ensured absolute punctuality.

At exactly 1:00 p.m. what must surely have been the biggest caravan of its type in the history of the West reached the Oakridge Shopping Centre and dispersed its luscious cargo among the Woodward chain.

At the 1974 United Fresh Fruits and Vegetable Association Convention in Las Vegas, Eadie won Produce Merchandising Man of the Year Award.

"What really captivated us," said *The Packers'* publisher in making the award, "was his general merchandising philosophy, which is: If someone says it can't be done that's the time to try it."

Woodward's had been exceptionally lucky or skilful, or both, in attracting and retaining for their lifetime the loyalty of some exceptionally talented people. Their pride in and devotion to the Company is its greatest asset.

At the 1972 Annual Awards dinners of the Woodwynn Club, an organization of employees with twenty years' service or more, two hundred and eighty-three employees received service awards. There were almost seven hundred persons present with an average of thirty years' service. One of them, Jack Branston of the Grandview Service Building, had worked at Woodward's for fifty years. He received $1,000 and an all-expense paid trip to any place in the world. (Two years later Bill Peacock of the Vancouver Credit Office matched his record and was also lavishly rewarded.)

In 1968 Puggy Woodward and his friend and colleague Bill Mann died. Their deaths were followed three years later by that of Courtney Haddock. The careers of these three pioneer developers of the Company have been described elsewhere in this history. In the early 1970's other directors who had made sterling contributions retired, having reached the retirement age for managers and executives of sixty. One of these was George Rennie, Divisional Manager of the Food Division and grocery buyer supreme. Others were Gordon Skinner, Vice-President Finance and Secretary, who had guided Woodward's financial policies with outstanding wisdom and Harold Joy, Vice-President Personnel, who knew more Woodwardites and had won more of their affection than any one in the Company. He had joined Woodward's as a parcel-boy in the Meat Division in 1929, one year after Tom Farrell. When the two young men were earning enough money to marry, they had married sisters.

Few companies could boast men of the calibre of Farrell, Skinner, Joy and Rennie: fewer still could retain their service for a lifetime.

Chunky had few relatives since only four of his paternal grandfather's nine children had had children of their own. Puggy's only son Douglas had died in his youth. Chunky was the sole male Woodward of his generation. One of his brothers-in-law, Robert White, became a director of the Company in 1963 and a cousin Grant Woodward McLaren, known as "Woody", joined it in 1957 becoming a Senior Vice-President seventeen years later. He was the grandson of Ann Woodward who had married Arthur Sanders and lived the rest of her short life in St. Thomas, Ontario.

Though brought up in Eastern Canada, Woody had wanted to work for Woodward's since his boyhood. In 1951, as soon as he was out of school, he presented himself to his great-uncle Billy and asked to be put to work. But Billy had other views.

"You must first make yourself independent," he told the 18-year-old youth, and arranged for him to be articled to the accounting firm of Price, Waterhouse. Six years later, Woody McLaren, by then a qualified chartered accountant, was employed in Woodward's General Office. Thence by talent and persistence, and not through nepotism, he worked his way to the Merchandising Division.

Like any big business worth its salt Woodward's is conscious of its civic responsibilities and meets them in many ways, in obvious ways such as providing financial support for charitable and cultural enterprises, in less obvious ways such as helping the disabled with employment or with shopping problems. When suitable jobs could be found, the deaf, the lame and the partially sighted have been put on the payroll.

Native Indians sometimes claim they are denied employment opportunities in British Columbia. So when Cyrl Keetch was appointed manager of the Kamloops Store he made friends with Mrs. Gus Godfreidson, first Indian to be named Woman of the Year by the Federal Government and sought her help in finding suitable Indian employees for his store. A young Indian leader, David Isaac, has been a salesman in the Sporting Goods Department of the Prince George Store since its opening.

Operation Wheelchair is another community project directed towards helping the disadvantaged. Farrell had noted the difficulty handicapped people have shopping in a crowded store and determined to do something about it. In Woodward's, Victoria, in 1970, an evening was set aside to give the blind and the handicapped a leisurely opportunity for Christmas shopping. A complete Woodward staff was on hand, augmented by many volunteers from off-duty staff members and service clubs. Hundreds of disabled people came to the Store and were guided individually through the various departments. Coffee and doughnuts, small gifts from Santa Claus and carol-singing were added to make a brighter Christmas for them.

Operation Wheelchair has become a Christmas tradition in many of the Woodward Stores in B.C. and Alberta.

CHAPTER THIRTY-FOUR

A New Decade

A new word was coined to describe economic conditions in Canada in the 1970's. That word was "stagflation" and it was used to imply a stagnant economy and a galloping inflation. Each year the rate of price increase leapt ahead. The 1975 jump in food costs was about 15% or almost double the 1972 increase of 7.9%. The price of gasoline rose in 1974 by 40%. Interest rates remained at a level that placed an almost impossible burden on people and put the buying of a home far beyond the reach of the ordinary citizen.

Trade unions, apprehensive of skyrocketing prices for every necessity of life, made wage demands that were in no way related to the productivity of the country. Canada became one of the most strike-ridden nations in the world with British Columbia the province with the most labour strife.

Like indulgent parents reluctantly chastising their errant children, the Federal and Provincial governments belatedly and half-heartedly set controls and guidelines which were promptly and strenuously opposed by organized labour and professionals alike.

It was a difficult time for a businessman whether he was operating a multi-million dollar chain or a corner grocery.

"Stagflation" or no, Vancouver marched boldly on. Before the 'Seventies were one month old, the Bloedel Conservatory which housed beneath its great glass dome a profusion of plants and flowers gathered from all over the world was opened and in the summer of the same year the only super-port in British Columbia was receiving super-freighters at Roberts Bank. The rejuvenation of Gastown and of the downtown waterfront area was followed by a new Georgia

Viaduct, and a bridge at the south end of Oak Street to accommodate Airport traffic and an ambitious plan to reclaim more of False Creek. (Charles Woodward would have liked that. As early as 1899 he had been harrying the Mayor and Aldermen of Vancouver 'to find ways and means to secure the upper end of False Creek.')

A splendid array of hotels and restaurants, of towering skyscrapers, luxurious office complexes and shopping malls, continued to crowd the centre of the city.

There was no sign of faltering in the plans of the developers or in the living style of many citizens.

There were of course many struggling to keep up with the ever-rising cost of living. Woodward's endeavoured to meet their needs.

The promotion of grass-fed beef was one method. Beef which hitherto had been on the dinner tables of Canadians at most levels of the social scale had suddenly become a luxury, doubling and trebling in price. The principal reason was the escalating cost of feed. So Woodward's promoted grass-fed beef which could be marketed much more cheaply than grain-fed. Another method was the establishing of several Bargain Stores where 'substandards' or merchandise with small imperfections might be sold.

Furniture Fair was opened in 1973 and pioneered a less costly way of selling furniture by which customers could buy it at discount prices if they were prepared to receive furniture in its original factory packaging, uncrate, assemble and deliver it themselves, thereby saving the cost of these services. They could if they preferred pay the "de luxe" price and have the complete department store service. The idea had revolutionized furniture merchandising in the United States and spread to Toronto and Montreal. Woodward's Furniture Fair was the first in Western Canada.

The premises in Burnaby comprised 100,000 square feet of warehouse and a showroom about half that size containing 250 decorated room settings. As each room setting was backed with inventory in the warehouse, customers might have any item they required within twenty minutes of purchasing it.

Furniture Fair was another of Woodward's "First in B.C." Others had been the one-price sale day: the self-service groceteria: the ban on use of comparative prices in advertising: the Shopping Centre, and the battle against fixed minimum prices.

Elizabeth Russ, elder daughter of Mr. and Mrs. W. C. Woodward.

All these merchandising practices had set trends which were widely followed. Shopping Centres and supermarkets had sprung up all over the country. The one-price sale day was the most copied sale day in the country. But the attempt to keep down the cost of living, which remained Woodward's most cherished policy, was never harder to implement in all the company's long history.

Between 1930 and 1973 British Columbia's population grew by 1,628,000 (240%), the largest population increase of any province in Canada. Alberta's was not far behind.

Woodward's expansion programme kept pace.

In Vancouver another Food Floor was opened in 1974 in Arbutus Village Square. A Shopping Centre had been on the City Planners' drawing-boards for the district of Arbutus for several years. Development had been held up since 1967 because residents feared congestion in a part of Vancouver which was mainly residential and where many of the houses were exclusive and expensive. The Arbutus Village Food Floor was different from other Woodward groceterias in that there was no department store beside it. In addition to the usual plethora of basic foods the taste of the most discriminating gourmet was catered to and a "complete variety of the unordinary" offered.

In 1975 the Company embarked on six new projects, three of them substantial shopping centres in new territory.

The first of these developments took place in Lethbridge and has already been described.

At intervals of one month, there followed Cherry Lane Shopping Centre in Penticton, central city of the Okanagan Valley, and Sevenoaks Shopping Centre in Abbotsford, both leased operations with the customary Woodward Department Store, Food Market and Auto Centre.

In Richmond, B.C., a shopping centre larger than any of these has been planned for opening in the fall of 1977. Its first phase was the construction of a Warehouse and Distribution Centre. A Bargain Store in Victoria and a Furniture Fair in Edmonton made 1975 a record year for construction completions.

Charles Woodward had presided over two department stores, Billy over five; by the end of 1975 Chunky was operating twenty-one.

Lew Phipps, who was responsible for seeing that the building programme throughout the chain was carried out, was the busiest man in the Company. He had worked his way from the bottom rung of the Engineers' ladder to Director of Store Planning and Buildings.

Our story started in Southern Ontario and has ranged all over British Columbia and Alberta. One senses the dawn of a new era. Douglas Lake Ranch now can be reached in a matter of minutes in the Company's Lear Jet. Stray cattle are sought by helicopter. Woodwynn Farm is the home of Elizabeth and Barney Russ. As Barney practises law in Victoria and Elizabeth is the mother of five daughters, some of the land and cattle are leased. Aberdeen Angus still predominate.

Charles Woodward's one-room shack at Bidwell, Manitoulin Island, has grown to be a big business. To some the words "big business" are a term of opprobrium denoting greed, ruthlessness and cold self-interest. But the Woodwards have operated within self-designed and persistent high standards of ethical conduct. In so doing they have adhered to such basic principles as:

"Integrity must be total and complete."

"Buy the best that you can, sell it for as little as you can and make a profit."

"A deal is a good deal only if it benefits all parties concerned."

"Advertise without exaggeration, innuendo or ambiguity."

"Make staff members partners in the profits and in the planning of the enterprise."

"Return a share of earnings to the community by supporting charities and culture."

Big Government has not always been equally scrupulous in observing these principles.

Some of the Woodward's concepts may today be considered old-fashioned; for instance the belief that remuneration should be graded according to merit and responsibility, that promotion should be from within the ranks of the organization and available to all and that loyalty between staff and management is a mutual affair. Yet these creeds have stood the test of time.

The story ends in Vancouver, favourite city of Charles, his sons William and Percival, and his grandson. On December 21, 1974,

LEFT TO RIGHT: *John Woodward, Elizabeth, his wife, C. N. Woodward, Mary Twigg White, Robert White at the opening of Sevenoaks, Clearbrook, B.C., on October 15, 1975, the last of the six new projects of 1975.*

John Woodward, third of that name and second eldest of Chunky's four children, took time off from his job in the Menswear Department of the Downtown Store to marry Elizabeth Taylor, also a member of a pioneer Vancouver family. By coincidence she became the third Elizabeth Woodward. One of his ushers was Michael McBride, whose grandfather Tom McBride held and father 'Pidge' McBride still holds an executive position and directorship at Woodward's. The church was full of Woodwardites at all levels. Gentle, modest Mary McGruer was a guest with a special interest. She had been Billy's secretary, was now Chunky's and still looked young enough to serve the next incumbent. She had given Woodward's a superb degree of competence for forty-five years.

Like his grandfather and father, young John Woodward had hesitated a while before joining the Company. Independently-minded, in the Woodward pattern, he was reluctant to leave his work as a fishing and hunting guide at Campbell River. Like his grandfather and father he eventually decided to go into the family business and, as fourth generation Woodward in the business, to begin his apprenticeship.

Not the least part of his inheritance is a set of working policies and principles which have guided the Woodward Stores to more than merely material success and made the Woodwards a distinguished Canadian family.

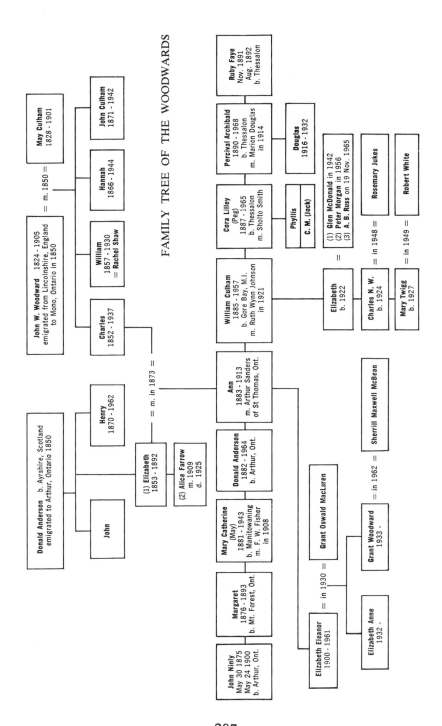

FAMILY TREE OF THE WOODWARDS

297

Chronology

1850   John W. Woodward came to Canada from Lincolnshire, England; worked as a wheelwright and as a farmer at Mono, Ontario. He married Mary Culham of Beverley Township.

1852   Charles, their eldest child, was born on the farm.

1863   John W. Woodward moved to Orangeville, Ontario.

1866   Charles Woodward left school and started work on his father's farm.

1873   Charles married Elizabeth Anderson.
He bought 42 acres with money given him by his father and began to work as an independent farmer.

1874   John W. Woodward moved to Arthur, Ontario, and purchased a 92-acre lot.

1875   Charles became an apprentice in a store, probably at Arthur, for $8.00 a month. Three months later he resigned. He bought 200 acres of Manitoulin Island at Bidwell, twelve miles from Manitowaning. His land was too stony to farm.
John N. Woodward, his first child, born.

1876   Charles became a trader at Bidwell and started the first Woodward Store in a small log cabin there.

1877   Charles moved to Manitowaning and started a store with a partner.
Margaret Woodward born.

1879   Charles faced with bankruptcy was rescued by his father.

1881   Mary Catherine Woodward (May) born.

1882   Charles sold the Manitowaning Store, by this time successful and well-established, in order to deal in oxen in Manitoba.
The Manitoba boom burst and Charles returned to Manitoulin Island where he bought a bankrupt store at Gore Bay.
Donald Woodward born at Gore Bay.

1883   Ann Woodward born.

1885   William C. Woodward born at Gore Bay.
Charles bought a second and larger store at Thessalon on the mainland and put a manager in charge.

1887   Charles found that the Thessalon store had accumulated liabilities of $30,000. He dismissed the manager, sold the store at Gore Bay and moved to Thessalon.

1888   Charles became magistrate at Thessalon.

1890   The Thessalon store burned and was a total loss.
P. A. Woodward born at Thessalon.

1891   Charles visited British Columbia and bought two lots for a store in Vancouver.

1892   In January Charles arrived in Vancouver with his eight children. His wife, who was both ill and pregnant, came two or three months later. In mid-January he started to build his store on Westminster Avenue and was doing business in it on March 1st.
Elizabeth Woodward died in July and the baby in August.

1893   Eldest daughter Margaret Woodward died.

1894   Charles bought a house at 401 Fifth Avenue in the Mount Pleasant district.

1895   Woodward's Drug Department established with John Woodward as manager.

1897   Mount Pleasant house rented. Family resided over the Store.

1900   Death of John N. Woodward.
        May (19) and Donald (18) joined the firm of Woodward's as book-keeper and salesman respectively.

1901   At the suggestion of lawyer J. E. Bird several small businesses combined and formed a group with Charles Woodward as the General Manager.
        Charles Woodward, without authority from colleagues, took option on a lot 66' x 132' on Hastings Street.
        William (16) left school and joined the Royal Bank in the Kootenays.
        Ann went to Winnipeg to train as a nurse, met A. Sanders and married him.

1902   SEPTEMBER 12   The Company was incorporated as Woodward Department Stores Ltd.
        The building of the Store on Hastings was commenced but delayed owing to labour trouble.

1903   MID-OCTOBER   Display goods moved into the Store.
        NOVEMBER   Woodward's Store was opened for business at 101 West Hastings Street, a 3-storey wooden frame building.

1904   FEBRUARY   Managers' salaries reduced to $75 including Charles Woodward's.
        APRIL   Extension of credit sought from trade creditors and Bank of North America.
        MAY 12   Fiery meeting at which R. G. Buchanan moved that Charles be replaced as manager and Receiver appointed.
        Circular issued stated that Charles Woodward had bought out Directors Davidson and Hyndman and sought resignation of Receiver Helliwell.
        Charles became Managing Director. Receiver Helliwell resigned.
        House in Mount Pleasant was sold.

1905   JUNE 15 Woodward's banking business was transferred to Royal Bank of Canada.
        Woodward family moved to 1240 West Pender Street.

1905   W. C. Woodward worked in Cuba as banker, later as stockbroker from 1905 to 1907.

1907   W. C. Woodward returned as bookkeeper for Woodward's.
        P. A. Woodward left school and joined Woodward's as salesclerk.
        May was a teacher at Seymour School.

1908   Donald Woodward made Secretary-Treasurer.
        Charles Wynn-Johnson bought Alkali Lake.
        May married F. W. Fisher.
        W. C. Woodward and P. A. Woodward attended Directors' Meeting for the first time on FEBRUARY 17.

1909   Charles Woodward married Alice Farrow.
        W. C. Woodward listed as "Floor Manager" and later as Secretary-Treasurer in place of Donald who had left the company.

1910   Woodward's first one-price Sale Day. *Twenty-five Cent Day.*

1912   Charles Woodward now a millionaire decided to retire to California and bought a walnut grove.
        Woodward's had twenty departments and a mail-order business.

300

AUGUST 1912 and MARCH 1913   Directors' Meetings chaired by J. W. Little. W. C. Woodward went to live at Glencoe Lodge.

1913   Woodward's had a fleet of 12 horse-drawn delivery wagons.
Vancouver's Real Estate boom collapsed.
MARCH 11   Directors' Meeting chaired by Charles Woodward back from "retirement". J. W. Little as Vice-President and W. C. Woodward as Secretary-Treasurer.

1914   85-ft. lot adjacent to Store on Hastings Street purchased for $350,000.
Outbreak of First World War.
Marriage of P. A. Woodward and Marion Douglas.

1915   FEBRUARY 8   P. A. Woodward appointed Vice-President and W. C. Secretary-Treasurer.

1916   AUGUST 14   W. C. Woodward resigned from the Store and was commissioned with First Canadian Heavy Battery (1916-1919).
Ruth Wynn-Johnson in Dublin with Mrs. Kenworthy, her aunt. (1916-1917).

1919   Opening of Woodward's Self-Service Groceteria.

1921   Marriage of William C. Woodward and Ruth Wynn-Johnson.

1922   Registration of C. Woodward Ltd., Edmonton, with Mr. and Mrs. Charles Woodward as sole directors.
J. W. Little died.

1923   A new building (designed for four more storeys), the Cordova Street Annex opened (Hardware Department).

1925   New Building from Hastings Street through to Cordova on Abbott, i.e., whole block, replacing Metropole Hotel, commenced MARCH 8.

1924   Charles Woodward elected Liberal M.L.A. (1924-28).
He headed Vancouver poll.
Death of Mrs. Alice Farrow Woodward (or 1925).
Attempt to extort $4,000 from W. C. Woodward.
Robbery at Woodward's. Store watchman knocked out.

1926   C. Woodward's opened in Edmonton, Alberta.

1927 $200,000 addition to Store on Cordova Street side.

1929   Store increased to six storeys.
W. C. Woodward elected President of Vancouver Board of Trade.

1930   Parking Garage built and pedestrian tunnel connecting it with the Food Floor.

1931   Vancouver Welfare Federation formed. W. C. Woodward chairman.

1934   W. C. Woodward appointed Hon. Lieut.-Col., 15th Field Regt. RCA.

1935   W. C. Woodward appointed director of newly-formed Bank of Canada.

1936   Vancouver's Golden Jubilee.
New City Hall opened.
Vancouver visited by Lord Mayor of London.

1937   Store increased to seven storeys with Lower Main and sub-basement on Cordova Street.
JUNE   Death of Charles Woodward. W. C. Woodward appointed President. W. C. Woodward appointed Director of Royal Bank.

1938   May Fisher's anonymous gift of $50,000 starts B.C. Cancer Institute.
"Sit-in" by unemployed men in Vancouver Post Office and Art Gallery. Windows smashed at Woodward's and David Spencer's Department Stores.

301

1939   Further additions to Vancouver Store.

Charles Woodward Memorial Auditorium opened.

SEPTEMBER   War declared against Germany.

DECEMBER   W. C. Woodward left Vancouver to serve on War Supply board in Ottawa. P. A. Woodward appointed General Manager of Woodward's.

King George VI and Queen Elizabeth visited Vancouver.

New Vancouver Hotel opened.

1940   APRIL   Department of Munitions and Supply organized with C. D. Howe, Minister, and W. C. Woodward, Chairman of its executive committee and Director-General of War Supply Board.

AUGUST   W. C. Woodward becomes C. D. Howe's Executive Assistant.

OCTOBER   350,000 food parcels supplied by Woodward's at cost and despatched overseas.

DECEMBER   W. C. Woodward torpedoed on liner *Western Prince* while on his way to England.

Hitler overran Denmark and Norway, Holland and Belgium.

France sues for an armistice.

1941   Two-storey addition to Edmonton Store commenced.

W. C. Woodward terminated duties in Ottawa and returned to Vancouver.

AUGUST   W. C. Woodward appointed Lieutenant-Governor of British Columbia.

1942   Staff Advisory Council formed.

1943   Wednesday closing commenced as a wartime measure.

APRIL   P. A. Woodward appointed head of Northwest Purchasing Company with headquarters in Edmonton.

C. N. Woodward resigned from the COTC and enlisted in Canadian Army.

1944   FEBRUARY   Hon. W. C. Woodward purchased Woodwynn Farm in Saanichton, V.I.

C. N. Woodward served in Northwest Europe as trooper with the 12th Manitoba Dragoons.

1945   APRIL   Hon. W. C. Woodward visited troops of 1st Canadian Army in Northwest Europe.

MAY   War in Europe ended.

AUGUST   Japanese surrender. End of the Second World War.

1946   AUGUST   W. C. Woodward retired as Lieutenant-Governor of British Columbia.

London Buying Office opened.

C. N. Woodward demobilized, joined staff of Woodward's.

1947   Addition to Downtown Store: 7th and 8th floors completed and 10-storey section added.

Groceteria enlarged.

Vancouver's Downtown Businessmen's Association revived and enlarged at instigation of P. A. Woodward.

1948   Port Alberni Store, Vancouver Island, B.C.

Marriage of C. N. Woodward to Rosemary Jukes.

1948 to 1957 were prosperous years in which Canadian Gross National Product more than doubled.

1949   Warehouse and Delivery Service Building, Vancouver.
       Toronto office opened.
       Marriage of Mary Twigg Woodward to Robert White.

1950   Park Royal Shopping Centre.
       Hon. and Mrs. W. C. Woodward, A. R. Mitchell and J. C. Haddock
       toured Europe and appointed agencies.

1951   Second floor added to Park Royal Store.
       Small store of specialized departments opened in Victoria, B.C.
       Hon. W. C. Woodward received the Freedom of the City of Van-
       couver.
       McQuarrie Commission declared itself opposed to resale price main-
       tenance.

1952   Agents appointed in Siam, Japan, Turkey, India, Malaya, Pakistan
       and Hong Kong, following round-the-world tour by Hon. and Mrs.
       W. C. Woodward and A. R. Mitchell.
       Mrs. W. C. Woodward adopted Aberdeen Angus cattle at Woodwynn
       Farm.
       Rt. Hon. Vincent Massey appointed first Canadian Governor-General.

1953   Woodward's Profit-Sharing and Savings Fund Plan inaugurated.
       The last of the old streetcars left Vancouver's streets.

1954   New Westminster Store, New Westminster, B.C.
       Woodward's decided to remain on a five-day shopping week in spite
       of lost plebiscite.

1955   Westmount Centre, West Edmonton.
       P. A. Woodward retired. Mr. and Mrs. P. A. Woodward Foundation
       formed.
       British Columbia Lions joined Western Football League.
       Woodward's sponsors Boys and Girls' Quarterback Club.

1956   Hon. W. C. Woodward appointed Colonel-at-Large of Canadian
       Militia.
       J. W. Butterfield retired as President of Woodward's.

1957   Hon. W. C. Woodward died.
       C. N. Woodward appointed President and Chief Executive.
       900-car self-parking garage opened.
       C. N. Woodward purchased Douglas Lake Cattle Company.
       C. N. Woodward turned the sod at the site of Oakridge Shopping
       Centre.
       Rt. Hon. John Diefenbaker elected Prime Minister of Canada.

1958   Hon. W. C. Woodward Scholarships inaugurated at U.B.C. and Univ.
       of Alberta.
       British Columbia's Centennial Celebrations.
       Woodward's published "The City and the Store".

1959   Oakridge Shopping Centre.
       Grandview Service Building extended to cover ten acres.
       Woodward's Marine Division at Coal Harbour.
       George Massey Tunnel opened.

1960   Chinook Centre, Calgary, Alberta.
       C. N. Woodward appointed Director of Royal Bank of Canada.

1963   Mayfair Centre, Victoria, B.C.
       Port Mann Bridge opened.

1964   Kamloops Store, Kamloops, B.C.
Woodward Library given to U.B.C. by Mr. and Mrs. P. A. Woodward.
Mrs. W. C. Woodward toured New Zealand and Australia with Western Canadian ranchers.
C. N. Woodward rode at the Royal Windsor Horse Show for Queen Elizabeth and Prince Philip and won Canadian steer-cutting championship.

1965   Northgate Centre, Edmonton.
New Canadian Flag adopted.
Marriage of Elizabeth and Bernard Russ.

1966   Guildford Centre, Surrey, B.C.
Parkwood Centre, Prince George, B.C.
P. A. Woodward's gift of $3½ million enabled U.B.C. to begin construction of Health Sciences Centre.

1967   Centenary of Canadian Confederation.
C. N. Woodward champion steer cutter at Horse of the Year Show, Vancouver.

1968   Woodward's joined Project 200, a project to develop Vancouver's waterfront.
P. A. Woodward died.
New Vancouver International Airport opened.
Problem of French-Canadian separatism came to a head. Emergency War Measures Act.

1969   Strathcona Distribution Centre, Edmonton, Alberta.
410-bed hospital and research centre opened on University Boulevard, a gift of the P. A. Woodward Foundation.

1970   Southgate Store, Edmonton.
Restoration of Gastown commenced.
Operation Wheelchair inaugurated.
Port Roberts Super-port opened.

1971   Market Mall, Calgary.
New Parking Garage, the Coggery and Maple Leaf House, Water Street, Vancouver.

1972   Farm to Family Express.
Woodward's returned to six-day shopping week.
Mrs. W. C. Woodward died.
G. D. Glanville retired as President of Woodward's.
Jack Branston first Woodwardite to complete fifty years of service.
Hon. W. C. Woodward Scholarships increased to 7 and to $600.00 per annum.

1973   Furniture Fair, Burnaby, B.C.

1974   Edmonton Centre, Alberta.
Arbutus Village Square, Vancouver.
Net sales topped 500 million dollars, quadrupled in past 15 years.
Marriage of John Woodward to Elizabeth Taylor.

1975   Lethbridge Centre, Lethbridge, Alberta.
Cherry Lane Centre, Penticton, B.C.
Sevenoaks Shopping Centre, Abbotsford, B.C.
Richmond Distribution Centre, Richmond, B.C.
Furniture Fair, Edmonton, B.C.
T. R. Farrell retired as President of Woodward's: Succeeded by C. R. Clarridge.

Acknowledgements
and Bibliography

The author wishes gratefully to acknowledge assistance received from the following sources and generous friends:

Provincial Archives of British Columbia, Victoria, B.C.

Vancouver City Archives

Provincial Archives of Alberta, Edmonton, Alberta

Edmonton City Archives

Charles Woodward's Reminiscences (unpublished)

Charles Woodward Merchandiser Extraordinary: Degree Thesis written in 1967 at the University of British Columbia by Ian B. McDonald

Orangeville, 100 Years of History

Historical Atlas of Wellington County, Ontario, 1906

Vancouver, From Milltown to Metropolis by Alan Morley

Vancouver by Eric Nicol

The History of British Columbia by Dr. Margaret Ormsby

A History of Edmonton by J. J. McGregor

Politics in Paradise by Dr. Patrick McGeer

Cariboo Cowboy by Harry Marriott

Ten Lost Years by Barry Broadfoot

Many Trails by R. D. Symons

Their Finest Hour by W. S. Churchill

Abraham Cristall by Robert Cristall

Very Far West Indeed by R. Byron Johnson

The Story of Douglas Lake Ranch by Campbell Carroll

Letters and Papers of the former Vancouver City Archivist, the late Major Matthews

Files of the *Vancouver Sun,* the *Vancouver Province,* the *Edmonton Journal,* the *Manitoulin Expositor, Thessalon Advocate, Twin Cities' Times, West Coast Advocate*

Articles on Woodward's by MacReynolds published in 1952 in the *Saturday Evening Post* and *Macleans Magazine*

Henderson's Directories for Alberta

Alberta, Where the Action Is — article by Paul Friggens published in the *Readers' Digest* January 1976

The Beacon, Woodward's Staff Magazines — 1945 to 1975 — and especially the current editor, Sita Crombie

Scrapbooks kept by the late Mrs. W. C. Woodward and lent by Elizabeth Russ

Roy Thomson of Fleet Street by Russell Braddon

Scrapbooks relating to Woodward's Port Alberni, lent by Hazel Ritchie

Diaries of the late Charles Wynn-Johnson

Minutes of Woodward's Staff Advisory Council lent by Rose Bancroft

Vancouver Board of Trade Reports

Archives and Files of the Royal Bank of Canada

Members of the Woodward Organization, past and present, and at all levels, who have provided more letters, diaries, scrapbooks, photographs, minute-books, and memories than could be enumerated

Bernard Russ, who read, checked, encouraged and advised from start to finish

Stewart J. Shaw of Belwood, Ontario who researched; Margaret Tallman of North Pender Island who typed; Tempest de Wolf who shared his memories, Harold Joy who proof-read

Geoffrey Rock, Canadian artist, whose highly valued contribution to this book has been the cover

My wife, whose support is unfailing, unstinting and, to the author, indispensable.

Awards

Mr. C. N. Woodward (left) is shown presenting Mr. William Peacock with his award for 50 years of service with Woodward Stores Limited. Mr. Peacock received an inscribed silver tray and scroll, a trip for two anywhere in the world and a $1,500 cheque.

On October 29, 1974, 590 Woodwynn Club members gathered to celebrate long service awards at a presentation banquet held at the Canyon Gardens in North Vancouver. Members were present from all Woodward's stores in B.C. and each has a minimum of 20 years service with the Company. The awards this year, which are given at 20, 25, 30, 35, 40, 45, 50 years and at retirement, went to 203 staff members and represented 4,675 combined years of association with Woodward's The standards set by these dedicated employees have contributed immeasurably to the public confidence that has lead to the steady growth of Woodward's in Western Canada.

308

TWENTY YEAR AWARD
1954 - 1974

Andersen, Al
Balzer, Max
Barteluk, Laurie
Berg, Emanuel
Biggs, Irene
Blanchard,
  Lucienne
Boyd, Doreen
Brisbois, Betty
Britton, Ronald
Brundin, Ivy
Burditt, Charles
Campbell, Cora
Cardno, Roberta
Carter, Constance
Cattermole,
  Richard
Christoff, Lloyd
Cooke, Jackson
Cox, Elizabeth
Cruickshank,
  Robert
Davies, Douglas
Den Daas, Ron

Disdero, Andrew
Eason, Walter
Filer, Stella
Fox, Albert
Gair, Kathleen
Galbraith, Neil
Gilliland, George
Gingell, Beatrice
Goodman, Cyril
Gray, Alex
Grundy, Ralph
Harbor, Stanley
Hesketh, Nancy
Howaniec, Anna
Howard, Robert
Hunka, Joseph
Jasbec, Mervin
Kellough, Walter
Kitching, Fred
Laing, Norma
Landstrom, Carl
Little, Jack
Love, Thomas
MacInnes, John

McIlwee, Peter
McKay, Peter
McLeod, Mary
Mann, George
Markham,
  Florence
Morgan, Bridget
Morris, Richard
Murdoch, Robert
Nesbitt, Leone
Newby, Reginald
Nickey, George
Nicklin, Peggy
Nielsen, Bruce
Nicolson, Fern
Parker, Viola
Pfeil, Astrid
Rashbrook,
  Gerard
Reeves, Jane
Richardson,
  William
Risley, Florence
Robertson, Joe

Roy, Josephine
Sault, Elizabeth
Scullion, Thomas
Sinclair, Edward
Sneddon, George
Springford, John
Strathern, John
Sutton, Patricia
Thicke, Alice
Thornton, Wally
Townsend, Harry
Unruh, Nicholas
Weelicome,
  Gerald
Westlake, Patricia
Wiggins, Harry
Worster, Hazel
Yaworsky,
  Mathilda
Yeaman. James
Young, Bernice
Yuskow, Walter
Zimmer, Norman

TWENTY-FIVE YEAR AWARD
1949 - 1974

Barr, Lawrence E.
Biltzen, Elsie
Bjelland, Agnes
Blair, James W.
Chapman, Rosa V.
Cronin,
  Gwendolyn
Dodman,
  Robert E.
Eckstein, Lorne
Farnsworth,
  Frank

Forbes,
  Kenneth R.
Gorst, Robert
Huthrie, Alfred R.
Hale, William G.
Hall, William
Hearst, Joseph P.
Horton,
  John H. M.
Johnson, Bjorn
Kennedy, Daniel
Lego, Joseph
Lendrum, Colin C.

MacDonell,
  Allan H.
McLardy, Ronald
Mason, Walter A.
Mayuk, Christine
Midgley, Jack N.
Miles, Thomas H.
Norum, Stuart L.
Nudd, Ian M.
Parsons, Thomas
Pottinger, Walter
Purvis, Robert T.
Reith, William T.

Rhodes, Harold L.
Roberts, Herbert
Sanders, James
Smith, Margaret
Steele, Hugh A.
Sullivan,
  Catherine
Thiessen,
  Susannah
Tymo, Pearl
Watt, David
Watson, Leonard
Wilson, Donald J.

THIRTY YEAR AWARD
1944 - 1974

Carle, Ralph C.
Evans,
  Norman G.

Creswell, Kay
Jacques, Roy
Muncy, Dorothy

Sturley, Lewis
Spencer,
  Duncan W.

Swanson, Bernice

THIRTY-FIVE YEAR AWARD
1939 - 1974

Aiken, Harry
Junker, Donald

Hodgson, George
Marsden, Clifford

Slade, Clifford
White, George

Warkentin, Ann

FORTY YEAR AWARD
1934 - 1974

Clarridge,
C. Reginald

Eden, Shirley E.

Ker, Miriam

McKenzie,
Alexander

FORTY-FIVE YEAR AWARD
1929 - 1974

Anderson, Gordon
Joy, Harold L.

Ellis, George

MacGruer, Mary

McMurdo, Margaret

FIFTY YEAR AWARD
1954 - 1974

Peacock, William

1974 RETIREMENTS

1951 Anthony,
    William L.
1955 Asemissen, Neva I.
1954 Berg, Emanuel
1953 Brigden, Ethel S.
1953 Bryce, George Y.
1944 Carle, Ralph C.
1940 Clarke, Mary A.
1954 Cox, Elizabeth
1947 Cummings,
    William M.
1933 Curtis, Ruth F.
1950 Dick, Margaret
1934 Eden, Shirley E.
1929 Ellis, George
1945 Evans, Dorothy
1952 Ethier, Edith
1950 Fawcett,
    Edward H.
1953 Foster, Joan E.
1946 Fraser, George W.

1926 Frew, Violet T.
1952 Gatenby,
    T. Norman
1954 Gilliland,
    George R.
1946 Howard, George S.
1954 Jasbec, J. Mervin
1929 Joy, Harold L.
1937 Kelly, Gordon
1934 Ker, Miriam
1955 Lyttle, Terence
1946 McLeod, John
1954 McLeod, Mary
1939 Marsden, Clifford
1955 Nelson, Olive
1950 Nuttall, Stanley
1950 O'Connor,
    Florence I.
1930 Oram, Harry
1952 Park, James P.

1924 Peacock, William
1948 Rezac, James
1949 Sanders, James
1941 Sim, Clarence L.
1931 Skinner, James A.
1948 Skinner,
    W. Gordon
1944 Spencer,
    Duncan W.
1946 Stevenson,
    Helen W.
1948 Stokes, Queenie
1953 Tait, James M.
1935 Vernon, W. Wesley
1950 Wills, Violet A.
1953 Wilson, Beulah B.
1937 Woodward,
    Kenneth
1947 Yashinsky,
    Stephen

Index

312

313

314

315

316